Henry Gouger

A Personal Narrative of Two Years' Imprisonment in Burmah

1824-26

Henry Gouger

A Personal Narrative of Two Years' Imprisonment in Burmah
1824-26

ISBN/EAN: 9783744752367

Printed in Europe, USA, Canada, Australia, Japan

Cover: Foto ©Thomas Meinert / pixelio.de

More available books at **www.hansebooks.com**

THE ROYAL PALACE AT AVA.

From a Native Drawing presented to the Royal Asiatic Society by Colonel H. Burney

PERSONAL NARRATIVE

OF

TWO YEARS' IMPRISONMENT

IN

BURMAH.

By HENRY GOUGER.

WAR BOAT.

WITH ILLUSTRATIONS.

LONDON:
JOHN MURRAY, ALBEMARLE STREET.
1860.

The right of Translation is reserved.

LONDON: PRINTED BY W. CLOWES AND SONS, STAMFORD STREET,
AND CHARING CROSS.

A

PERSONAL NARRATIVE

OF

TWO YEARS' IMPRISONMENT

IN

BURMAH,

1824-26.

BY HENRY GOUGER.

With Illustrations.

LONDON:
JOHN MURRAY, ALBEMARLE STREET.
1860.

[The right of Translation is reserved.]

LONDON:
PRINTED BY WOODFALL AND KINDER,
ANGEL COURT, SKINNER STREET.

PREFACE.

Several friends, to whom I have from time to time related fragments of the story told in the following pages, expressed an opinion that a connected narrative would possess sufficient interest to engage the attention of a class of readers who seek for amusement, and who might not think it the less exciting because it is true. These friends have often urged me to prepare such an one for the press. Perhaps I might have adopted their suggestion, but never having followed literary pursuits, I was naturally diffident of my powers of description, and of my ability to convey to the minds of others the impressions which the events related had very forcibly imprinted on my own, or even of relating the facts themselves in a sufficiently engaging manner.

Recently, however, during an attack of illness which confined me several months to my couch, I overcame this diffidence, and attempted the task for my own amusement. The occupation proved a very efficient aid to the physician, and many a weary hour was beguiled of its sadness as the story proceeded. If my friends derive half as much pleasure in reading as I did in writing it, I shall be amply satisfied.

Should this book chance to fall into the hands of any persons who have become acquainted with Burmah and the Burmese of late years, especially since the last war in 1852, it is possible they may not recognize a very strong resemblance. I must therefore beg such persons to keep in mind that I am not writing of Burmah as it is, but as it was at a time when to the inhabitants of the interior a white man was a novelty; when the arts and sciences, the habits, sentiments, and opinions of the nations of the West were altogether unknown to them.

After reading the interesting book of Major Yule, and there finding the King and his Court discussing the merits of treaties with some appearance of common sense, holding disputations on nice questions of government and civil policy, giving good dinners, criticizing paintings, manifesting good faith in compacts, getting rid of bad customs, abolishing degrading compliances at Court, correcting its institutions, and, above all, coming to understand the map of the world, and the necessity of treating other nations with consideration and respect, I must confess it is with some difficulty I do myself recognize the ignorant, conceited, and arrogant Power it was when I became acquainted with it. Most nations have undergone great changes during the last forty years, and the Burmese seem to have kept pace with them.

H. GOUGER.

Frogmore House, Blackwater,
  October, 1860.

CONTENTS.

CHAPTER I.

The object and origin of my expedition.—I embark in the *Alfred* for Rangoon.—Escape from wreck on the Preparis Rocks.—Arrive at Rangoon.—Official "Visit" on board the *Alfred*.—Mr. Lanciego, the Akoupwoon.—Duties levied in kind.—My investment attracts attention.—I engage an interpreter.—Pagoda lake.—First impressions of the Burmese.—Preparations for pursuing my voyage.—Visits to the Viceroy.—I secure his protection.—Boats' crews.—Their honesty.—Food.—Ngapwee.—Departure for Amerapoorah.—Favourable prospects 1

CHAPTER II.

Delta of the Irrawuddi.—Musquitos and jungle.—The great river.—Voyage up the river.—Fleets of native boats.—Inland trade in rice.—Safety of the river.—Hilly country.—Picturesque sail beyond Prome.—Monasteries and monks.—Their habits.—Education general among the people.—I acquire the language.—Arrival at Amerapoorah.—Tolls and transit dues abolished.—Safety of the river 16

CHAPTER III.

The King removes from Amerapoorah to Ava.—The population in a state of transition.—Amerapoorah.—No exactions on landing.—I take a house.—Gain easy access to His Majesty.—Abandon the use of shoes.—The King's temporary Palace.—Apparition of an Englishman.—Mr. Rodgers.—I am introduced to the chief Queen.—Her character and influence.—Musical-glasses.—The Queen's present.—Betel-chewing.—The King's practical joke . 25

CHAPTER IV.

A day in the Palace.—Ladies of Her Majesty's household.—Their demeanour.—Bargaining.—Strange salutation.—Honesty in the Palace.—The Queen's present.—Constitution of the household.—The Men-tha-mees.—The King's dinner.—Flattering reception.—Factions at Court.—Visit to the Prince of Tharawudi.—Men-tha-gee.—Their characters and mutual hostility.—Tharawudi's embarrassing familiarity 28

CHAPTER V.

Visit to various Chiefs.—Their occupations.—The Hlut-dau.—Burmese law-courts.—Bribery and corruption.—The Loo-byo-dau.—Their visits.—I am accused of stealing the King's sheep.—His Majesty's adjudication.—Slaughter of oxen.—I am protected by Tharawudi, who participates.—Wretched bazaar.—I attend the Royal Council.—The Yoong-dau.—Facility of acquiring information.—Absence of amusements.—Salubrity of climate . . 49

CHAPTER VI.

Mercantile prospects.—Export trade.—General system of prohibition.—Astonishing profits on imports.—Prospects of immense fortune.—On what circumstances depending.—Difficulties.—How to be overcome 59

CHAPTER VII.

Mr. Rodgers.—His history.—Irascible character of the King.—His attack upon his Council.—New Palace at Ava.—It is injured by lightning.—Consequent execution of the architect.—I take leave of the King.—His commands.—I return to Rangoon under convoy.—Kyouptaloung Thegee.—Gross treatment of Europeans at Rangoon.—An instance.—Singular escape of a Lascar . . 68

CHAPTER VIII.

Arrival in Calcutta.—Hesitation about returning.—I determine to follow our scheme.—Disgraceful neglect of the Bengal Government.—I engage Mr. Richardson.—We sail for Rangoon.—Mr. Stockdale.—Return to Ava.—Explosion of a priest.—"Red Rat" and "Red Gold."—I make myself independent of interpreter.—Death of Mr. Stockdale.—A boatman drowned.—Escape from drowning.—Alligators.—Strange habit.—A boatman of Dr. Price taken by one.—Anecdote of Wellesley Province . 78

CONTENTS. vii

CHAPTER IX.

Our arrival in Ava.—No European settlers.—Mr. Cabral, his fate.—Ava occupied.—Mr. Lanciego lends me a house.—Audience of the King.—Present him with the dog.—Absence of all love of sports among the Burmese.—Sale of investments.—Mercantile proceedings.—Mr. Rodgers.—Arrival of Dr. Price, a missionary.—Anecdotes of the old King.—His character.—He forces Mahomedans to eat pork.—His astrological whims.—Brahmin astronomers *versus* Burmese.—Prediction of eclipse.—The King consigns a section of his Court to the horse-pond.—Escape of Mr. Rodgers.—Rebellion at the accession of His Majesty.—Complicity of Mr. Rodgers.—How he cleared the Irrawaddi of pirates 90

CHAPTER X.

First indications of war.—Causes assigned for it.—Opinions of Tharawudi.—Popular feeling in favour of war.—Bundoola crosses the river with an army.—War boats.—Magnificent regattas.—Dr. Judson arrives.—Bundoola's army marched for the British frontier.—Accusation about Mr. Stockdale's property.—I accompany the King to the Shwai-dyke.—Tempting exhibition of silver.—Attempt to walk off with it.—My failure therein.—Growing dislike and suspicions.—I confine myself much to my house 102

CHAPTER XI.

Perplexities.—Departure of Mr. Richardson, who escapes in safety.—Taking a wild elephant.—Mode of taming him.—Royal pugilists.—My last interview with the King.—Scheme for escape with the Sakkya Woongee.—Defeated by delays.—Might have been worse 114

CHAPTER XII.

Rangoon bombarded.—Effect of the news.—Hopes and plans of the Americans.—Mr. Rodgers.—Lanciego.—I confine myself to the house.—State of the city.—Message from Tharawudi.—Cure for cholera.—I am shunned by every one.—Summoned to the Byadyke.—Arrival of Mr. Laird.—I am accused of being a British spy.—Examinations.—I am committed to the custody of the Taing-dau, and remanded 124

CONTENTS.

CHAPTER XIII.

Changed prospects.—My guards accompany me home.—Our flight discovered.—I am taken back to prison at midnight.—Another examination lasts all night.—I am again committed to the Taing-dau, and consigned to the stocks.—Punishment of my keepers.—Corruptibility of the Taing-dau.—I am stripped and carried to the Death Prison.—Some account of that establishment.—Let-ma-yoon.—Terror of its name.—I am loaded with three pairs of fetters 136

CHAPTER XIV.

I find Mr. Laird in irons before me.—Mr. Rodgers taken.—Apprehension of the American missionary, Dr. Judson.—His ill-treatment.—Dr. Price arrested.—The "Red Rat" entrapped.—We are prohibited the use of the English language.—We are put on the bamboo.—Prison discipline.—Our first night.—How passed.—Starvation of prisoners.—Alms-giving in the prison.—I am taken from my companions.—Torture of a man accused of robbery.—Its result 150

CHAPTER XV.

I am examined about my property.—Hour of execution in the prison.—A Greek and an Armenian arrested.—Arrakeel's escape from Tharawadi.—Our second night in prison.—Dr. Judson examined about his property.—The "Rat" and Mirza released.—Mrs. Judson visits her husband in prison.—She gains us some comforts.—We are lodged in an outside shed.—Examinations by torture.—How practised.—Our growing apathy at beholding these scenes 163

CHAPTER XVI.

Some account of our prison party.—Dr. Judson.—Remarks on the Baptist mission to Burmah.—Missionary misrepresentations.—Some account of Dr. Price.—And of Mr. Rodgers.—His superstition.—Some account of Mr. Laird.—Constantine, the Greek.—Arrakeel, the Armenian 174

CHAPTER XVII.

We are shut up in the inner prison again.—Our property is seized.—Impure state of the inner prison.—How to change our dress.—We are released from the bamboo.—News from Rangoon.—Signal-guns.—Prison thoughts.—Thunba Woongee made General.—Prison disclosures.—Superstition.—Execution of a native for stepping over the King's image.—Strange treatment of a man who fancied he could fly.—Arrival of an Irish soldier.—His treatment.—News brought by him 185

CHAPTER XVIII.

We are transferred to the cells.—Description of them.—Plan of the prison.—Plague of rats.—Murder in the prison.—Its cause.—Frailty of a Menthamee.—How punished.—My house being burnt down, I am accused of arson.—Narrow escape.—Fortunate destruction of my journal.—Providential interferences.—Anecdote of escape from a tiger 196

CHAPTER XIX.

My utter destitution.—My servants abscond.—Fidelity of my Mahomedan baker.—Defeat and death of Thunba Woongee.—We are thrust into the inner prison again.—A prisoner brought in with smallpox.—We escape infection by tobacco.—Its universal use.—Prison recreations of Dr. Price.—I play chess with Dr. Judson.—Chess in the Palace.—Amusements of Mr. Rodgers and of Mr. Laird.—Laxity of prison regulations.—My dangerous illness.—Barbarity of the gaolers.—I recover unexpectedly . . . 208

CHAPTER XX.

Bundoola is recalled from Arracan to command the army.—Runaway soldiers.—Their superstitious reports.—Captured sepoys arrive and are imprisoned with us.—We escape suffocation.—I am chained to a leper.—Native officers starved to death.—Their want of endurance.—One man saved.—News of Mr. Richardson.—Accusations revived.—A gang breaks out of prison.—Oppressions in prison.—Father Ngalah's system.—Uncomfortable dispute between the missionaries.—A mother and daughters in irons 219

CHAPTER XXI.

Our fetters are increased to five pairs each.—Increased severities.—Orders given for our assassination.—Why not executed.—We are not allowed to be seen.—The Governor's communication to Mrs. Judson.—Bandoola's victory.—His defeat and death.—The King's Horse in prison.—Advance of the British army.—The crowing hen.—Superstitions.—Nostrum to ensure longevity.—Prison museum.—Pacahm-woon in irons.—He is appointed Generalissimo.—His hatred of the English.—Mr. Lanciego arrested and put to the torture.—Our wretched condition . . 230

CHAPTER XXII.

We are removed from the Let-ma-yoon, and taken to Oung-ben-lai.—Our sufferings on the journey.—My terror.—Dr. Judson.—His intense suffering.—Murder of the Greek.—The ringed men leave us.—Night at Amerapoorah.—We are carted to Oung-ben-lai.—We are in fear of being burned.—The prison described.—We are put in the stocks.—Contrivance for hoisting them.—Musquitos.—We are chained in couples.—My baker's fidelity.—Mrs. Judson follows her husband.—The Governor's warning to her 242

CHAPTER XXIII.

Some comforts at Oung-ben-lai.—Our anxious position.—Ignatius Brito, a Roman Catholic priest, is arrested and imprisoned, and goes mad.—A lioness in prison with us.—Our conjectures and terror.—The lioness starved to death.—Object of the Pacahm-woon.—Insalubrity of Oung-ben-lai.—Mrs. Judson takes small-pox.—Judson takes fever.—He inhabits the lion's den.—Plague of snakes.—We kill great numbers of the cobra capello.—Nandau snakes.—My marvellous escape from a cobra . . 254

CHAPTER XXIV.

British army goes into quarters at Prome.—The Talain race join and assist it.—Preparations of Pacahm-woon.—His intention to bury us alive in Oung-ben-lai.—He is suspected of treason, and put to death.—Causes of his fall.—Doubt about the plot.—We escape by his death.—Summoned to Amerapoorah.—Translation of letters.—Offer to negotiate for peace.—Negotiations.—Judson taken from prison.—Bad faith.—Melloon stormed.—Judson protected by a Chief.—Ava put in a state of defence.—The Burmese are routed at Pagan.—Dr. Sandford deputed to the British General.—Returns to prison.—Burmese incredulity.—Dr. Price is released and employed 265

CHAPTER XXV.

The British army advances.—Rumours.—The King prepares for flight.—Kindness of Dr. Sandford.—I am supplied with arrack.—Doubtful policy of the Court.—I make preparations to escape.—Koh-bai gained over.—Major Jackson.—His munificent present.—Another strange cage of prisoners.—Liberated on the 16th February, and carried to Ava.—Interview with the Myo-woon.—I embark on a war-boat and start for our camp.—Passage down the river.—Stopped by the Kaulen-mengee.—Remains of the Burmese army.—Its dejected state.—Interview with Burmese General.—I am allowed to proceed 277

CHAPTER XXVI.

Arrive at the British camp.—My joy at regaining my liberty.—Alarm of my crew at the steamer.—I am kindly received by Major Armstrong.—I report myself to Sir A. Campbell.—His hospitality.—The army advances to Yandabo.—Timidity of the Indian Government.—Their anxiety for peace.—Translation of the Treaty.—I save the Government £70,000.—The Commissioners refuse to admit my claims.—Treaty of Peace.—I leave Yandabo with Sir A. Campbell 289

CHAPTER XXVII.

Voyage from Yandabo to Rangoon.—A dispatch received by Sir A. Campbell to proclaim Pegu independent.—Too late to act on it.—Delightful voyage.—An unexpected adventure.—Capture of a war-boat.—I am appointed police magistrate for the Pegu district.—Its disturbed state.—Burmans and Peguers.—Instances of Burmese revenge on the revolted Peguers.—Massacre of a boat's crew.—Attack on a Talain village 301

CHAPTER XXVIII.

Famine in Pegu.—Depredations of tigers.—One shot in the town of Rangoon.—Payment of the money under Treaty.—Mr. Crawfurd appointed Envoy to Ava.—Dr. Judson accompanies him.—Death of Mrs. Judson.—The Burmese secretly collect arms in Rangoon.—Their seizure.—Crowded state of my gaols.—Woongee arrives in Rangoon.—Sir A. Campbell honours him with a State dinner.—Some account of it.—How the Woondouk enjoys it.—Other amusements at table.—Embarkation of the troops.—Evacuation of Rangoon.—I proceed to Amherst.—Some notice of it.—I go in search of teak forests.—Depopulation of the country.—Interesting sight of a herd of wild cows.—Conclusion . . 313

LIST OF ILLUSTRATIONS.

ROYAL PALACE AT AVA	*Frontispiece.*
WAR BOAT	*Title-page.*
A BURMAN OF RANK	To face page 31
EXTERIOR OF PRISON, AVA	,, 144
INTERIOR OF PRISON	,, 154
A BURMESE GIRL	,, 198

NARRATIVE

OF A

TWO YEARS' IMPRISONMENT

IN BURMAH.

CHAPTER I.

The object and origin of my expedition.—I embark in the Alfred *for Rangoon.—Escape from wreck on the Preparis rocks.—Arrive at Rangoon.—Official "Visit" on board the* Alfred.—*Mr. Lanciego, the Akoupwoon.—Duties levied in kind.—My investment attracts attention.—I engage an interpreter.—Pagoda lake.—First impressions of the Burmese.—Preparations for pursuing my voyage.—Visits to the Viceroy.—I secure his protection.—Boats' crews.—Their honesty.—Food.—Ngapwee.—Departure for Amerapoorah.—Favourable prospects.*

The year 1822 found me residing in the district of Bauleah in Bengal, where, for two or three years, I had been following the hazardous occupation of producing raw silk in competition with the commercial Resident of the East India Company. I say *hazardous*, because the arbitrary power which that Government possessed was intrusted to its servants, who used it in the most unscrupulous manner to crush the spirit of private adventure, and to retain in their hands the virtual monopoly of a branch of industry which by an act of the British legislature, in 1813, had been declared open to all its subjects, under certain restrictions.*

* The days of monopoly are now happily at an end, but it may not be uninteresting to look back to those times, and to rejoice in the change. The East India Company competed with the private trader in the production of raw silk. They had their commercial Residents established in different parts of the silk districts, whose emoluments mainly depended on the quantity of silk they secured for the Company, who permitted these agents (or *residents* as they were termed) to charge them a certain commission on its value.

The system pursued by both parties was this :—Advances of money before each bund or crop, were made to two classes of persons—first, to the cultivators who reared the cacoons; next, to the large class of winders who formed the mass of the population of the surrounding villages. By the first, the raw material was secured; by the last the labour for working it. These advances were regarded as legal earnest money, or as pledges by the receivers to confine their dealings to the party disbursing it.

The larger the quantity of silk the resident provided for his masters the greater was his remuneration,—a state of things which naturally created a jealousy between the functionary and the private trader, as their interests clashed. But there was no equality in the competition, the one being armed with arbitrary power, the other, not. I will state a case of every-day occurrence.

A native wishing to sell me the cocoons he produces for the season takes my advance of money; a village of winders does the same. After this contract is made, two of the Resident's servants are despatched to the village, the one bearing a bag of rupees, the other a book, in which to register the names of the recipients. In vain does the man to whom the money is offered protest that he has entered into a prior engagement with me. If he refuses to accept it, a rupee is *thrown into his house*, his name is written down before the witness who carries the bag, and that is enough. Under this iniquitous proceeding the Resident, by the authority committed to him, forcibly seizes *my* property and *my* labourers even at my own door.

Nor does the oppression stop here. If I sued the man in Court for repayment of the money I had thus been defrauded of, the judge was compelled, before granting a decree in my favour, to ascertain from the commercial Resident whether the defaulter was in debt to the East India Company. If he was, a prior decree was given to the Resident, and I lost my money.

In the year above named I was attacked by an obstinate complaint which baffled medical skill, and was advised, as a last resource, to try a change of climate as affording the only means of recovery. This advice I was the more disposed to follow, as the expiring efforts of the East India Company to retain its ascendancy in the silk districts seemed likely to bring about my ejection at no distant time, with great damage to my fortune. I therefore arranged my affairs as quickly as possible, and went down to Calcutta, quite undetermined in what part of the world to seek the restoration of the health I had lost.

While in this state of uncertainty, an intimate and dear friend,* now no more, first suggested to me the idea of a voyage to Rangoon, the chief seaport of the Burmese dominions, and thence by the river Irrawuddi to Amerapoorah, then the capital of the Empire.

At that period the Burmese Empire might truly be styled *terra incognita*, for, with the exception of three or four traders at Rangoon, who had rarely penetrated beyond a few miles from the town, this vast country was destitute of European inhabitants, and its capacities for commerce almost totally unknown. The published narratives of two missions,† from the Bengal Government to the Court of Ava, contained all the information

---

˙ Another weapon in the hand of the Resident was the settlement of prices to be paid to the cultivators at the close of each season, the East India Company's price regulating that of the private trader. The higher the price, the greater his commission,—the money was not his own, and his masters had a long purse. Under a system like this my willingness to escape ruin cannot be wondered at. Yet this was called in those days *free trade*.

* The late John M'Kenzie, Esq., of Calcutta.

† That of Colonel Michael Symes, Envoy in 1795, and of Captain Hiram Cox in the year following.

we could collect. These I read with the deepest interest, but I cannot say there was much in them to encourage the undertaking, for they both, especially the later one by Captain Cox, were records of a tissue of ignorance, insult, and caprice, such as would render commercial dealings on a liberal scale utterly impracticable. On the other hand, although haughty and jealous to the representative of a foreign power, I might find them quite the reverse when it was discovered that my objects were purely mercantile. Many abortive attempts to form trading establishments among the Burmese had been made during the last century, not only by the English East India Company, but also by the French and other western nations. In every instance they appear to have failed through the treacherous conduct of the Government, and long before the East India Company had ceased to be a trading corporation, all further efforts in this direction were abandoned by them. Even private individual enterprise, which, especially in commercial affairs, often succeeds in effecting what a Government or powerful Corporation would attempt in vain, had apparently been frightened from the field, for I could not learn that a single person deserving the name of a merchant had ever the hardihood to embark capital to any extent in dealings with a nation whose security was so questionable.

My friend, an intelligent merchant, in whose judgment I placed great reliance, said he had reason to believe that a highly lucrative commerce might be established with Amerapoorah and the regions beyond, especially in the introduction of British cotton manufactures, which were at this time beginning to supplant the native fabrics in most of the markets of the East. To ascertain the wants of the population in this particular, and to acquire a knowledge of the various products of the country suitable for export, were the main objects of the proposed expedition, while at the same time an equally important question might be set at rest, whether, under such an arbitrary government, life and property would be sufficiently secure to justify the attempt. My choice lay between accepting this proposal, and undertaking a dull routine voyage with no other object than the fulfilment of the doctor's injunction, and the reader will have little difficulty in deciding which of the two offered the strongest attractions, when I add that, at this time, I was barely twenty-three years of age. The love of novelty and adventure quickly settled the question in my mind, and I at once entered enthusiastically into the views of my friend, who, on his part, manifested his confidence in the success of the scheme by engaging to supply me amply with the means necessary to carry it out.

I soon found a ship sailing for Rangoon, the *Alfred*, Captain Dolge, and in her I embarked at the end of June, 1822, having supplied myself with a few suitable presents for the King and his Court, which, it appeared from the books before alluded to, would be almost indispensable to my success. My friend, Mr. Mackenzie, also expended a few thousand pounds in furnishing me with such sorts of British goods as he thought best adapted to the purpose of testing the wants of the people. Meanwhile, my health continued so precarious that it was deemed prudent to associate with me a gentleman,* whose services happily were not long needed.

* The late Mr. A. Tainsh, who remained at Rangoon, and subsequently had the good fortune to escape with his life when the town was captured by our troops.

He proceeded with me no further than the port of Rangoon, where I left him.

The weather, from the time the pilot took his leave, was a constant succession of squalls and rain, for which, at this season of the year, the Bay of Bengal is noted. While this lasted we kept our course by dead reckoning, for the clouds were so dense and the rain so continuous, that we had nearly traversed the bay before we obtained a sight of the heavenly bodies. As he neared the land, Captain Dolge became rather anxious. One afternoon, at three bells, as we were seated at dinner, the rain pouring down in such a deluge that nothing was visible fifty yards from the ship, it suddenly ceased,—the weather, for the moment, became clear, when the terrible shout, "Breakers ahead!" quickly brought us from the table to the deck. We now discovered that the breakers were not only ahead, but also on either bow, forming the shape of a horse-shoe, into the hollow of which the ship was fast ploughing her way. Had the rain lasted ten minutes longer, every soul on board must have perished. As the wind fortunately was free, we had still time to clear the outermost reef, but near enough—to use a nautical phrase, rather hyperbolical—to pitch a biscuit on it. Once out of danger, our captain found the occurrence most useful, as it gave him a correct knowledge of our position, and told him we were on the Preparis shoal, well known to mariners, and much dreaded by them. Two or three days more brought us abreast of the town of Rangoon, where we anchored about the middle of July.

Rangoon has, no doubt, undergone great improvement since it became a dependency of the British Crown, but at that time it was a miserable, dirty town, containing

8000 or 10,000 inhabitants, the houses being built of bamboo and teak planks with thatched roofs,—almost without drainage, and intersected by muddy creeks, through which the tide flowed at high water. It had altogether a mean, uninviting appearance, but it was the seat of government of an extensive Province, ruled over by a Viceroy, a Woongee of the Empire, in high favour at the Court.

On the day after her anchoring, the *Alfred* was to receive what was technically called the "Visit," previous to which, according to custom, she was not permitted to commence the discharge of her cargo. This official visit was conducted by the Akoupwoon, or Collector of the Customs, the only office under the Crown held by a European. At this time it was filled by Mr. Lanciego, a Spaniard by birth, who had resided many years in Burmah, which he had made the country of his adoption by marrying a lady of the Court, the sister of a favourite Queen. As this gentleman will be frequently mentioned, I may here remark that he was a man of liberal education, having been brought up in his own country to the medical profession. He was about fifty years old, of a somewhat irascible, but generous temper. The changes and chances of the French revolution threw him on this coast, where it was said he was wrecked while privateering against British commerce. Although no lover of my nation, he once generously interfered at a critical moment to save my life, as will appear hereafter in these pages.

In the train of the Akoupwoon came a rabble of twenty or thirty native followers, who were allowed to range over the ship at their pleasure, and to devour whatever provision they might find, while their Chief was occupied with a more civilized repast prepared for him in the great cabin. A Burman is not very particular in his food—he will eat almost anything. Mr. Lanciego told me that on one of these visits his followers observed him eating some cheese, and in prowling about the ship they presently came upon what they took to be a similar delicacy, but which to their grief turned out to be a bar of yellow soap. They did not discover their mistake, nor discontinue their attacks upon it, until their mouths were foaming with the lather, and in utter astonishment at their master's predilection for such nastiness. The visit was ostensibly to examine the ship's papers and manifest, but in reality it was a mere pretext for the extraction of a present.

In order to place the ship entirely at the mercy of the authorities, Captain Dolge was required to unship and to send on shore the vessel's rudder; but this degrading demand he was allowed to evade by giving a bribe to the Akoupwoon.

When these ceremonies had been gone through, the ship was permitted to send her cargo on shore to a large brick building, where the Royal duties were taken in kind. They consisted of one tenth part of every article imported which was capable of division, and the heterogeneous mass of stuff of all kinds collected by this barbarous process, fit only to stock a marine store, was annually escorted to the capital by the Akoupwoon, there to be presented to his Majesty. Even pieces of cloth were torn asunder when the number of them was insufficient to permit a tenth piece to be taken, giving to the customhouse, for the time, the appearance of a large haberdasher's shop. After my goods had thus passed through the King's warehouse, excised of one-tenth, I was allowed to remove them to my temporary residence until I had provided boats to convey me up the river. It was ominous of good to observe that while they were thus exposed to public view in the King's warehouse they excited the eager curiosity of a crowd of native dealers, who flocked to see them, and who urged me to sell them all at once, offering enormous profits as an inducement; but, as this would have defeated my main object of making it a voyage of discovery, I declined every offer, much to their chagrin.

My first business on shore was to engage an interpreter, who, at the same time, was able to assist me in matters of business. He was a native of the Malabar coast, who had passed all his life in Burmah, and had adopted, as usual, a Burmese name, Shwai-ee. He could not speak English, but communicated with me through the Hindostanee language, the common field of intercourse between Europeans and the various races of India.

As there was no particular cause for my immediate departure, and as my health was rapidly improving, I determined to remain at Rangoon for a month, picking up what information I could gain to smooth my way on the voyage which was before me. Each morning before sunrise, when the weather permitted—for the rain falls in torrents during the south-western monsoon—I rode out to a secluded little lake, two or three miles from the town, beyond the celebrated Shwai-tukoon pagoda, where, tying my pony to a tree, I enjoyed a delicious bath, the tall gilded dome and spires of the temple towering above me. This lake was well concealed from public view by magnificent trees and brushwood, and, strange to say, was so little frequented that I was rarely disturbed by an intruder. How was I grieved, when I repeated my visit after the war, to see its dilapidated banks; its luxuriant trees cut down, and its clear sparkling waters converted into a filthy slimy pool! It seemed to have been made the common washing-pot for the whole British army.

I soon found that I had left behind me all the comforts and luxuries which Europeans enjoy in British India; the large, richly-furnished houses, the handsome equipage, the luxurious, well-served table, the convivial party, the comfortable palanquin, the phalanx of appropriate servants, the civilized society,—even my umbrella to shield me from the sun and rain, I was obliged to carry myself, for in this country the long umbrella carried by a servant, figures as an important article among the insignia of rank. Money could not purchase any of these luxuries. Such a state of things might well appal an *old Indian*, and one item perhaps beyond all others, the free-and-easy bearing of the natives, contrasting so harshly with the obsequious cringing and the polished insincerity to which he had been accustomed in Hindostan. Here, there was no aristocracy of colour, or rather none that is not involuntarily accorded to the higher civilization of the white races. The conditions of society were reversed; the dominant race was the native, whose Nobles and Governors exacted the same tokens of respect and submission from the European, who casually dwelt among them, as they did from their own subjects. I confess, at first, it seemed strange to me to ascend with unshod feet the house of some magnate of the land, and there, in his presence, to twist myself into a constrained contortion of body, half sitting, half kneeling, while the great man before me was enjoying his ease on some cushion of honour. But I soon got accustomed to these little disquietudes, and descended into the rank of the homage-paying class with less of the feeling of wounded pride than I had thought possible.

To make amends for this there was the never-failing compensation of living among the common people on terms, in some respects, approaching to equality. Even between me and my Burman servants there was as much of liberty and equality as would have satisfied the pride of an American "help," without degenerating into disobedience or insolence. The exemption of these people from the prejudices of caste, the freedom allowed to their women, who are never secluded, even among the highest class,—their good-nature and rude hospitality, their inquisitive characters, and the total absence of anything like servility or flattery—all tend to create a favourable impression on any stranger whose mind has not been vitiated by the obsequious manners of the natives of British India.

I am now speaking of their manner and bearing towards each other and to foreigners, who, like myself, had no official rank to maintain. On the other hand, it must not be supposed that this freedom extends to their intercourse with the governing classes, towards whom there is certainly no lack of servility. Submission, even to obsequiousness, is inflexibly demanded by the one, and yielded by the other from motives of fear. The possession of power is ruin to the Burmese character; so much so, that the governors and the governed seem to possess almost different natures. It is rare to find a man in authority who is not oppressive, corrupt, crafty, and cruel. A plebeian advanced to power leaps from one nature to the other at a bound, and exercises the pride and tyranny of office with as much apparent ease as if it had been his birthright.

My excursions into the country were bounded by the thick jungles which covered it at a short distance from the town, leaving few roads practicable even for horse exercise. For the same reason there was little amusement for the sportsman. The fallow deer abounded in the plains of Pegu, but were difficult to get at. The Burmese having no love of sport kill them by decoy for the profit of selling them in the market of Rangoon, which at some seasons is pretty well supplied with venison. Wild fowl and snipe were abundant, but they could not be followed while the monsoon rains kept the country under water. I saw also a few of the jungle fowl. My promenades, therefore, resembled those of a horse in a mill; every accessible part of the country was soon known to me. In one of my walks I came unexpectedly upon the bodies of two men who had just been executed for robbery. They were lying on the roadside with their backs upward, their decapitated heads being reversed and fastened to the ground by wooden pins driven through their mouths. No one was on the spot, nor did the circumstance seem to cause any sensation in the town.

The work of fitting out boats, and engaging crews for a voyage to Ava, was a very dilatory affair. It was not the custom to let out boats on hire; it became necessary, therefore, to purchase them. After a long and fatiguing search along the banks of the river and the muddy creeks, two sound strong canoes were found, and while these were being fitted out with masts, sails, oars, &c., I made several visits to the Viceroy of the province.

He was a tall, gaunt old man, of dignified bearing, who wasted very few words on his visitors, but had a kinder disposition than his solemn features at first led me to expect. He had an ugly habit, unknown to me when I made my first visit, of using a long spear as a walking-stick. I was seated with my interpreter on the floor of a long gloomy apartment in his palace when this stately old Governor entered from a door at the extreme end of the hall, stalking towards me with the aid of the formidable spear, the point of which glittered above his head. He had to walk a long distance before he reached the spot where I sat, which he traversed slowly and silently as a ghost, never stopping until he stood over me in most uncomfortable proximity. I thought the old man was mad, and did not at all like my situation, but he soon broke silence, and before we parted he became quite affable. Meeadai Mengee, for such was his title, had done good service to His Majesty, when, at his accession, the Throne had been contested by his two uncles,* securing immense influence at the Court thereby. When I unfolded my plans, and stated my desire to proceed to Amerapoorah to settle there under the protection of the Golden Feet, he encouraged the idea, and promised to address the *Hlut-dau* (the chief Council of State, of which he was a member), to secure me a good reception; warned me of the dangers of the river, and offered me his special passport, which he said would protect me on my voyage if I got into any difficulty or needed assistance. He was as good as his word, and the document proved to be of great value in extricating me from exactions and delays and suspicions in various parts of the river. I considered myself fortunate in gaining the goodwill and countenance of this powerful minister.

Early in August, my two boats, "well fitted, victualled, and manned," were ready for service. The decks were thatched with cadjan leaves, well laced together by a

---

* The Princes of Prome and Toungoo, who were reported to have been put to death in a manner too revolting to describe.

strong netting of split bamboos. At the stern of one of them a comfortable cabin was built for my accommodation of the same materials, quite impervious to the weather. The crews consisted of sixteen stout boatmen and a *hle-thegee*, or helmsman, to each boat, making thirty-four in all, besides my interpreter and four Hindostanee servants. Most of the men were armed with spears, or swords, and as I was well provided with firearms for my own use, we mustered altogether a formidable force. The men were engaged for the voyage up to Amerapoorah, where they were to be discharged, at the rate of fourteen ticals of flowered silver each man, equal to about thirty-five shillings; the pay of the steersman, who had likewise the authority of captain, being double. To their credit be it said, that although nearly all this money was paid to them in advance before the boats left their moorings, there was not a single instance of desertion throughout the voyage, an example of good faith for which I was little prepared. The commissariat also was supplied at my cost, but the Burmese, as before observed, not being a dainty race, the expense was trifling, and they were easily satisfied. Their rations consisted merely of rice and *ngapwee*, a kind of preserved fish, used rather plentifully as a condiment. Although the rank scent of this delicacy is certainly not agreeable to the fastidious European at first, yet in the course of time, after this prejudice has been overcome, many use it with great relish; and, at the risk of being laughed at, I am not ashamed to confess that after the lapse of thirty-eight years since I first made its acquaintance, I do, up to the present time, enjoy it as a luxury when my friends are kind enough to supply me with it, as they sometimes do. If a man be content to live under the tyranny of his nose, he may for ever lose the enjoyment of some of the most *recherché* fruits of the East.

I had grown tired of the monotony of Rangoon, and it was with pleasure I saw my boats loosed from the shore at noon-day, the crews joining in a loud and cheerful song, keeping time as cleverly with the stroke of their oars as if they had been long practising rehearsals.

The short stay I made at Rangoon tended to encourage me in the mission I had undertaken. The general and eager demand for manufactures of the descriptions I had brought, very few of which had yet found their way into the country, clearly proved that my far-sighted friend had neither miscalculated the extent to which this trade might be carried on, nor been much mistaken in the character of the goods he had selected. The friendly reception accorded to me,—the absence of all unauthorized exactions,—the good-will of the Viceroy, and his ready and cordial assent to my proposal to settle at Amerapoorah, were all encouraging signs, and gave promise of security in my operations. It is true the lazy, desolate appearance of their chief seaport was disappointing, as almost the only export trade which could be discovered there was in the article of teak timber, which strewed the banks of the river in innumerable rafts. The value of this trade, however, was insignificant in amount, and the poverty of the place indicated no small difficulty in finding adequate means of exchange for extended commerce with foreign countries. Still, on the whole, I had reason to be satisfied with this first stage in my work, and I set forward on my voyage with ardour and in high spirits.

CHAPTER II.

Delta of the Irrawaddi.—Musquitos and jungle.—The great river.—Voyage up the river.—Fleets of native boats.—Inland trade in rice.—Safety of the river.—Hilly country.—Picturesque sail beyond Prome.—Monasteries and monks.—Their habits.—Education general among the people.—I acquire the language.—Arrival at Amerapoorah.—Tolls and transit dues abolished.—Safety of the river.

EVERY one who has been to sea knows the discomfort of a ship at the beginning of a long voyage until she has sent away her pilot, ceased her communication with the shore, stowed away her tackle, and finds herself at last in blue water. Even so, to a certain extent, it was with my boats,—every one of my crew had forgotten something, or had something else to do, or had some friend to see; so, to accommodate all parties and begin the voyage in good humour, I proceeded only a short distance up the river with the flood-tide, and spent the remainder of the day at a village a few miles above Rangoon, called Kemindine. Having shaken ourselves into our places, and found a hole or corner for the stowage of every one's baggage, we commenced our voyage in earnest on the following morning.

And here, before my boats start from the shore, I must remind the reader that he has to expect nothing more than a personal narrative of events which happened to me as a pioneer attempting to open a commerce with the interior of the country. Had this book been written at the time those events occurred, it would, no doubt, have been far more interesting, as possessing the charm of novelty. It would then have been unpardonable to have neglected the various topics of information usually given by travellers passing through a country but little known. Some notices of the history, government, productions, employments, and habits of the people might have been expected; but the two wars which followed, and the published accounts of the missions * they gave rise to, have so opened the heart of the country to those who read for information, that were I now to advert to them on all occasions these pages would be merely a repetition of the observations and researches of men far more capable than I am of doing them justice. I shall therefore make no further allusion to such subjects than may serve to illustrate my story or to render it intelligible, and I mention this to avoid the reproach of passing through a country with my eyes closed, as it were, to all the objects of interest it presented.

For two days after leaving Kemindine we threaded the windings of this, one of the chief channels of the delta of the Irrawuddi. The country seemed hopelessly abandoned to a state of nature, bringing to the imagination the accounts we read of the feverish swamps of the Mississippi, or of parts of the West Coast of Africa. Either bank was covered to the water's edge with thick reed and bush jungle, the resort of wild animals, the recess of the tide leaving exposed numerous banks of slimy mud. Of course, such a wilderness was almost destitute of inhabitants, though here and there a few wretched huts were

* The mission of Mr. Crawfurd, Envoy to the Court of Ava in 1826, and of Major Phayre in 1857, narrated by Major Yule.

seen peeping through the jungle, which threatened to entwine them as part of itself. At one of these miserable hamlets on the verge of the mud, and in a dank, steamy atmosphere, we prepared to pass the first night, but directly the sun was down my boatmen were attacked with swarms of musquitos, so venomous that, finding sleep out of the question, they again got the boats under way, preferring to pull throughout the night to the alternative of being eaten up by insects. Walking on shore, I found the interior of all the huts and cattle-sheds filled with the smoke of smouldering cow-dung, the only mode of rendering existence possible.

My boatmen told me that not long since a criminal was put to death by being exposed, during a night, to the attacks of these insects. It is unaccountable that human beings should make choice of such a desolate habitation, when healthy plains are not far from them.

On the third day we emerged from these dense, unwholesome jungles, which the breath of heaven could scarcely penetrate, and opened the broad expanse of the noble Irrawuddi with the feelings of those who are exchanging a noisome dungeon for the pure air of freedom. The boatmen had now little use for the oars at which they had hitherto been labouring, but, unfurling their sails to the strong south-westerly winds, stemmed the rapid current of the river, now swollen by the waters of its tributaries to its extremest bounds. When the wind failed us, which was not often the case, my powerful crews took to the rope rather than the oars, tracking the boat at a slow walking pace wherever the banks were practicable. Each night, when a town or village was within reach, we sought its protection, and when no such friendly shelter could be found, we selected some open spot, clear of cover or jungle, to prevent surprise and set our watch for the night. A long line of laden boats fringed the bank of every town at night, as the inhabitants were held responsible by law for their safety from gang robbery while made fast to the shore under their protection. In any suspicious neighbourhood I took the middle watch myself, and whether it was from the knowledge of my being well armed (for I always discharged my fire-arms in the evening by way of advertisement), or whether the river was at the time unusually quiet, we pursued our voyage to the end in perfect safety. At several places, it is true, attempts were made by the local authorities to detain me by rumours of gangs of pirates, at others to attempt to enforce illegal exactions on many frivolous pretences; but in all cases a judicious use of the Viceroy's passport, and representing that my boats contained presents for the King, relieved me from such molestations.

Our progress now became as cheerful as it had hitherto been dreary and monotonous. Large fleets of boats under full sail, laden with rice and *ngapwee* for the supply of the capital and the upper provinces, enlivened the scene, increasing in numbers as we proceeded. Some of these boats were of considerable tonnage, capable of carrying from 100 to 200 tons of cargo. Their sails were of immense spread, but of clumsy construction, and would not draw unless the wind was free. They lost much time, therefore, in waiting for a fair wind, or in tracking up the unfavourable reaches of the river, rendering it impossible to compass more than one voyage to Ava in the season. The lands enclosed in the delta of the great river, and the fertile plains which are inundated or partake of the heavy periodical rains, are not only the most productive in the kingdom, but yield a quality of grain superior to that grown in the higher districts, and the enhanced price it commands in the capital amply repays the expense of its transit. Often I could count more than 100 of these boats in view at the same time. With some of them we amused ourselves by challenging to an animated race, and were frequently beaten from the immense width of canvas they carried. The ardour of my men when they entered into these races could not be restrained,—the boats, having no keel, were not fitted to bear an unusual press of sail, and more than once their rashness brought us to the verge of destruction.

In a few days we came in sight of the distant hills of the Arracan range on the right bank, some of their spurs extending to the river, and affording a cheering sight to one who for some years past had not seen a rising ground higher than an ant-hill. Long before I got to Prome—looked upon usually as the half-way town between Rangoon and Ava—and for many days after leaving it, I found myself sailing among picturesque well-wooded hills, rising abruptly from the river on each bank. I have ever looked back with great delight on this part of my voyage. The view was enlivened by numerous towns and villages, most of them adorned with monasteries and pagodas, the pretty white spires of the latter rising in the distance among the rich foliage, and recalling to my imagination the village churches of my own happy country.

In choosing my evening walks I was seldom mistaken or disappointed when I took the path which led from the village to the neighbouring monastery. These ecclesiastics had almost invariably displayed good taste in appropriating the prettiest locality for their residence, in which particular I believe the monks of the Buddhist persuasion are by no means singular. Although the life led by these priests is on the whole an idle one, yet it is impossible not to be struck with the value of the order in one most important particular—the very general diffusion of education through their instrumentality among the common people. By *education* I mean simply the art of reading and writing their own language. At a very early hour in the morning the convent is alive, when a division of the brethren sally forth as mendicants to collect from the neighbouring community their voluntary gift of provisions for the day's consumption. These offerings are in all cases ready-cooked for use. I was much amused at watching the morning perambulations of these mendicant friars as they passed through the villages. Covered by a long yellow robe, his crown shaven and exposed to the weather, he pursued his walk in solemn silence, looking neither to the right hand nor the left, and carrying before him a large lacquered tray, into which those who were religiously or charitably disposed placed their contributions. When, as was usually the case, the contributor happened to be one of the fair sex, far from acknowledging the gift, he averted his face in a most ungallant manner, as though the glance of a female carried with it a contaminating influence. How far this public parade of chastity is borne out in private life one may be inclined to doubt, though, to do them justice, common report gave them a better character in this respect than it does to the monks of other religious orders nearer home. This system of removing temptation rather than overcoming it, appears to be carried out by this religious order as a general principle. They are forbidden to possess or even to touch the precious metals, as a guard against avarice—to taste anything stronger than water, to avoid intoxication; enjoined to shave the head, as proof against personal vanity—to have no *cuisine*, to prevent luxury—all which, no doubt, may prevent positive crime, but, even if effectual, are practicable only by an idle priesthood.

While a part of the brethren are thus employed in providing for the daily sustenance of the community, the Convent they have left resounds with a loud clatter commonly made by beating the boarded floor with small wooden mallets. This is the call of the village children to their lessons, which are imparted gratuitously to as many as are sent by their parents to take advantage of them. Thus, as this simple education costs nothing beyond the time it occupies, vast numbers avail themselves of it, and my impression was, that a larger proportion of the common people could read and write in Burmah than could be found among similar classes in our own country.

Having much leisure time during this six weeks' voyage, I now set myself with great industry to acquire the language. My fat, indolent Malabaree proved but a very indifferent instructor, but I was fortunate enough to possess a little vocabulary, prefaced by some useful hints on the construction of the language, printed at the Serampore press, by Dr. Judson, and this I found to be a great assistance. I soon mastered the written character. As the language is essentially monosyllabic, there is hardly a combination of two or three letters which has not its appropriate signification, and it was my daily amusement to put together a number of these at a venture, and then ferret out their meaning from my interpreter. Words gained by this process became indelibly fixed on the memory, and it surprised me to see how soon

I became possessed of a large stock of them. My ear, too, was rarely greeted by any other sounds than those of the Burmese, an advantage in acquiring this language beyond most others, as it possesses a peculiarity of emphasis and intonation and a nice precision of sounds most difficult to attain by any one living among Europeans, and taking up the language as a mere study. I have heard even Dr. Judson, whose grammatical knowledge of it was perfect, but whose ear was not good, lament that he had never been able to conquer this difficulty, and that he never expected to do so. For want of this peculiarity of emphasis, or intoning, his addresses to the natives lost much of their power. By the time I reached Amerapoorah I had the gratification to find that I could express myself on common topics with some degree of fluency and correctness.

I gave myself no holiday, so to speak, on this voyage. I had a great desire to visit various places on the river where objects of interest were to be seen, especially the celebrated earth oil wells at Yainangyoung, and to wander among the ruins of the ancient temples of the city of Pagan; but I denied myself all such excursions of pleasure, as they would have carried me away to a distance from my boats, which I thought it prudent constantly to protect by my presence. I believe I might have done so, however, with perfect safety.

It was late in September when the tall spire of the Royal palace at Amerapoorah came into view, the voyage having been accomplished in about six weeks, the ordinary time for boats laden like mine at this season of the year.

Another doubtful point, of no small importance to the success of my project of settling at Amerapoorah, was now satisfactorily set at rest. From this first experiment I had good reason to believe that with ordinary precautions my boats would be able to make the voyage to and from Rangoon without much danger. Nor, so far as I could discover, were there any annoying exactions or tolls to impede them on their passage. Some years back transit dues had been levied on the native inland commerce at various stations on the river, but these, and the far greater exactions they gave colour to by the rapacious local authorities, so interfered with the supply of the necessaries of life at the Capital, that it was found necessary to abolish them altogether to avoid starvation. The entire passage of this noble river from Rangoon to Amerapoorah might now be said to be free from any hindrance or molestation whatever.

CHAPTER III.

The King removes from Amerapoorah to Ava.—The population in a state of transition. — Amerapoorah.—No exactions on landing.—I take a house.—Gain easy access to His Majesty.—Abandon the use of shoes.—The King's temporary Palace.—Apparition of an Englishman.—Mr. Rodgers.—I am introduced to the chief Queen.—Her character and influence.—Musical glasses.—The Queen's present.—Betel-chewing.—The King's practical joke.

THE epoch of my arrival at Amerapoorah was rather an unfortunate one; for the King, who had succeeded to the Throne of his grandfather only three years, with the usual caprice of Burmese monarchs, had determined to abandon his stately Palace, and to build a new one on the site of the ancient city of Ava, five miles lower down the river. This city had met a similar fate in a former reign, and was, until the late order to restore it, a deserted heap of ruins. The removal of the palace means, in Burmah, the removal of the entire population of the Capital. The nobles did not care about it, as they were repaid for the little inconvenience it caused them, by filling their pockets from the corrupt distribution of the building sites of the new city, and the frequent litigation it gave rise to. To the people it was the source of ruinous loss and discomfort, to which none but an unfeeling despotism would have dared to subject them. It was melancholy to see them breaking up their old habitations, and seeking new ones at great cost and labour. This senseless custom of changing the Royal residence is by no means uncommon. I have since read, that when this present wayward King was a few years later deposed by his younger brother, a similar freak possessed the brain of the usurper, who, in his turn, gave up his brother's newly-built city and palace at Ava to the owls and the bats, for the whim of again restoring the seat of government to this now half-demolished town. Such is Despotism!

With the exception of a few of the principal streets where the houses boasted of tiled roofs, Amerapoorah was constructed entirely of teak wood, bamboos, and thatch. For a town built of such fragile materials, it must have presented a respectable appearance before the work of demolition commenced. The houses, according to the usual plan of their domestic architecture, were supported on strong poles of teak timber, the floor fronting the street being laid two or three feet from the ground, forming a kind of enclosed verandah, which served for the shops of the traders. At the back of this, a staircase or a short ladder leads to the dwelling-rooms, which, from their increased height of floor, leave an enclosed room below, used as a store, or for various purposes; but where this is not required, a free passage is left under the whole building. This plan of building is peculiarly well suited to a country liable, like Amerapoorah, to frequent shocks of Earthquake. One of these occurred while I was there, but, though it was rather a severe one, no damage was done; the houses merely rocked backwards and forwards without injury, and it seemed to cause very little alarm to the inhabitants. I have since read that a remarkably severe shock occurred in 1839, which converted many substantial pagodas into heaps of ruins, and caused great damage to the new Palace then building at Amerapoorah, though the severest shock could do little injury to houses such as I have described. The duration of this earthquake, or rather of this series of earthquakes, was most remarkable. A respectable witness of them says, after describing the terrific violence of the first shock, "For four or five days we had nothing but earthquakes, every fifteen or thirty minutes, and, *for six months after*, scarcely a day passed without one." He estimates that 300 or 400 persons were killed in the first shock.*

The main streets were wide and cheerful, dotted here and there with noble tamarind trees, affording an agreeable shade, though the natives hold it to be unhealthy to live under the shelter of these trees. The town was surrounded by a high brick wall with battlements, and a wide ditch; this was nearly half a mile from the river, which,—above an island that has formed in the stream opposite the town, appears to be a mile broad. A large proportion of the population lived between the wall and the river, and it was in this suburb, on the river side, that I hired a house.

The day after my arrival, my property and effects were carried up from the boats without having sustained any damage by weather, or loss by pilfering. No Royal or municipal dues were demanded; no troublesome official appeared to obstruct the course of business; my boats' crews were discharged quite satisfied with their treatment, and I found myself comfortably established in my new quarters, with less vexatious annoyance than I should have encountered in any town in Europe. All this was gratifying.

* Yule's Embassy, page 350.

The news that a white foreigner had arrived, with a prodigious amount of goods for sale, spread like wildfire through the town, and the state of chaos into which everything was thrown by the unhappy exodus did not prevent a crowd of traders from flocking around my interpreter, urging him at once to open his stores. Cheering as this symptom was, he thought a little delay would only tend to sharpen their appetite: besides, it was imperative that I should first bow before the Golden Feet, to present my offerings and solicit the Royal protection. I therefore sent Shwai-ee to inquire of one of the Attwenwoons, whether I might have that honour on the following day. He returned with a gracious answer.

After breakfast the next morning, I mounted one of their beautiful little ponies, and, accompanied by Shwai-ee, set forth on my Royal visit with alacrity, as to a holiday treat. I had first to go to the court of the Attwenwoons, called the *Bya-dyke*, dismount at the gate, and take off my shoes before I entered the building. And here I cannot help stopping a moment, to exclaim against the folly of my countrymen generally, in raising a senseless clamour against a custom so truly agreeable in a tropical climate. I found the comfort of it so great, that from that day forth I never wore our detestable foot-gear of stockings and boots so long as I remained in the country. The cool light sandal of the native, slipped on and off with facility, was quite a luxury after the foot became trained to the use of the strap that binds it to the sole. The entering a house barefooted, or walking abroad in sandals, carries with it an idea of degradation to the European, which is quite foreign to the mind of the Burman. They did not object to my retaining the stockings, nor the hat, but I did not wish either of them.

Our Envoys have always complained of vexatious delays before they could secure a reception at Court. Nothing of the kind was experienced by the foreigner who had no state dignity to uphold. As for myself, I found far less difficulty in gaining an audience of his Majesty than I should have had in getting an interview with our Secretary of State in Downing Street; a few questions were asked at the *Bya-dyke*, and in less than an hour I was in the presence of the King.

For some astrological reason, His Majesty had vacated his gorgeous Palace, and was inhabiting a temporary one near to it, constructed of bamboo and thatch. Of course no attempt had been made to decorate such a building. The apartments were large, and the Royal style of raising roof upon roof had been attended to, a huge bunch of straw crowning the whole, as the gilded *tee* or umbrella did the finished building; but it was so slightly put together that the floors creaked and bent uncomfortably under our weight as we walked over them.

My ideas of the Court of His Majesty of Burmah were derived from the descriptions of our former Envoys.[*] I

---

[*] "We had been seated little more than a quarter of an hour, when the folding-doors that concealed the seat opened with a loud noise, and discovered His Majesty ascending a flight of steps that led up to the Throne from the inner apartment. He advanced but slowly, and seemed not to possess a free use of his limbs, being obliged to support himself with his hands on the balustrade. I was informed that this appearance of weakness proceeded from the weight of the regal habiliments in which he was clad; and, if what we were told was true, that he carried on his dress fifteen viss, upwards of fifty pounds avoirdupois of gold, his difficulty of ascending was not surprising. On reaching the top, he stood for a minute as if to take breath, and then sat down on an embroidered cushion with his legs inverted. His crown was a high conical cap, richly studded with precious stones; his fingers were covered with rings, and in his dress he bore the appearance of a man cased in golden armour, whilst

left my house, expecting to gain a momentary glance at a personage dressed up like a heathen idol, before whom all people were bowing in profound adoration—whose glory was too great to permit him to unbend, and to whom I should not be suffered to address a word in person. My imagination was filled with the idea that I was merely to go through a needful ceremony which I might not be permitted to repeat, and it was with the sensation of one who had to witness a curious and splendid show rather than to secure any tangible and permanent advantage, that I appeared before the Palace gates. From what I had read, I could not disconnect the King's human nature from the pageantry and exclusiveness with which it pleased his Court to invest it.

Filled with these misconceptions, judge of my surprise, when, on entering a spacious apartment used as an Audience Hall, the floor creaking in a most uncourtly manner at each step, I beheld at the end of it a young man, about thirty years old, with a pleasant, good-humoured countenance, seated cross-legged on a gilded arm-chair of European make, manifesting no sign or symbol of state other than the chair he sat in, which rested on a stage very slightly raised from the floor. This was His Majesty! His costume did not vary from that of his courtiers, except that the silk cloth worn

a gilded, or probably a golden wing on each shoulder, did not add much lightness to his figure." After the presentation of presents, the Envoy adds,—" His Majesty remained only a few minutes longer, and during that time looked at us attentively, but did not honour us with any verbal notice, or speak at all, except to give the order before mentioned. When he rose to depart, he manifested the same signs of infirmity as on his entrance. After he had withdrawn, the folding-doors were closed, and the Court broke up."—*Embassy to the Kingdom of Ava*, by Lieut.-Colonel Symes, 1795.

A BURMAN OF RANK IN UNDRESS COSTUME.

Extracted from a group in 'Yule's Embassy.'

To face page 31

round the loins was a bright scarlet check, a colour confined to the use of the Royal family. This, and a light jacket tied with strings in front, made of white muslin, with a handkerchief of the same material twisted round the head to confine the hair, completed the costume of both the King and his people. There were probably forty or fifty persons assembled before him on the floor, in a posture half sitting, half kneeling, their bodies bent forward, their eyes fixed on the ground, and their hands clasped as in an attitude of respect, with some of whom His Majesty was apparently conversing on rather familiar terms.

The presents intended for His Majesty were borne in gilded trays by some of the attendants in the Royal household, and, being numerous, they formed rather an imposing procession. They consisted of a large, richly-cut crystal dish, selections from the best portions of my British manufactures, and twelve stands of capital muskets and bayonets, which were, no doubt, used against us with effect in the war which followed. These last attracted the greatest notice, and were examined with attention. These offerings were carried forward and placed in front of his Majesty for his inspection, while I followed, bending forward as I walked, and took my seat on the floor in a spot pointed out to me in advance of the assembled company, imitating, as well as I was able, the attitude of those whom I saw near me. My interpreter, Shwai-ee, was crouching behind me.

The disease of Court favour is very contagious. I caught it at once; though it cannot be denied there is a mixture of fear in the gratification one feels at being in favour with an uncontrolled Despot. I could not but reflect that the man sitting before me, cross-legged, on that arm-chair, was indeed an object to be feared, and by no means to be trifled with, though at the present moment clothed with smiles. How soon might this calm surface be lashed into fury by an unguarded word or an untoward circumstance! It is at such a time, when the lives of human beings are mere toys in his estimation, that the unbridled power of an irresponsible Despot shines forth in its true and hateful colours, and to such sudden changes and paroxysms this smiling Monarch was far from being a stranger. Well might those who sought his favour, crouch in his presence! At the present moment, however, kindness and good-humour were in the ascendant.

After some inquiries about my country, and the objects I had in view in coming to Ava, His Majesty addressed a few words to some one in the ranks behind me, which, to my no small astonishment, elicited an address to me in clear, good English accent—"Are you, sir, an Englishman?" Robinson Crusoe's surprise at the celebrated footprint in the uninhabited island could hardly have surpassed mine, for I thought myself 500 miles away from any of my own race. I turned my head to the quarter where the voice came from, and shall never forget the whimsical figure the speaker presented to my view. He was a large, strongly-built man, slightly bent by age, attired after the fashion of the natives, already described—a long, ample silk cloth round the waist, a loose muslin jacket, tied with strings in front, covered his body, but did not conceal the white skin beneath, barelegged of course, and his long grey hair twisted into a knot at the crown, where it was confined by a strip of white muslin. His long grey beard was so thinned, according to the native fashion, that that portion only which appertained to the middle part of the chin was preserved, and this being of a texture stiff as horsehair wagged backwards and forwards in a most ludicrous manner whenever he attempted to speak. He spoke Burmese fluently, and might well have passed for a native, had not his fair complexion, his light-blue eyes, and prominent nose, of such shape and colour as I have never seen except among my own respected countrymen, unmistakably attested his origin. He was addressed as "Yadza" (the nearest approach the Burmese language admits to " Rodgers "), and I now recollected that when in Rangoon I had heard of such a person residing at Amerapoorah, who had formerly held the office of Collector of the Port, now filled by Mr. Lanciego. His history is a melancholy one, and I will give it hereafter as I heard it from his own lips. The King was highly amused at hearing a conversation in the English language for the first time, and encouraged us to continue it, though I fear some of the free remarks his aged servant was imprudent enough to make, would not have gone unpunished if they had been understood.

The King was extremely affable, permitting me to take many little liberties which would not have been tolerated for a moment in his own subjects. Finding, from my awkward and undignified twistings, that I could not accomplish the native feat of sitting on one half of my body only, he desired that I should be at my ease, when, to the horror of all present, I proceeded to change my posture to a cross-legged seat, such as a tailor uses on his shopboard. I was not rebuked for this, nor when I sat upright, nor when I had the audacity to stare His Majesty in the face. It was evident he was pleased at the idea of my settling at the capital, by the protection he promised, in a manner that left no doubt it was intended. After liberty had been given to present my offerings to the chief

Queen, and to come to the Palace as often as I liked, I was allowed to withdraw, backing out, as I saw others do, on all-fours for a few yards before rising.

I had now to be presented to a more powerful person in the State even than His Majesty. The chief Queen had been raised to the Throne from the humble condition of chief gaoler's daughter. Although some years older than the King, and far from possessing any personal charms, she had, by the judicious use of her influence, and a certain determination of character, obtained complete control over the mind of her easy husband. By corrupt means she had acquired immense wealth—her intrigues had filled most of the important offices in the Kingdom with her creatures, and through the instrumentality of her only brother, a fit agent for the purpose, she was enabled to carry on a large traffic in bribery and extortion. As avarice, backed by unlimited power, naturally leads to cruelty, this venal pair were as unscrupulous and vindictive as they were avaricious. They were equally feared and detested by the people.

On our first acquaintance her Majesty was pleased to be unusually gracious. I was ushered into her reception-room without much ceremony, the presents which I had prepared being borne in front as before. She was seated on a square cushion laid upon the floor. Several persons were crouching before her, apparently engaged on business, while a few female attendants behind had charge of her betel-box, golden cup, fan, &c. She did me the honour to order a rush mat to be spread for me on the floor, which was considered to be a mark of great condescension. Unlike the King she examined the presents carefully, and was so much enamoured of the fine muslins and prints of Manchester and Glasgow that, on being told that I had a large quantity of them for sale, she expressed a wish that I should send forward several packages and repeat my visit on the morrow, when a great many of the ladies of the Palace would like to buy them. Here, indeed, was a piece of good luck I had little expected! Her Majesty could not have made a proposition more exactly suited to my taste. No one was there to taunt me with becoming the Court Haberdasher,—or even if they did, or ten times worse, such an opportunity for a day's amusement would not have been allowed to pass neglected. I gladly promised obedience.

Her Majesty then condescended to present me, as a mark of her especial favour, with a pawn from her own box. It was a leaf enclosing a combination of substances at which my stomach revolted,—areca-nut, tobacco, terra japonica, lime, and spices, and I know not what besides. What was I to do? I could not chew all this nastiness to a pulp, as was evidently required of me, so with great deliberation I put it into my waistcoat-pocket. A burst of laughter followed from the young ladies behind at what they supposed to be my ignorance; another peal, when I told them I should keep it for ever as a mark of Her Majesty's distinguished favour. The present of a pawn in its crude state is not much amiss, but the exhibition of it in a different shape quite sickened me. Her Majesty, after some chewing of one of these delicacies, took it from her mouth and handed it over to a pretty girl behind her, who, esteeming herself highly honoured by the gift—*horribile dictu!*—popped the nasty morsel into her mouth, and completed its mastication. How fortunate an escape that her Majesty did not so far honour me! I have witnessed a more unceremonious transfer of this delicious quid than even the one related, but I spare my reader the disgusting detail.

Among my presents to the Queen was a handsome box of musical glasses, and while I was explaining to her the method of using them, His Majesty unexpectedly entered the apartment. He asked me if I could play upon them. I answered that I would attempt to do so (for I had amused myself with them in my voyage up the river), but that it would be necessary to provide me with a cup of water for the purpose. A large cup of water was brought. His Majesty seized it from the attendant *in transitu*, and dashed it with great force over the ranges of cups, deluging the musician, and sprinkling the great Lady besides, as she was seated not far off. As His Majesty laughed heartily at this Royal practical joke, it was of course expected that the company should join in the merriment, and we all did so. After putting my glasses in order again, I had the honour to entertain them with " God save the King," performed in very tolerable style for an amateur, in a place where it certainly had never been heard before.

It is not, however, altogether prudent for a man to parade his accomplishments at the Court of His Majesty of Ava. I saw there a band of adroit but unfortunate jugglers, who had crossed from Madras, on speculation, to exhibit their feats before the King. They were so successful that he issued his Royal command that they should be kept at his Court, on an allowance of a basket of rice to each person monthly. I was told that they had suffered this detention for two years, and were still not allowed to depart.

On returning home, and thinking over the events of the day, I confess I was very much bewildered. All my

preconceived notions of the dignity and exclusiveness of
this great Monarch had been suddenly blown to the
winds. It is true that when a private merchant only had
to be presented, some descent from the formality of state
might reasonably be expected,—but that I should have
been laughing and joking with the King and Queen, and
that I should have been invited to what was pretty sure
to be a repetition of it to-morrow on a larger scale,
seemed almost incredible. My interpreter, Burman
though he was, seemed equally astonished. In the
mean time this footing of intimacy with Crowned Heads
was far from disagreeable to think on, and I looked
forward with pleasing anticipations of amusement in
repeating my visit to the Palace on the morrow.

CHAPTER IV.

A day in the Palace.—Ladies of Her Majesty's household.—Their demeanour.—Bargaining.—Strange salutation.—Honesty in the Palace.—The Queen's present.—Constitution of the household.—The Mentha-mees.—The King's dinner.—Flattering reception.—Factions at Court.—Visit to the Prince of Tharawudi.—Menthagee.—Their characters and mutual hostility.—Tharawudi's embarrassing familiarity.

I EXPECTED an amusing day, and I was not disappointed; howbeit the picture my imagination had formed of the Royal household was nearly as far from the truth as that of yesterday, when I looked for a proud Monarch half concealed from vulgar gaze by a cloud of exclusiveness, and found instead, a man, affable, inclined to unbend, and throw off the trammels of Royalty so far as a Despot may. I now painted a galaxy of Burmese beauties, sought throughout the breadth of the land for their superior charms, and living a life of luxurious indolence within the Palace walls; in fact, the harem of a Sultan improved by the infusion of a spice of liberty. What puzzled my brain was to account for my easy access to such a company, for it looked very much like an unwarrantable invasion of the sacred privacy of Royalty. I will relate the circumstances of this visit, as it will give some idea of the domestic state of the Royal household.

Several packages were sent away from my house early according to the Queen's command, and I followed them to the Palace about two o'clock, just after Her Majesty had taken her noon-day nap. Female curiosity, however, was there before me. How could it be expected that fifty or sixty ladies should do violence to their feelings by submitting to unnecessary delay, when unheard-of finery lay hidden in the iron-bound boxes before them? The chests had been opened, and their contents strewed about in wonderful confusion. One young lady had attached herself to twenty or thirty yards of Manchester chintz, in which she was strutting about for the amusement of the rest, the superfluous length trailing on the ground behind her. Others glided about like ghosts enveloped in endless white Glasgow muslins. Many dispersed themselves into little coteries of two and three, passing their remarks on articles for dress perhaps new to them. The clatter of tongues was great, and no effort was made to restrain laughter and fun. The moment I entered, many left the goods to talk to the merchant, a still greater curiosity. The unfortunate interpreter was worried with questions much faster than he could answer them, and, as it was evident I was the subject, my deficiency in the language was a sore trial. As tongues went faster, and practical jokes with the contents of the chests increased, there was some danger that these pleasantries might extend into rather riotous proportions, when the entrance of the chief Queen set matters to rights and restored order.

While Her Majesty was engaged in asking me questions about myself and my country, the ladies completed their selections. Her presence did not seem to impose more than a salutary restraint, for it did not prevent the conversation of the rest, which went on in a more subdued tone. Presently the King entered the apartment as if by accident. When he saw me seated on the floor he came forward rapidly, and gave me a smart slap on the head by way of recognition. Corrected as my ideas had been about the Regal dignity, I was yet little prepared for such a flattering mark of familiarity as this, and the dread Monarch was fast descending in my estimation to the level of a buffoon or a man of weak intellect. In this, however, I was quite mistaken; it was merely an indication that His Majesty was in a good humour, and might be approached with safety. When informed how his ladies had occupied themselves the last hour, His Majesty commanded each one to come forward in turn to give me an account of what she had taken, thus affording me an opportunity of saying a few words to each Lady of the Court singly, a gratification for which I was duly thankful. The female dress of the Burmese does not admit of much taste or variety. A heavy silk cloth of gaudy colours is wrapped round the body, completely enveloping it from the neck to the feet; it is open in front, overlapping considerably, and is fastened by a peculiar twist above and below the breast. Females of rank wear this garment of greater length than the common people,—those worn in the Palace trailed on the ground fully six inches or a foot. This is exclusively a native manufacture, and cannot be successfully imitated,—it is therefore only the upper garment or loose jacket in which any room is left for the display of taste, and it was for new material for this that they had so greedily dived into my chests. Not being sufficiently skilled in the language to write their titles correctly in the Burmese, I made use of the Roman character, which seemed to puzzle them all excessively, and they were surprised when at His Majesty's command I read the list aloud with tolerable accuracy. A hearty laugh followed any glaring mistake in the pronunciation of their titles, and no doubt I left a *sobriquet* to many a fair one that stuck to her long after I had departed.

So far everything went on agreeably, but now came the painful duty of telling each of the fair purchasers how much she had to pay, and the still more difficult one of assessing the value of the gold and silver she presented for payment. The King's command, however, must be obeyed. Each lady must again be paraded in turn to make payment for what she had taken. His Majesty remained to see fair play, and entered into the spirit of the trafficking, laughing heartily at every dispute which subsequently occurred.

Scales and weights were now introduced, but this I could not stand; my *amour propre* rebelled against it. I thought of Shylock the Jew, and though the two cases bore no similarity beyond the apparition of the weights and scales, he was present to my thoughts, and I insisted on making over this part of the play to Shwai-ee, who never having read Shakespeare had no such fancies to get over. I professed my ignorance of the touch of gold and the face of silver, an avowal that no doubt relieved the apprehensions of the ladies, who were looking for a grasping creditor, and who, with all their good-humoured smiles, were not free from a spice of avarice, or it might have been only a love of bargaining. Never was a man so baited as the poor Malabaree. Whenever he gave his honest opinion of the value of the gold, he was instantly assailed, accused of cheating, threatened, coaxed, bullied and called very hard names. When I was appealed to, I always gave judgment in favour of the lady, for finding the gentle creatures were, by their own unbiassed and voluntary assessment of prices, paying five or six times as much as the goods cost, I could well afford to be generous. The easy indifference I manifested in submitting to what they knew to be attempts at imposition gained me high favour, while it conferred also perhaps the character of a greenhorn. I felt a great disposition to gain immortal renown by making them a present of all they had chosen, which would not have been a very extravagant gift after all, but I feared the precedent might be a troublesome one. With all their eagerness to take petty advantages, honesty was enforced in the main, and no one was allowed to evade the payment of her debt.

My factotum put up his gold and silver into bags, and I thought the day's amusement had drawn to a close, when I found that I was not to be released without another mark of the Queen's favour, far more embarrassing than that of the pawn, which had been so dexterously evaded; in fact, one would think she selected her honours purposely with the view of plaguing me. Two pieces of rich silk tartan were produced in two shades of bright scarlet colour, extremely beautiful, and such as I should have valued had the gift been unshackled by absurd conditions. It was doubtless with the view of enhancing the value of the present, that Her Majesty desired I should wear one of these gay cloths whenever I made my appearance at the Court in future. The pattern and colour were such as none but the Royal family were permitted to wear: the intent, therefore, was evident; but what was to be done? I could not submit to dress like a native, with a red wrapper round my waist, and yet it was plain this was intended. Though much mortified, I was compelled to receive them with thanks, and to promise compliance, as there was no mode of escape without giving offence. But on reaching home my mind was relieved by a hint from Shwai-ee, that although

Her Majesty had commanded me to *wear* them, she had not prohibited me from *cutting* them! The thought was a bright one; they were passed into the hands of my tailor, who soon converted them into a complete suit, of jacket, waistcoat, and trousers, and thus attired in bright scarlet silk from head to foot, like a mountebank, I was obliged in future to parade through the city whenever business or pleasure called me to the Palace. Fortunately, there was no one to ridicule me in my distress.

This visit gave me a pleasing impression of the freedom allowed to the inmates of the Palace. The hilarity, good-humour, and cheerfulness exhibited by the ladies of the Royal household were sufficient evidence that no excessive strictness of discipline was exerted to mar their happiness. But there was one thing unaccountable and grievously disappointing. Where was the blaze of beauty that my imagination had conjured up? It is true the Tartar features, which are strongly developed in the Burmese physiognomy, are not, in our estimation, favourable to beauty; but, still, youth and comeliness have charms in all races, and here there seemed to be a total disregard of them. There were not more than six or eight really pretty girls in the whole company. Many of them were older than the King himself, and could have had no pretensions at any time to personal charms. The use of the abominable betel-nut had stained the whiteness of their teeth, and the liberal application of sandal-wood ground into powder and dusted over their faces and necks, though it might divert the attention from the incipient wrinkles of those who had passed their prime, certainly did not add to the attractions of the younger and prettier, who needed no such foil. I felt a deep contempt for the taste of the young Monarch, and thought, with such a field to choose from, what a much more satisfactory selection I would have made myself. On relating my disappointment to Mr. Rodgers, he pointed out to me clearly my mistake. In the choice of the females of the Royal household beauty is of little or no account. The Palace unites the character of a harem with that of an honorary prison. Whenever a post conferring great power or confidence is bestowed on a subject, especially if it be that of Governor of a distant province, the jealous feeling of the King is awakened. It is thought necessary to secure his loyalty either through gratitude or fear, and with this view his nearest female relative, usually a daughter, is taken into the Palace in some sense as a hostage for the father's fidelity. If a daughter cannot be given, a sister is taken, and this accounts for the number of ladies of mature age among them. When introduced into this new honour, the revenue of a town or district is granted them for subsistence, from which also they derive their title. This title clearly indicates their position—Men-thamee (Governor's daughter) being applied indiscriminately to them all.

It was late when I got away from the Palace. As I was leaving, the remains of the Royal dinner were being carried out on covered lacquered trays. Many neat little cups and plates, some gold, some porcelain, were filled with salads and a variety of strange substances of doubtful character, requiring prudent investigation before being admitted to closer acquaintance. Being already a favourite, I was permitted to gratify my curiosity by tasting one of the most suspicious-looking dishes. It was a kind of sand-cricket fried crisp—nice enough, except in name, as a condiment, with boiled rice. Another favourite insect with the Burmese—though I did not see it among the King's dishes—is one which I would not offend the stomach of my reader by calling it a *maggot*, if I could find another word equally appropriate. It somewhat resembles a nut-maggot, magnified to three or four inches long, and is found embedded in every joint or sprout of a species of palm, close to its insertion into the main trunk of the tree. When fried and spread on a toast, it is not to be distinguished from marrow, though I never could altogether overcome my repugnance to its shape and its large black head, with which it was brought to table entire in undisguised hideousness. A wonderful stride in luxury must have been made since those days, when I read of a British Envoy being entertained at breakfast by a Woongee of the Empire, who displayed an array of fifty-seven different dishes, some of them being by no means contemptible specimens of the culinary art.*

Altogether, on weighing the events of these two days, my reception at the Court could not be considered otherwise than highly successful, and such as gave promise of my being protected in carrying out my plans, so far as it rested with his Majesty. But Despots are seldom their own masters. They are generally in their turn ruled by favourites or factions, and so I found it in Ava. There were two powerful parties at the Court, both in favour with the King, but fiercely hostile to each other. I must say something of the leaders of these factions, as their influence will be seen as the story proceeds. One of them was the Prince of Tharawudi, the younger brother of his Majesty, a daring, reckless young fellow, about twenty-five years old, whose thoughtless extravagances

* Yule's Mission, page 101.

did not deprive him of the wit to perceive that if his brother's Throne became vacant, there must be a deadly fight for it, which, according to custom, could only end by the total destruction of one party or the other. The rightful Heir, a youth of fifteen, the son of the King by a former marriage, was little regarded by either party. He was kept back from power, and looked on only as an obstacle to be removed when necessary. Tharawadi surrounded himself with bands of daring ruffians, bandits, pugilists, and such like, who lived near his Palace, formed a kind of body-guard, and were ready at a moment's call for any desperate undertaking. As his vices were of a Royal kind, he was a favourite with the people, in spite of the violence and oppression resorted to to support his extravagance.

The other faction has been already indicated. It possessed all the material power of the Kingdom through the influence of the chief Queen. Her brother, styled Menthagee (the great Prince), was reputed to be a man possessed of every vice which can debase human nature— proud, rapacious, oppressive, vindictive, and cruel—and such, when times of trouble came, I found him to be. The sure road to office was bribing the Menthagee, who secured his influence throughout the country by the very means which filled his coffers. He was equally hated and feared by the people, and his designs on the Throne formed a topic of general conversation, apparent to all except the indolent and misguided King.

Another day was devoted to my visits to these great men, with presents as usual. I found them occupied in conformity with their reputed characters—the Prince surrounded by courtiers, dancers, and wrestlers—the Menthagee, in dispensing justice, or, to speak more correctly, in taking bribes to defeat it; the one had a frank, easy manner, the other was the picture of an unscrupulous miser.

Both were civil enough—in fact, the wild Prince quite embarrassed me with his familiarities. He besought me, when I came to see him again, to bring with me some bottles of beer (how he acquired the taste, or even the name, I cannot tell), that we might drink together, and then sent a man to show me over his stables and dog-kennels. In one of the latter I found a noble English mastiff, made furious by being kept chained in a solitary shed, so that no one, but his keepers who fed him, dared to approach within the range of his chain. The moment I entered he flew at me to the extent of his tether like a tiger, but in less than a minute, by whistling and talking to him, I could see that the creature had old associations. One knows almost instinctively whether a dog may be safely trusted, and as this one appeared to recognize me as a countryman, I put faith in him, and, to the astonishment and alarm of the keeper, we were instantly caressing each other like old friends. The King and his brother are both dog-fanciers; the Prince prided himself on having the larger and better kennel of the two, but both keep them as mere objects of curiosity, and not for sport or amusement. Before he parted with me, His Royal Highness proposed a frolic, which brought to my mind the recreations of Prince Hal, recorded by our immortal poet. I was to provide him with a suit of my white linen clothes, and, thus attired, we were to burst forth, like Tom and Jerry, on a nocturnal ramble through the suburb, where peace and order were supposed to be maintained under the protection of his magistracy. No doubt it was a most promising adventure after a few bottles of the beer he coveted, and I felt every inclination to fall in with his humour, and should have done so, but for the remonstrance of my more prudent Moonshee, who became alarmed for his own safety if his master became involved in a row. His contrivance for extricating us from the doubtful consequences of refusing the Prince's suggestion was more ingenious than true. He represented to the Prince that my clothes were all sewed together by women—a fatal obstacle to his projected fun, as a Burman of rank has a superstitious repugnance to wearing any garment stitched by the other sex.

To the Woongees, also, I thought it prudent to pay the compliment of a visit, and was, in every case, well received.

CHAPTER V.

Visit to various chiefs.—Their occupations.—The Hlut-dau.—Burmese law-courts.—Bribery and corruption.—The loo-byo-dau.—Their visits.—I am accused of stealing the King's sheep.—His Majesty's adjudication.—Slaughter of oxen.—I am protected by Tharawudi, who participates.—Wretched bazaar.—I attend the Royal Council.—The Yoong-dau.—Facility of acquiring information.—Absence of amusements.—Salubrity of climate.

THESE necessary preliminaries being completed, I had leisure to attend to the more immediate objects of my voyage; but as I intend to devote the next chapter to the unfolding of my mercantile projects, which, it will be seen, opened out prospects of wealth, brilliant beyond my most sanguine expectations, I shall first say a little on the manner of life this novel seclusion entailed on me. Cut off from all European society, I was necessarily thrown on that of the natives. My *visiting list*, as it would be called in England, sounded magnificently—King, Princes, and Nobles were glad when I called on them, and those who treated me with the greatest affability had the largest share of my attentions.

In their private houses I was allowed to sit and hear the various business the multitude of callers had to transact. Petitioners, litigants, dependants preferred their memorials, causes, and reports,—gave information, craved assistance, claimed advice, applied persuasive bribes (where

D

they were not in the gross form of bullion, which was reserved for the secret chamber); and gradually, but rapidly, I became conversant with the state of society and its secret workings, which I should have sought in vain by any other means.

Sometimes I attended the *hlut-dau*, the great Council of State, where the Woongees of the Empire sit to decide causes, and carry on the business of the country. All legal proceedings here were public. Petitions were presented in the first instance, but the investigation and evidence were taken verbally. The number of these Woongees depends on the pleasure of the King; at this time there were five, four sitting in the hlut-dau, and one residing at Rangoon—the old Viceroy, Meeadai Mengee, already noticed. The pressure of the war that followed increased their number to seven. Each Woongee hears causes separately, and some, more affable than the rest, would allow me to approach near them for the convenience of hearing, as a Judge in England will invite a distinguished visitor to sit beside him on the bench. Here I would sit at the feet of the great Gamaliel, and watch the rocks and shoals and under-currents of the perilous navigation of Burmese law, bringing on its victims all the evils we deplore in England. But the fountain of justice is by no means so pure. Though no money passes openly, unmistakable indications of the horseleech constantly peeped out,—delays, doubts, hints, quite comprehensible to the litigants and their lawyers. In fact, it may be said, once for all, that bribery is the mainspring by which all manner of business is moved throughout the country. Nothing could be done without it—few things fail to be accomplished by its aid. This is so well understood that the best cause is lost unless the Judge is primed. It is not only in litigation that bribery is practised—it pervades society. No power of any sort can be obtained without it. The chiefs of these bribery shops have favourites who act as touters. Do you want Menthagee's influence? Bribe his touter, arrange the price, and he will secure it. Finding this hateful system was universal, and that it was ridiculous to expect to get on without it, I became in time as expert a briber as the rest, and more successful, as I had an unfathomable pocket. Conscience prevented its being resorted to for an unjust purpose, but I was absolutely compelled to look upon it as the legitimate means of securing anything which I could conscientiously demand. To refuse the use of this national custom would be like a traveller kicking willingly against every asperity on the road when the path round it was easy,—so, as I did not come to Burmah to teach them a purer code of political or judicial morality, there was nothing for it but either to adopt theirs, or give up my object of pursuit altogether.

At the Palace, of course, I was a frequent visitor. My standing well there was indispensable, and the groundwork of my safety. If I failed to appear for many days together, the King would ask for me.

Although Princes and Ministers of State would have thought their dignity compromised by returning my visits, there was a class of the junior nobility, called *loo-byo-dau* (Royal youths), composed chiefly of the sons of men in high office, who did not so consider it, and many of these were frequent visitors at my house. They passed most of their time in the Palace, ministering flattery to the King, watching opportunities to wriggle themselves into office through his favour, and, unfortunately for me, too glad when they could attract His

Majesty's notice by any kind of news-bearing, be it ever so mischievous. As I encouraged this kind of intercourse, in common with every other means of gaining local information, their visits became rather troublesome, especially when the rogues found out my hour of dining. Still it aided me in acquiring the language, and it was with some pride I began to find I could walk alone without the aid of Shwai-ee, who had hitherto been as indispensable to me as a walking-stick to a cripple. I could never move without him. Two of these ungrateful youngsters, who had been enjoying my hospitality, brought me into a scrape, which might have been attended with serious consequences, and put the favour of his Majesty to a severe test.

It is well known that the Burmese, being followers of Boodh, do not rear animals for food, though they do not object to eat the carcases of such as die a natural death. Sheep, therefore, are not to be found in the kingdom, except on the banks of a lake near to Amerapoorah, where a flock of several thousands, the property of the King, may be seen feeding.

It was long since I had tasted mutton, so long that the temptation was irresistible, and yet I could not bring myself to eat it after it had become carrion. A negotiation was therefore opened between the chief shepherd on the one part, and my man of business on the other, which terminated in half a dozen of the flock being transferred by night, and deposited safely in the enclosed room under my house. So far all was well. For some days I rejoiced to see mutton on my table, though, to the disgrace of His Majesty, it was lean and tough. It so chanced that when two of these *loo-byo-dau* were sitting in my verandah, one of these unlucky creatures, most vexatiously, began to bleat. The unusual sound was not lost on the quick ears of my guests, who, like shabby fellows, carried the news to the King that the white foreigner had been stealing his sheep! The next day an officer from the Palace came to explore, found my little flock (now reduced to five), took possession, and drove them away for His Majesty's inspection. In a like scrape a Burman would have bribed the whole party; but, nothing daunted, I mounted my pony and rode after them to the Palace to protect my interests. It was noon—His Majesty was taking his siesta, and the sheep were below, waiting his waking. I took my seat in the hall, in an almost ungovernable rage with the tale-bearers who confronted me, and passed an uncomfortable half-hour, wondering what the end of this affair might be. I could see by their manner that the rascals thought me in a bad way.

When at length the King entered after his nap, he saw me and the sheep at a glance, and asked me what I wanted them for. My politic but mendacious Malabaree wished to tell the King that I was going to domesticate them for amusement; this, of course, I would not allow, but, proud of my growing proficiency in the language, I blurted out the whole truth at once, and informed His Majesty that it was impossible for an Englishman to live in sight of mutton without tasting it. He burst into a hearty laugh, gave me back two of them, which were black-faced (the best for my purpose), and ordered the remaining three, with white faces, back to his flock. The courtiers were astounded at my escape. The chief shepherd, no doubt, made a good profit by his flock, which *die* at convenient times, as wanted by his Majesty or by his other customers. My mistake was in buying them alive.

The shepherd escaped of course by a bribe, and always afterwards contrived a *death* among his flock whenever I gave him notice, though I was obliged to abandon the idea of fattening them.

It was not without an unpleasant twinge that I read in an unpublished manuscript, lent to me for perusal some years ago by the late Colonel Burney,—in which he gives a graphic description of the Revolution which placed Tharawudi on the throne,—the following butcher-like paragraph:—" On this day the King ordered a poor man, who had killed a sheep, to be put to death and quartered in the same manner as he had quartered the sheep." And who was this King, but the very man who was now my confederate in setting at defiance the laws of the Boodh and the King!

I soon found out that my jovial friend, the Prince Tharawudi, was as great a lover of beef and mutton as myself. No doubt he made good use of his brother's flock on the lake, but, by some strange process of casuistry, these pious Buddhists appeared to weigh the enormity of the crime by the size of the animal that suffers, and I question whether even *he* dared to incur the iniquity or the odium of slaughtering an ox, or even a calf. I saved him both the trouble and the sin. Among my servants were four Mahomedans, willing agents in obtaining beef and veal. We used to slaughter them at night in an out-building, but though all secresy was used, it was impossible to say whether accidental discovery might not entail unpleasant consequences. We were living in a quarter of the town under the Prince's immediate jurisdiction; complaints would therefore go to him. This facilitated matters wonderfully, as my compliments always went to His Royal Highness, with a quarter of an animal which "*had unfortunately died in my yard last night.*" We perfectly understood each other, and the Prince being *particeps criminis*, we could eat our beef without fear of the consequences.

Unpleasant as it was to run counter to the prejudices of the natives in the supply of my table, the state of their shambles justified it. Joints of carrion ponies, oxen and cows,—rats, snakes, and pigs (the scavengers of the streets), could not be tolerated, and a daily mess of boiled rice, with *ngapwee* and wild vegetables, formed a meagre fare to one who had been long used to a generous one. Ghosts of poultry and eggs were certainly to be had, with now and then some indifferent lake fish. Much might be done for health and comfort on a future voyage, by the precaution of having a good supply of preserved meats; but that I had unluckily neglected to provide.

Captain Cox says, "This filthy custom of eating the flesh of diseased animals is the cause of a dreadful disorder which attacks the extremities with ulcerous sores, which soon mortify, and leave those who survive disgusting and mutilated objects."* I have known a horse, which died of disease in the stable of a friend, to be cut in pieces on the spot and carried away for food, the operators eagerly contending for the best portions of the delicacy.

One of the most interesting sights at the Court was the meeting of the Royal Council. Although it is not usual to admit strangers to it, an Attwenwoon, named Moung-tsa, whose acquaintance I had made, relying on the favour shown me by the King, ventured to take me there, an unauthorized guest, under the shadow of his

---

* Mission of Captain Hiram Cox, page 192.

wing. No clock was needed to summon this assembly. It was held every morning punctually as the sun peeped above the horizon, at which time it was expected that every high functionary would be in his place, waiting His Majesty's appearance, a condition, I trow, which, however salutary, would damp the aspirations of many of our senators at home.

Nothing could exceed the order and solemnity with which business was transacted, for although I very imperfectly understood what was going forward, and although bribery and corruption might be at the root of every subject discussed, yet it was evident that there *was* a discussion, that rival interests were represented, and that the semblance at least of a certain amount of freedom of opinion was preserved. The usual form of introducing a topic was by a written document, which was read, or rather sung or intoned, by an officer of the Court, called a *Thandausen*, and before the Royal order was given on it those present were permitted to express themselves. Few opened their lips, however, except the Woongees and the Attwenwoons, unless appealed to, and on their representations the Royal order was given and registered by the same officer who had chaunted the memorial. No dresses of state were worn, nor decoration, except a simple belt of a few thin cotton cords thrown over the left shoulder, the number of these cords indicating the rank of the wearer. Colours were avoided in the robe and head-dress, both of which were of white muslin. No seats or mats were allowed; all sat on the boarded floor, arranged according to their respective rank, nearer to, or more distant from, the Throne, the gilded arm-chair I before alluded to. His Majesty, on recognizing me, said a few words to my protector, but did not address me directly. The sight was altogether an imposing one, calculated to inspire confidence in a stranger by the strict order and apparent deliberation that prevailed in the assembly. The retiring of His Majesty was the signal for the breaking-up of the Council.

There was another Court of Justice in the city called the Yoong-dau, presided over by the Myowoon, or Governor of the town, answering to our police-courts. It took cognizance of all criminal cases occurring within the precincts of the town. I was surprised at the few instances of robbery or other great crimes that came before the court, but after-experience too clearly explained this, when the secrets of the dread *Let-ma-yoon*, or deathprison, where the terrible inquisition into crimes of this nature was conducted, became unfolded to my view in all its cruelty.

What with frequently dropping into their Courts, visiting the chiefs at their houses, encouraging the society of such as chose to call on me, constant familiar intercourse with the more respectable portion of the traders, and, above all, keeping habitually on the alert to lose no opportunity, I acquired, in two or three months, a pretty correct insight into the people and their institutions. The general publicity pervading all affairs of business or of State, as well as the free domestic habits of the common people, much aided me in gaining this knowledge. If I happened to stop at a decent shop, the chances were that I should be asked to go inside and chat with the wife and children. Their worst habit was an utter disregard to truth where an object could be gained by lying. This was a vice common to all classes, practised, too, with such little skill or adroitness, that it was easy to detect truth from falsehood at the first glance.

Of amusements there were few beyond those created by novelty. Unlike Rangoon the country round Amerapoorah was open and accessible for horse exercise by decent roads; but this solitary riding I soon found wearisome, and cared little for it. There was a woful lack of game within a reasonable distance from the town, and I could not but foresee that if a love of lucre should tempt me to make this my place of residence for any lengthened period, I must be content to make the pursuit of gain for the time almost my only solace.

That the climate was salubrious, the robust condition of the population sufficiently testified. During the cool months, from November to March, the temperature was delicious. In the morning I often found the roads hard with frost, thin ice covering the puddles. I was told, however, that in the summer, before the periodical rains set in, which here are far from heavy or constant, the heats were very intense; but, altogether, I saw nothing to fear from the climate.

CHAPTER VI.

Mercantile prospects.—Export trade.—General system of prohibition.—Astonishing profits on imports.—Prospects of immense fortune.—On what circumstances depending.—Difficulties.—How to be overcome.

It is now time that I should advert more particularly to the prime objects of my enterprise. The disclosure of the golden harvest which lay ready to the sickle of any one who saw his way to reap it, and to surmount the various obstacles in his path, will not fail to astonish the reader, as it did me. It is, however, more surprising that so recently as the year 1823, after many years of active search by a host of adventurers for new markets in which to extend British commerce and force her manufactures, so important a field as Burmah should have been overlooked or neglected, than that the first person who thoroughly explored it should discover a mine of wealth to work to his own advantage. No doubt there were frightful difficulties in the way of establishing an extended commerce, that must be overcome before success could attend these efforts, and very likely the knowledge of these difficulties may have hitherto deterred any one from making the attempt. But my observations led me to believe that some of the most formidable might be removed by judicious management, and if they were so removed, the way to untold wealth was plain and certain.

In those days Burmah may be said to have had almost no external commerce at all. The only traffic worthy the name was that with the Chinese, who carried off large quantities of cotton by the highway of the Irrawuddi, for the supply of their southern provinces, giving in return many articles fit for home consumption, which arrived annually in caravans, transported by mules and other beasts of burden, at a village called Medai, a few miles to the northward of Amerapoorah. The article of the greatest value in this caravan was raw silk.

There was also another mart for barter with the Chinese higher up the river, but too distant for me to attend it.

From their sea-port of Rangoon little else was exported than teak timber, which their extensive forests furnished in boundless quantity. The money value of it, however, was insignificant, and quite inadequate for purposes of exchange. As the encouragement of commerce was not thought of, the industry of the country had not been directed to produce or to manufacture articles for export, and even those which existed—such was the ignorance of the Government—were prohibited from exportation, under the absurd idea that the country would be drained of useful commodities, and become impoverished thereby. Such, for instance, was the case with the silk imported by land from China. It was not to be exported, for fear sufficient should not remain for the clothing of the population! Rice, the most abundant product of the country, often raised in such inexhaustible quantity that men and cattle conjointly could not consume it, was under a similar law. The precious metals, the produce of native mines, which, for want of the requisite skill among the Burmese, were farmed to and worked by Chinese, were guarded with still greater jealousy, under the mistaken notion that gold and silver constituted the wealth of a nation. Their spirited little ponies were vainly considered so valuable, that means were adopted to perpetuate the breed in Burmah alone, taking care that foreign countries should not participate in the benefits. Their beautiful marble, for which there might possibly have been a foreign demand, was also prohibited, being sacred to the manufacture of their idols. Thus, from one cause or other, almost every product of value was fettered, and industry crushed by legislation such as prevailed with our ancestors in by-gone times, but which has been gradually abandoned as its folly became apparent. Rubies and sapphires of the finest quality are found in abundance; but even precious stones, a commodity which, from its small bulk, would seem to be beyond the reach of fiscal laws, partook of the restriction. In fact, one would argue, from the state of the laws, that the Government had the definite object in view completely to exclude any commercial intercourse whatever with other countries.

Such an unpromising state of affairs existing, one may naturally ask how I could indulge a ray of hope? Whence the extravagant prospect of success held out at the commencement of this chapter? I answer, that the very conditions so depressing and forbidding to the multitude are precisely those by which an *individual* may profit, and which he may turn to the greatest advantage. Not that I contemplated evading their laws by entering into illicit trade, which, irrespective of the unanswerable moral argument against it, might have led to dangerous consequences; but perhaps my ideas may more clearly develope themselves if I first pass to the other side of the question, and show the marvellous success that attended our little trial adventure in the import trade.

It is necessary I should remind the reader that I had brought with me from Bengal a variety of the cotton manufactures of Manchester and Glasgow, such as my friend there thought most likely to suit the wants of the people. The cost of them in Calcutta was £3000. With the exception of a few chests sent to the Palace at the Queen's desire, these were all now at my house. When the formalities of presentation at the Court had been gone through, Shwai-ee gave notice to the eager traders that I was now ready to dispose of these goods. They came—and a scene ensued that opened my eyes at once to the fortune which might be rapidly amassed by the pioneers in this field. The contention among these men as to who should be the fortunate buyer ran so high that I began to fear a fight would ensue; therefore, as prices had been already offered that might have satisfied the greediest extortioner, the strife of the battle-field was calmed down by the assurance that each should participate in the purchase. The almost incredible sum of about £8000 was the result of this negotiation! But even these figures do not represent the enormous profits disclosed to my wondering view. Many of the goods were ill chosen and unsuitable to the market, a mistake inseparable from a first essay with uncertain means of information, but which it was easy to avoid in future. Without entering into uninteresting detail, it is enough to say, that the more favoured selections might be represented by the figures $5s.$ or $6s.$ on the one hand, and $35s.$ on the other; the first being the cost at the place of manufacture,—the last, the selling price at

Amerapoorah,—or about six or seven times their first cost.

It was impossible to say to what extent this trade might be carried, or how long such astounding prices would continue; but this was quite certain,—that the demand would be beyond what I had the power to supply, and that prices would not fall until the restrictions on exportable produce should be removed. Competition would then step in as the knowledge of the commerce became generally known, and prices and profits would as usual conform. The population of the Capital was not the only one to be supplied. These goods would find their way into the northern provinces of the Empire, which could not be supplied from any other source.

The next day my friends came with bags of silver and gold in bullion to pay for their purchases. Some, not so wealthy, I suppose, as their brethren, asked me to grant them credit. As I had made up my mind to remain at the least two months, for the purpose of acquiring information, and wishing to test the honesty and trustworthiness of the dealers, I willingly consented to do so, and it spoke well for the people that none of them failed in their payments. One delinquent hesitated, but on my threatening to tell the King how he endeavoured to defraud a foreigner, the money was immediately paid. Their very loose manner of committing engagements to writing astonished me. A coarse thick paper, like pasteboard, made of bamboo macerated and pulped, and rendered black by a preparation of charcoal and other substances, is written on with a stick of soap-stone, just as we use our slate and slate-pencil, the writing being as easily obliterated by a damp sponge. On this the bond is written, the names of the witnesses being inserted, and without any signature, either of the party bound or by the witnesses, is placed in the possession of the creditor. In fact, it partakes only the character of a memorandum. At first, I demurred to such a frail document, but on being assured it was their custom, and that the debt could be established by the witnesses, I submitted, though it must be confessed a less binding document, or one more liable to evasion, can hardly be imagined. They seemed to have no idea of proof by signature, or by the recognition of handwriting. Perhaps the continuous sameness of formal circles constituting the Burmese writing does not admit the same facility of identification as the more varied forms of the Roman character.

But now the difficulty before contemplated comes prominently into view. It is true I have got £8000 in gold and silver, but what am I to do with it? It seems to be about as valueless as the same weight of iron. I want to transport it, or its equivalent, to Calcutta, but how is this to be accomplished? The simple mode would be to send the bullion itself, but that is illegal. The next impulse is to buy the productions of the country suited for exportation, but I am met by the same obstruction, except in the staple of teak timber and a few articles of even less value. Besides, how many huge ships will it require to carry away £8000 worth of timber, and what the loss and delay in effecting it? The thought is indeed disheartening, but can no mode of relief be hit upon? It is certainly clear enough that if a man residing in Bengal worth £10,000 wishes to emigrate, and become a denizen of Burmah, he may in effecting the change convert his £10,000 into £25,000 or even £30,000, but there he must remain for the remainder of his days—at least his property must. But the worst has not yet been stated. So jealous was the Government of the drain of the precious metals from the country, that it objected to my removing so large a sum from the capital to their own port of Rangoon, under the conviction that I should do so merely for the facility it afforded of smuggling it on board ship. Altogether this was indeed a maze of embarrassment and perplexity, and unless I could find a pathway through it, the only alternative was to spend my money as quickly as possible, and then decamp.

As I was not at all disposed to do this, I began to act in the spirit of the well-known adage which advises us to fall in with the customs of the country we happen to live in; and what would a Burman do under such circumstances? What but extricate himself by bribery? If ever doubtful means were not only admissible but justifiable, they were so here; so I opened my batteries against the strongholds of prohibition, by sending balls of gold and silver into Menthagee and the Woongees with such effect that the outworks were soon demolished. First fell the refusal to permit me carrying my treasure to Rangoon, then (bringing heavier metal to bear) the liberty to buy and export a little raw silk. I dared no more for the present; but I left off firing with this conviction, viz. that if I chose to bribe high enough, and in the right quarter, there were few privileges that were beyond my reach. If I determined to follow up this first essay by a permanent residence at Ava, a few thousand pounds spent among the Princes and Ministers annually—a sum which would hardly be felt where the gains were so large—would suffice to secure the whole Court in my interest.

It thus appears that one, and only one, serious impediment stood in the way of any individual seizing the tempting opportunity to make a gigantic fortune, and that, too, in a very unexpected manner, in times when every corner of the world was supposed to be overrun and explored by hosts of indefatigable fortune-hunters. This one impediment was how to get the profits out of the country after they had been made. For the precious metals there was no hope; the prejudice was too deeply rooted to be assailed with any chance of success. But there was another article of commerce, already slightly adverted to, which would serve my purpose far better, and at the same time was not so likely to meet with opposition. If I could only succeed in shaking the obstinacy and ignorance of the Hlut-dau, the wanting link would be supplied, and the chain of commerce made perfect. I allude to Rice. My information led me to believe that in the luxuriant plains of Pegu and Arracan it was a common thing in some years of plenty to allow the excess of production of grain, after supplying the demand for home consumption, to go to destruction, the cultivators not deeming it worth the labour to clean the grain from the husk, when no certain market could afterwards be found for its sale. I thought, by representing the folly of this waste (liberally backed by that without which no good could be effected), I might get the Hlut-dau to grant an order to the Viceroy to allow me to purchase it for export. When the cultivators once saw that they could depend on a market, the production would rapidly increase, and it would form a monopoly in my favour of incalculable value. The course of events subsequent to the war go to prove the accuracy of my calculations, for in a few years after the cession of Arracan to us, those prolific plains alone, raised such an astonishing quantity of grain as actually glutted for a time all the markets of Europe, after providing for their own sustenance. It was a subject, however, which required delicate handling, as their prejudices were strong on this point, so I left it for future diplomacy, contenting myself on this occasion in following the old beaten path, with such little variations as lay within my reach.

Before concluding this chapter (in which it will be seen from my remarks that I have anticipated and made use of information acquired during subsequent months), a few figures embodying the opinions I had arrived at may still more astonish the reader. They may have been sanguine, but even now, on a retrospect, I am not at all sure they were so. It must be remembered that a commerce, which now supports numerous flourishing mercantile establishments, was at that time unfolded to me alone, and lay at my feet, a huge monopoly, requiring only dexterous management to be converted into a mine of wealth. I say, then, that £50,000 embarked in the trade annually would readily find a market, and produce three times that sum, or £150,000, leaving an apparent gain of £100,000 per annum. If the prohibition could be sapped in the articles of grain and raw silk, and assuming that the latter was of a quality saleable in the European markets,—which I was now in the way of proving,—there would be little difficulty in remitting this sum to India or to Europe, and in thus securing the profit. On the contrary, should my diplomacy in this matter fail, and I was cast upon the unmanageable timber trade alone, one fourth part of that sum would hardly find remittance— even this perhaps at a loss; and the whole enterprise might then be regarded as a failure, scarcely worth the anxiety and risk which must necessarily be encountered.

CHAPTER VII.

Mr. Rodgers.—His history.—Irascible character of the King.—His attack upon his Council.—New Palace at Ava.—It is injured by lightning.—Consequent execution of the architect.—I take leave of the King.—His commands.—I return to Rangoon under convoy.—Kyouptaloung Thegee.—Gross treatment of Europeans at Rangoon.—An instance.—Singular escape of a lascar.

As Mr. Rodgers, the old gentleman whose acquaintance I had made in so singular a manner, was the only European within reach, we naturally saw a good deal of each other, and most valuable to me his long experience of the country proved in forming my conclusions as to the security to be enjoyed at the Capital. I was curious to know by what train of accidents he had been brought to spend his life in this rude country, and he gave me an outline of his history, which, as he and all the actors in it must long since have passed away, there can be no objection to my giving, as nearly as I can recollect it, in his own words. A useful moral may be drawn from his sad story.

"In the year 1782 I was the fourth officer in one of the ships belonging to the East India Company, trading to Calcutta. On the outward voyage complaints were made by the crew of the bad quality of the salt provisions served out to them, and I had the misfortune to discover, when I was sent below to get up some fresh casks, that the chief officer was dishonestly feeding them with tainted meat which belonged to himself, intending to replace it by so many casks from the ship's stores. He was much exasperated when, on returning to the upper deck, I taxed him with the fraud. An altercation ensued, then blows. For this, being the junior officer, I was placed under arrest, from which I was not released when the ship anchored in the river Hooghly. I was allowed, however, to go on shore for exercise occasionally at Fultah, where there was a solitary tavern at which the officers used to regale themselves.

"Here I hid myself until an opportunity offered of meeting my oppressor as he was walking alone in a garden behind the house. I then approached him with two of the ship's pistols, taxed him with his ill-usage, and demanded satisfaction, offering him his choice of the pistols. This he refused, when, urged on by the desire of revenge, I attacked him with a Penang lawyer,* which I had provided for the purpose, intending only to inflict a severe chastisement; but each blow seemed to increase my fury, which, as my injuries arose to my mind, became quite ungovernable. At last I left him insensible, I feared, perhaps, dead. What was to be done? Return on board my ship I dared not, so I got into a dingy, and taking the flood-tide paid the men to pull me with all speed to Barrackpore, a place some miles above Calcutta, where the cadets who came out as passengers in the ship were quartered. I cast myself on their protection, which was readily granted, as the chief officer was by no means a favourite, and they knew the provocation I had received. Here I lay hidden by them for some weeks, and then, sup-

---

* A thick cane, so called.

plying me with money, they sent me forward to Chittagong, whence I made my way across the British frontier into Arracan, and eventually to Rangoon, where, in an unknown foreign country, I found a safe asylum. From that time I have never once quitted the Burman territory, though I might have done so with safety, as I heard afterwards that the man I had so unmercifully punished happily recovered, and made subsequent voyages in the service of the East India Company."

It is much to be feared that this melancholy story will not admit even the alleviation noticed in the sequel, but that the subject of it fell into the common delusion of believing that which he so earnestly wished to be true. If the crime was great, so was the retribution; it was life-long, and terrible enough almost to justify the exclamation of the first murderer, "My punishment is greater than I can bear." For more than forty years had this unhappy man (by no means destitute of kind and benevolent feelings) been a fugitive from justice, banished from civilized life, suffering alone the pangs of remorse, the constant victim of oppression from which he dared not fly, and harassed by the continual fear of being claimed as a criminal by the Indian Government. He had long ceased all communication with his family, but had heard that he had a younger brother, a teacher of music at a town in Lincolnshire, which report, singularly enough, I was able to confirm, as I had been in his company some years before at the house of a friend where he attended professionally. It was impossible not to be drawn into sympathy with such a sufferer, while I listened with wonder to the incidents with which his strange life abounded. Mr. Rodgers had married a native Portuguese woman, by whom he had a son, about twelve years old—of course nearly native in all his habits and ideas.

Once in conversation I alluded to the good-humoured, condescending manners of the King. "Pretty well at times," was the reply, "but he is not to be trusted, sir. He gives way to sudden bursts of passion, when for a little while he is like a raging madman, and no one dares to approach him. I was once present at a full durbar where all the officers of Government then at the Capital were assembled. The King was seated on a gilded chair as you have seen him, to all appearance in his usual good temper, when something was said by one present which irritated him. His Majesty rose quickly from his chair and disappeared at a door opening to a private apartment behind the Throne. The Council looked all aghast, not knowing what to think of it, but when he re-appeared armed with a long spear, the panic was universal. *Sauve qui peut.* We made a simultaneous rush to the wide flight of steps leading to the Palace-yard, like a herd of deer before a savage tiger; down the stairs we went pell-mell, tumbling over each other in our haste to escape, without respect to rank or station. His Majesty made a furious rush at us, chased the flying crowd to the head of the flight of stairs, and then, quite forgetting in his frenzy who was the delinquent, launched his spear in the midst of us at a venture. It passed my cheek, and stuck in the shoulder of an unfortunate man on the step before me without doing him any very serious injury. The only man who remained in the Council Hall was the old Sakkya Woongee, who could not escape because of his infirmity, however much he might have wished it. He had the cunning to crawl up to a huge marble image of Guatama always erected in the Hall, ready to receive His

Majesty's devotions, pretending to offer up prayers for the averting of the King's wrath. He might have saved himself the trouble, for it was already appeased by his mad attack upon his Council, and he spoke kindly to the old Minister for not having joined in the flight. If ever you see him getting into a passion, I advise you to keep out of his way."

I had not to wait long, to witness a more tragic instance of this unbridled temper, verifying the words of our poet,—

"How wretched
Is that poor man that hangs on princes' favours!"

I have said that the King was demolishing his old Palace at Amerapoorah, and was building a new one at Ava, four or five miles down the river. This new structure was designed to eclipse the old one in its size, and in the splendour of its decoration, and was now far advanced towards completion. It was, indeed, a remarkably beautiful building. The tallest of the teak trees of his forests had been hewn and carved into pillars, long, elegant vistas of which, richly gilded, already marked its noble proportions. The tall spire, consisting of a number of roofs tapering one above the other, in the well-known Chinese style, had just been crowned by the golden *tee*, or umbrella, regarded as the glory of the Palace, the use of it being confined to the Royal residence and to sacred edifices. This spire is erected over the Hall of Audience, and the sacred "*tee*," on its pinnacle, with its hoop of sonorous bells, is placed as nearly as possible over the Throne itself. The architect who planned the Palace, stood deservedly high in his master's favour, for it was admired by every one as a perfect specimen of good taste. The King was so much pleased with it, that he often amused himself by going to inspect the progress of the works. On one of these excursions the town was visited by a terrific thunder-storm, the sacred *tee* was struck by the lightning, the massive iron stanchions supporting it bent nearly to a right angle, and the ill-fated umbrella of course reversed. It was indeed a melancholy spectacle to behold the fragments of this beautiful pinnacle, suspended at an immense height, a mark for all the fury of the storm. But the tempest was nothing in comparison with that which raged in the breast of the Tyrant when he beheld his glory blown to shreds, and an omen of evil brought upon his Throne. As he could not vent his fury on the elements, he turned it on the able but ill-fated Architect. I did not see him at the moment, but was told his rage was like frantic insanity. The poor man was hunted up and dragged to the place of execution, the Tyrant ejaculating every few minutes, "Is he dead?" "Is he dead?" as if grudging a prolonged existence even of a few minutes.

But on the execution-ground a scene was enacted that illustrates my remarks about the universality of bribery. It is common, when the executioners have a victim of rank, or one able to pay, to suspend the blow till sunset, to give time to his friends to negotiate for his pardon. This chance was offered to the dejected Architect, who, almost as mad as his master, refused the boon, and insisted on their performing their office instantly; they complied, and the expected reprieve arrived too late. It is a pity that Despots do not always show themselves in this guise, without redeeming their character by any lucid interval. The genus would then soon become extinct.

Many amusing and many alarming anecdotes were

told me, by Mr. Rodgers, of the King's vagaries; but those I have related will give a pretty correct idea of the fickle and hasty character of the Monarch whose favour must be the groundwork of my safety, and indispensable to the success of my enterprise. Sometimes his anger would take a more ludicrous turn. A youth in the Palace had incurred his displeasure, but being a prime favourite, and not wishing to degrade him in the eyes of the public, His Majesty possessed himself of a sugar-cane, and belaboured the delinquent with it in a Princely style with his own hands, and with such severity as to leave no doubt about the reality of the punishment. Still this King, notwithstanding his violent and irritable disposition, was generally regarded as a mild and merciful Sovereign, and possessed the affections of his people. He was certainly partial to foreigners, or a different fate would have attended me and my companions in our subsequent captivity.

After passing two months under the Golden Feet, and feeling my way to a satisfactory solution of the queries which were the object of my voyage, I began to think of returning to Calcutta, to relate my adventures to the friend who had provided the means for the exploration. My boats were prepared, my crews engaged, my treasure and effects embarked, when I presented myself at the Palace to take my leave. The King was exceedingly gracious, asked if I had been well treated, and was apparently gratified when he heard that I intended to return the following year to live under his protection. When I asked whether there was anything my country produced that would be acceptable to His Majesty, he thought for a few moments, and then said, "My brother, Tharawudi, is always crowing over me about his dogs; it is very improper that he should have a larger one than me. Can you bring me a dog taller than any in his kennel?" I replied that I would do my best to take the conceit out of the Prince. "But," added he, "do not let him know what I tell you." The Prince was to be kept in profound ignorance of the humiliation he was to undergo, and the King was as delighted as a child at the idea of quietly outwitting his brother.

I then went to leave my P.P.C. with the Prince of Tharawudi. Here, in an outbuilding, I found the Chief of Kyouptaloung, a village on the river side a few miles below, who had fallen under the Prince's displeasure, and had been sentenced to a degrading and painful punishment. He implored me to intercede with his exasperated master, and, like a very frail Buddhist, promised to have an ox ready to put on board my boat when we passed his village, as a recompense for my good offices. I obtained the poor fellow's pardon, but did not delay my boats to claim the promised reward.

It happened that at this time the Prince was despatching a war-boat to his province of Tharawudi, which he offered to me as a protecting convoy. The large amount of treasure on board was likely to prove a temptation to the gangs of robbers who always more or less infested the river;—I therefore thankfully accepted his offer. The Chief of the war-boat faithfully executed his orders; indeed, he went beyond them, for he never lost sight of me until he had escorted me down to Rangoon.

I left Amerapoorah early in December, in company with this war-boat, rowing about sixty oars. The water in the river had much diminished, many islands and sandbanks, which we had sailed over in the rainy season, were now dry, rendering our progress circuitous and tedious; the current was comparatively sluggish, and the monsoon winds having ceased, we had to depend only on our oars. Nine or ten days brought me again to Rangoon, after an absence of five months.

Here I made my dispositions for transferring my money to Calcutta, which, with all the energy I could use, took two or three months to accomplish. I then followed as quickly as possible in the good ship *Alfred*, the same that brought me from Calcutta the previous year.

After the very kind and liberal treatment I had experienced at Amerapoorah, it was with regret I noticed that a system the very reverse was practised towards the few Europeans who were living at Rangoon. This was, no doubt, partly their own fault, for it must be admitted, that the unruly conduct of some of them tended rather to invite oppression than to inspire respect. An instance happened under my own eye, and may serve, not as a singular case, but as a sample of the little consideration usually shown them.

Captain Daniells, the master of a British ship called the *Aram*, was sitting in my house late in the evening, when a man arrived with the intelligence that a native lascar of his crew had jumped overboard to avoid a threatened punishment by one of the mates, and was unhappily swept away by the rapidity of the tide, and, in the darkness, was drowned. No sooner did the accident reach the ear of the Viceroy than an order was issued to seize the unfortunate mate, who, without inquiry, was thrust into a filthy prison, called by the foreigners the "firehouse." Here the poor man remained the whole of the night in the stocks, and a heavy fine would have been imposed, had not the strange disclosure of the following morning brought him relief. The innocent cause of this mischief then, to the surprise of every one, reappeared on deck. He had saved himself unperceived, by catching hold of some timber made fast to the stern, and re-entered the ship by the open raft port. He remained concealed all night in the hold, fearing the threatened punishment, while the anger of his oppressor was evaporating in the horrors of the "fire-house." This kind of extortion, carried to excess, brought about the second Burmese war in 1851, and the very act for which compensation was demanded and refused—in fact, the *casus belli*—was almost as insignificant as the one I have here related.

The lascar alluded to seemed to carry a charmed life. Although it has nothing to do with my story, the anecdote is so strange that I cannot resist giving it as it was related to me by Captain Daniells. The man fell overboard by accident from the *Aram*, on a former voyage, in the Bay of Bengal, on a dark, squally night, in which no effort to save him was practicable. Of course every one concluded he was drowned. Some days afterwards, however, Captain Daniells fell in with a vessel, which spoke him, and asked, "Have you lost a man overboard?" On the answer having been given in the affirmative, "Send a boat for him, we have picked him up." On his being restored to the ship, it was found that the poor fellow had been all the night the sport of the waves, and at daylight on the following morning he was literally almost run over by the ship that saved him.

CHAPTER VIII.

Arrival in Calcutta.—Hesitation about returning.—I determine to follow our scheme.—Disgraceful neglect of the Bengal Government.—I engage Mr. Richardson.—We sail for Rangoon.—Mr. Stockdale.—Return to Ava.—Explosion of a priest.—"Red Rat" and "Red Gold."—I make myself independent of interpreter.—Death of Mr. Stockdale.—A boatman drowned.—Escape from drowning.—Alligators.—Strange habit.—A boatman of Dr. Price taken by one.—Anecdote of Wellesley Province.

ONCE again arrived in Calcutta, I made my friend, Mr. M'Kenzie, acquainted with the details of my interesting expedition, and the fair fortune which lay exposed to view, but which, like the rich clusters of grapes the fox gazed at, was yet out of my reach. The only ladder likely to lead to its possession was a frail one, each step fraught with danger, and if it gave way, not only would the prize be lost, but the adventurer would hazard life or limb by the fall. There it was, however, a glittering bait sure enough, but provokingly obscured by clouds and mist. I began to consider, too, that, even if successful, I should be paying rather a heavy penalty. A few years' banishment from civilized life, and the being cast for society on the semi-barbarous natives, might go far to transform me into a savage like themselves; and much as I was in love with novelty and adventure, and with no dislike to the golden harvest it might produce, I could not help hesitating. Then I might be mistaken in my estimate of the efficacy of the means by which alone I could grasp the prize; though in this I had great confidence, yet if I was mistaken, it must, as I have before remarked, be a complete failure. Again the idea would present itself of ignobly abandoning a project so successfully begun. At last the urgent desire of my friend that I should persevere, and his promise to afford whatever assistance I might want, settled the question. In an evil hour I consented, little dreaming of the disasters which were to follow.

Had the wholesome publicity which is now generally given to political affairs through the medium of the press been the practice of those times, the disputes of our Government with the Burmese would have been known, and its subjects would have been saved from hazarding their lives by placing confidence in a barbarous Power likely soon to be at war with us. To the disgrace of Lord Amherst's Government be it said, that down to the time when the war was declared, and the expedition to Rangoon determined on, no timely warning, no merciful hints of danger, were thrown out to deter the unwary merchant or traveller from the hazard he was incurring. I know not whether it is considered among Governments the bounden duty of the Ruling power to give such reasonable notice; but this I do know, that the omission of it nearly cost the lives of several British subjects,— and that whether it be considered an official duty or not, the *moral* responsibility rests on him who has the power to give such friendly caution, and cruelly neglects to exercise it. I feel that I have a right to attribute all my subsequent sufferings to the thoughtlessness or the cruelty of Lord Amherst's Government. Be this as it may, the trap was open, and the incautious bird flew into it.

Having once resolved, no precious time was to be lost. As we now contemplated embarking a large amount of money, prudence suggested that I should have an assistant who could assume charge of the property if any ill fate befel me, and, when at leisure, protect our argosies up the Irrawaddi. I made choice of Mr. Richardson, a young man who afterwards had the wisdom to escape by a timely flight the waves of trouble that overwhelmed his less fortunate master. That he might not enter on his duties a complete novice, I took him with me in the first instance to Amerapoorah.

We sailed from Calcutta together, with a larger investment than before, in the *Anne*, a ship which I had chartered, and reached Rangoon early in July without incident. The port is easy of access. Captain Gibson, who had been there only once before, finding there was no pilot available at the mouth of the river, did not think it worth while to wait for one, but took the ship drawing fifteen feet of water up by the lead, and anchored her abreast the town of Rangoon without accident.

A few weeks sufficed for all I had to do in Rangoon. This time I had to equip three boats, of which I took the command of one, put Mr. Richardson in charge of another, and the third we kept well up between us. A Mr. Stockdale, residing at Rangoon, had some business up the river, and asked leave to join my fleet for protection, a request readily granted, as I found him a well-educated, companionable person, whose society enlivened our evenings when we assembled to make all safe for the night. He had a little boat of his own.

Just as we were embarking, a crowd of people in their holiday suits were seen pressing out to a little open plain in the suburbs. Curiosity induced me to join the concourse. I found they were going to blow up a priest of Boodh who had recently died, and was deemed of sufficient sanctity to cause some noise in the world he had just quitted. A small pagoda-shaped shed made of thatch had been erected, and contained the corpse surrounded by gunpowder and combustibles. At this target a number of rudely-constructed rockets on wheels, carrying grotesque figures, were fired one after another, at the distance of 100 or 150 yards, not only without success, but to the imminent danger of the assembled crowd, upon whom many of them seemed inclined to turn round and expend their fury. They were more successful at last in firing one of these projectiles directed to the object by a strong rope, along which it glided to its mark, when the ceremony terminated by the explosion of the edifice.

The obese Malabaree, my aide-de-camp on the former voyage, having departed this life during my absence at Calcutta, I had to look out for a substitute. This time I engaged two native Mahomedans, not that I wanted two, but because they were such sworn friends that they flatly refused to be parted. The name of the one was Kewet-nee (*Anglicè* "Red Rat"), while his *fidus Achates* bore the more dignified appellation of Shwai-nee ("Red Gold"). Nothing in the character or the appearance of the one or the other verified the nomenclature, unless indeed "red gold" might have typified *fidelity*. It is well known that, as a race, the Indian Mahomedan is proverbially unfriendly to the Englishman, but I cannot deny that these two friends, so long as our intercourse lasted, were found to be "as true as gold."

Who that has travelled in a foreign country, being ignorant of its language, has not endured torment from the insufferable tyranny which existed mutually between himself and his interpreter? The organ of speech is just as useless to you, when he is absent, as if you were born dumb. You must speak with his tongue, hear with his ears, believe what he tells you, form your judgment from his representations,—in fact, without him constantly at your elbow, you feel yourself to be little better than an unreasoning beast. He must follow you like your shadow, though never trusted. His exacting master is as much a tyrant to him, as he to his master. How happy was I now to find myself able to walk through the villages and streets, talk to whom I would, command my own men, do my own work, without this everlasting incumbrance sticking to one like an "Old Man of the Sea"! The country and all it contained assumed a new interest. I talked for the sake of talking, like one who has discovered a new faculty, and it was only on a rare or important occasion that I troubled either the "Red Rat" or the "Red Gold."

Nothing could have been more agreeable than our progress up the Irrawuddi, until we had passed the half-way town of Prome. Every day we spent singly, each one in his particular boat, following out his own reading or amusement, and ever alert to prevent danger by the propensity of the steersman to carry too much sail, or to enter too ardently into races with other boats; which seclusion during the day served only to render our evening rendezvous the more refreshing. We knew neither anxiety nor sorrow, each doing his best to beguile the tedium of the long evenings, until death invaded us, and we had to mourn the illness and death of our poor friend Stockdale. He met his death in the following manner.

When we had ascended the river a day or two's sail above Prome; my boatmen told me of a natural curiosity to be seen less than a mile from the bank of the river, in a secluded spot, where there was a beautiful example of a dropping well. The day was intensely hot, when we imprudently sallied forth in the afternoon, to gain a sight of this freak of nature. One of the boatmen, who knew the way, led our little party, by a narrow pathway, through the jungle. The tall, rank grass, towering many feet above our heads, closed upon the footpath on either side, so as to admit our advancing only in Indian file, and rain having recently fallen, the tangled jungle was steaming with the heat of the sun, and swarming with insects. Neither was our march rendered more cheerful, when we were told that the place was infested with tigers, a report which greatly accelerated our speed. It is difficult to explain why a man should walk quicker when he dreads the chance of being sprung upon by a tiger, but it is certain he does so. I have read of fear giving *wings* to flight, but in our circumstances no wings could have afforded us safety, unless by enabling us to soar above the danger. We soon found ourselves following the leader in a state of dripping perspiration, at a pace continually mending, until at last it amounted almost to a trot.

We reached the cavern in a deplorable state of heat and exhaustion. Its coolness was at first refreshing, and the large basin worn into the rock below, by the dropping water from the high, overhanging roof, through many ages, stood before us, invitingly filled to the brim with sparkling water of icy coldness. The temptation was not to be resisted. We each indulged in a fatal draught, the folly of which was brought home to our senses in a very few minutes.

At the first sensation of a chill, I beat a rapid retreat, not stopping long enough even to examine the secrets of this gloomy cave; but it was too late. We hurried back, thinking a like exertion might counteract the effects of our imprudence. In this we were mistaken. Stockdale and I were seized with shiverings, but Richardson escaped. Not knowing exactly what was best to be done, I thought the most sensible thing was to swallow a wineglassful of brandy, and to this I attribute my preservation. Mr. Stockdale preferred waiting an hour till dinner was ready. He had received his mortal stroke. Fever ensued. We had medicines of all sorts, but none of us knew how to administer them. Nevertheless, seeing it must end fatally, unless some active steps were taken, I strongly urged the use of calomel. Poor Stockdale, however, had such an antipathy to medicine, that he steadfastly refused; therefore, all that could be done to alleviate his sufferings was limited to good nursing, and attention to his comforts, which we did not fail to administer to the best of our ability. They proved unavailing; he sank under the disease, and died a few minutes after my boats anchored at Ava. The next day I saw him decently buried in the native cemetery, outside the walls of the town. I have been thus particular in relating the circumstances of this gentleman's death, because it is not at all likely his relations in this country, with whom I am not acquainted, can ever have heard of his fate, and it is possible this account, if it should meet their eye, may be the first authentic tidings they may have of it. His death was the cause of some trouble to me, as will be seen hereafter.

It is said that "misfortune rarely comes singly." It was so with us; for, a few days afterwards, a gloom was again cast over our spirits by the loss of the merriest of my crew, by drowning, in a somewhat singular manner. My boat was being towed within a few feet of the bank, when this man, wishing to go on shore, jumped into the water, thinking to reach it by one or two strokes of swimming. He had leaped into an eddy so strong, that he could not stem it even that short distance, and was carried, with wonderful rapidity, into the stream. As nobody thought he was in any danger, a fatal minute was lost before putting the boat round to his rescue. A quarter of this minute so lost would have saved him. When our fears were at length aroused by the rapidly-increasing distance between the unfortunate man and the boat, we followed as quickly as our oars would take us, and were within a few yards, preparing to extend the hand of safety, when the last remains of strength were exhausted, and the waters closed over his head so near, that the boat shot over the very spot where the last struggle for life had been made. It is a fatal mistake, under such circumstances, for a swimmer to endeavour to stem the current. The man was not a bad swimmer, and if, instead of exhausting his powers by vain efforts to regain the boat, he had turned round and gone with the stream, he could have landed himself a mile or two below without any difficulty.

About the same time I had myself, too, a narrow escape from a watery grave. One evening, while my crew were cooking their evening meal on shore, I sauntered alone a little way into the country for a walk, and coming upon a retired spot where a small tributary stream was making its way into the main river, the desire arose of a refreshing swim. Some years had passed since I last put my powers to the test, but after carefully eyeing the breadth of the rather sluggish stream, I felt no doubt of my ability to cross it, as I could easily have done in former times. So I stripped and plunged in, but when about two-thirds over, I became a little doubtful of the prudence of the attempt. Still, it was too late to think of returning, and I pushed on, till, finding my strength failing, I thought I would sound for a bottom, and on doing so, what was my relief to find I touched the ground about chin deep! I waded on shore, took a minute's rest, and then, seeing I must either perform the feat again, or wander naked in the jungles nobody knows how long, I took to the water with more confidence, from my having done it once, and regained in safety the envied spot where my clothes were deposited. It taxed my powers, however, to the utmost.

Bathing in the rivers of India is at all times a hazardous and foolish practice, especially in the Irrawuddi, which is teeming with alligators of huge size and terrible voracity. They are often known to take a man from the stern of his light canoe, depressed as it is almost to the water's edge by his own weight, offering a tempting bait to these ravenous creatures. I have seen them at times basking on the rushy bank, apparently asleep, with their horrid jaws wide open, and distended almost to a right angle. The natives say that while they are indulging in this way, their pestiferous breath attracts the swarms of flies and insects abounding on such sedgy banks, and that when their mouths are well lined with them a single snap secures the prey. This is not at all improbable, and must form rather a pleasant mode of taking a delicate dessert after a glutting meal of putrid carrion. A few years after, when my boat was once gliding noiselessly down the Saluen river, the men resting on their oars, I came unexpectedly upon one of these hateful reptiles as he lay extended in the cooling attitude just described. He was either asleep, or too intent upon his interesting amusement of fly-catching to notice my approach, until a charge of a very different description went down his nasty throat. A loud plash in the water followed, almost as quick as the report from my gun, and I saw him no more. There is no doubt he died, for the alligator rarely recovers from a severe wound.

Dr. Price, an American missionary, whose acquaintance I afterwards made in Ava, told me that when he was ascending the Irrawuddi, one of his crew having something to do over the boat's side, which necessitated his immersion in the water, was seized by an alligator of extraordinary size, and was, in the first instance, dragged quietly under water in sight of his comrades. While Price and the crew were staring at each other in mute consternation, the head and shoulders of the monster reappeared close to the boat's side, bearing the unfortunate man, probably still living, in his jaws. The alligator had seized his prey by the waist, the man lying across like a stick grasped in the middle. Rising with his prey several feet above the water, he brought it down with great force and a loud crack upon the surface, as if to facilitate the operation of breaking up the body—the red stain in the calm river marking with what fatal effect the object had been accomplished.

I can never think of an alligator without associating in my mind the providential escape of a very dear friend, whose intimacy for more than thirty years has been one of the most solid pleasures of my life. To those who only take their daily walk through one of the parks, the anecdote may be interesting, and, moreover, may tend to reconcile them to wandering on the banks of the Serpentine, even though they should occasionally incur the trouble of pressing their handkerchiefs rather closely to their noses. They will find that there are more unenviable promenades in the world than that.

My friend, then, was in the Civil Service of the East India Company on the Penang establishment, and the duty to which he was appointed was the magistracy of a tract of country on the adjacent coast of Malacca, called Province Wellesley, under the same Government.

Not far from his house was a lake or swamp, the banks of which in places were lined with rank grass and rushes, the favourite resort of these amphibious reptiles. On the banks of this lake my friend was in the habit of wandering alone in the evening to enjoy the cooling sight of the water, accompanied by a favourite dog of the fast-disappearing breed of the English bull-dog. One evening he was incautiously walking nearer to the reedy bank than prudence would warrant, playing a game of romps with his dog, who, in his ecstasy of play, was performing a series of leaps at his master,—he in his turn receiving his favourite on a walking-stick held by the two ends, thus throwing him over on the recurrence of each of these mimic attacks. Taking advantage of his helplessness after one of these tumbles, a giant Alligator leaped with the rapidity of lightning from his hiding-place among the reeds, and in a moment disappeared with the dog! No doubt he would have been "happy with either," but the poor dog was first, and my friend, fearing a fresh dash from another member of the family, if any remained, was fain to retreat with the loss of his pet. One's blood curdles in trying to realize such a scene. Among all the horrid forms of death none can be more revolting to the imagination, than being ground down under water by such an ogre; and grateful am I to the merciful Disposer of human life that such a frightful fate was averted from my friend.

CHAPTER IX.

Our arrival in Ava.—No European settlers.—Mr. Cabral, his fate.—Ava occupied.—Mr. Lanciego lends me a house.—Audience of the King.—Present him with the dog.—Absence of all love of sports among the Burmese.—Sale of investments.—Mercantile proceedings.—Mr. Rodgers.—Arrival of Dr. Price, a missionary.—Anecdotes of the old King.—His character.—He forces Mahomedans to eat pork.—His astrological whims.—Brahmin astronomers *versus* Burmese.—Prediction of eclipse.—The King consigns a section of his Court to the horse-pond.—Escape of Mr. Rodgers.—Rebellion at the accession of His Majesty.—Complicity of Mr. Rodgers.—How he cleared the Irrawuddi of pirates.

Our little fleet had been so impeded in its progress by the strength of the freshes setting down the river, that seven weeks passed away before it reached its destination. Throughout this long voyage, with a solitary exception, we had not seen a single European—a pretty good proof, if any were wanting, that, away from the centre of power, no protection for property could be relied on, or many an adventurous spirit would have been found pushing his fortunes on the rich banks of the Irrawuddi. This one exception was a Portuguese, named Cabral, who, for some cause or other beyond conjecture, had buried himself among the natives at Prome. It could not be for the sake of trade, for he had none; nor from misanthropy, for his amiable physiognomy and manners forbade the supposition. Whatever the cause, he met an evil fate. When troops were levying for the subsequent war, the poor man, not aware that the Burmese had superstitions somewhat in keeping with those of ancient Rome, unwittingly crossed the path on which a small body of them were marching, and was instantly cut to pieces by the leading soldiers, converting an augury of evil into an auspicious one.

At length, after an absence of nearly a year, the tall spire of the Palace at Ava again came into view. An architect, more fortunate, it is to be hoped, if not more skilful than his predecessor, had been found bold enough to replace the golden *tee* which now shone on high in glittering splendour. His Majesty had finally abandoned the Capital of his grandfather, and was now holding his Court in the place of his choice. His people had followed him, and had rebuilt the ancient town, little dreaming that ten or twelve years later a new Despot would inaugurate a fresh exodus. The place now began to assume a busy appearance, at the expense of its nearly-deserted rival. As it was also the residence of the Court, and was likely to become the great internal mart of the kingdom, I judged it advisable to settle there at once, rather than return to the fading old town above. The most difficult subjects to move were the Chinese settlers, of whom there are several thousands at Amerapoorah, who seemed to prefer clinging to their old homes, and who remained there long after the Court had withdrawn.

It happened most opportunely that Mr. Lanciego, the Rangoon Akoupwoon, was now on his annual visit to Ava, to present the Port duties to the King. But for the kindness of this gentleman I might have found it impossible to get a house in this half-finished town. He gave me the use of one, run up in his own allotment, which, although of the usual fragile material, had accommodation enough both for myself and Mr. Richardson. It was on the river side, and had a fine view of the noble woods and hills of Tsagain, with its nests of white and gilded pagodas on the opposite bank, the only feature of the country the eye could rest on with pleasure. It was otherwise a hot, dusty plain, with few fine trees even to recommend it.

Having consigned the remains of my unfortunate fellow-traveller to their mother earth, in a spot where none of his own faith before, and probably none since, have rested beside him, and having taken undisturbed possession, as before, of my new abode, it became high time that I should again assume my scarlet, and present myself before my Royal protector. No time indeed was to be lost, for the ever-curious eyes of the loo-byo-dau had caught sight of a personage of more interest for the moment than myself, who, concealed from vulgar gaze, I vainly hoped had eluded their prying propensities. This was the famous dog which was to bring glory to the King and confusion to the younger brother.

The Prince's mastiff was a giant, quite safe to be unmatched in inches, so, failing in point of size, I had turned my attention to rareness and beauty. As I knew they had not got an English greyhound, I purchased in Calcutta a white one, of rare size and beauty, whose company had solaced me on my voyage, and was now to be parted with, not without a pang. But he was going to a good master, too good in fact, for he soon killed him with kindness. His fame had gone before me, and if a sharp look-out had not been kept, he would have gone too, for be it known that the custom at this Court was to gratify the King without reference to the means. If a man could steal my dog, and present it to the King, the rogue would, to use a native expression, "*gain face*," which means that His Majesty would not fail to associate the giver with the gift, and in this it cannot be denied they exercised an intimate knowledge of human nature. Here I was their match, and, wishing to *gain face* myself, I carefully guarded my treasure, and kept him securely from their grasp, until we appeared together, side by side, in the Royal presence.

"Dart" exhibited a wonderful sense of propriety, in quietly taking his seat beside me, with all the gravity of a senator, but in a little while he forgot his manners, by a yawn wide enough to engulf a rabbit, which seemed to intimate, in very plain language, "I am tired of your Majesty's company." Then, with an intelligent look at me, quite as easily interpreted, he asked, "Can't we be off?" Notwithstanding his uncourtly manners, he became, on the instant, a prime favourite, was clothed in scarlet like his old master, and died a year or so afterwards, the death of an Alderman, from the effects of inactivity and high living. I suggested to His Majesty, in order that he might comprehend his worth, to try him at a hare, but the Burmese monarchs, unlike those of Hindostan, have no fancy whatever for sport, nor could I discover much of the true spirit of field sports among any of his subjects, who rather estimated the value of a stag by what he would bring in the shambles, than by the amusement he afforded in the stalking. Their faith as Buddhists is not the cause of this, for, strange as it may appear, the destruction of wild animals is not viewed with the same horror as the slaughter of those domesticated. Being very fond of field sports myself, I looked with an eye of covetousness on the King's group of noble elephants, and thought of the crashing line they would form in the tiger-haunted jungles of India, and wondered how a Prince, who had all the best appliances within his reach, could be so stupid and apathetic as to place no more value on them than he did on his flock of sheep. There is no accounting for taste!

Nothing could have been more satisfactory than my audience on this occasion. Far from discovering the seeds of discord which were at this very time vegetating on the British frontier, and, indeed, almost producing fruit, I found the King kind and cordial, and condescending almost to familiarity, as formerly. Promises of protection were repeated; the haughty Queen even joined in them, as did also the Prince of Tharawudi, in spite of the eclipse given to his kennel. Everything conspired to make me confident of good usage, and of liberty to concoct and to carry out my ambitious schemes of fortune without fear of interruption.

In a few days my investment of goods brought from Calcutta was again sold, with as great success as before, and I began to think of sending Mr. Richardson down to Rangoon, to wait there the arrival of others, and see them safely forwarded to me; but I was anxious before doing so to see what business could be transacted in the annual fair held by the Chinese at Medai. The caravans did not usually begin to arrive before the new year, and I had reason to believe that many of the commodities they brought would be of the greatest value to me as means of exchange. Besides raw silk, there was one which I had hopes of gaining the privilege to export, a valuable one indeed, and likely to extend my commerce immensely. It was the gold-leaf imported by the Chinese for the gilding of the sacred edifices, &c. As the Burmese did not beat out their own gold for this purpose, it could easily be distinguished and identified so as not to be confounded with the native metal, and on this ground I might hope for success, by a judicious use of the usual instruments of negotiation before adverted to. If I could acquire this privilege, Mr. Richardson might carry the intelligence to Calcutta, and prepare my friends for a large extension of their commerce. No occupation could be more absorbing than the one I was engaged in at this time. It was not the mere making of money by drudgery in any of the old beaten tracks, in which the act of accumulation itself in most instances forms the only recompense for the labour. It was the pleasure of discovering new sources—weighing the advantages—compassing the means—removing impediments—surmounting difficulties—and this in an unexplored field, where treasure lies concealed in many places, but where no human being who knew their value had yet sought for them.

I was glad to find my aged acquaintance, Mr. Rodgers, still in good health. The old gentleman was busily engaged in compassing the means to supplant his rival, the Spaniard, in the office of Akoupwoon of Rangoon, the only appointment under Government open to the ambition of a white man. The post had alternated from time to time between these contending parties, the tactics of each being as openly known to the other as those of Whig and Tory when contending for power in England. Bribes were the means always used. Unfortunately for me, their rivalry had at last descended to personal quarrel, which prevented me from enjoying their society together. As I was uninterested in their jealous bickerings, I kept aloof, and, by carefully avoiding the subject of contention, maintained a friendly footing with both.

Another recent arrival had thrown animation into the

European community of Ava, in the person of Dr. Price, an American citizen and missionary from the American Board of Baptist Missions. Mr. Rodgers had no faith in missions, nor, to say the truth, had I much myself at that time; but this was a prejudice arising from want of opportunity for information, or rather perhaps from a careless want of observation which was totally removed by later experience. " What do you think he would do," said the old gentleman, " if he were put to such a test as I once saw a number of Mahomedans subjected to ?" He then told me a story of abominable cruelty, but assuming rather a ludicrous form, which, as it is characteristic of Burmese despotism, I must relate.

The old King, grandfather of the present one, was by turns a bigot and a heretic; at one time slaying his subjects because they were not orthodox Buddhists; at another unfrocking their priests and confiscating their monasteries with as little remorse as our own " bluff King Hal," his subjects also following the lead with equal obsequiousness. At one period, when the heretical mood was in the ascendant, His Majesty was troubled in mind while in search of the true Religion, which he had the sagacity to see that Buddhism was *not*.

Once launched on the ocean of speculation, the currents drifted the uneasy Monarch hither and thither, until at last they set him on the shoal of Mahomedanism. His Majesty hit upon a very curious method of taking the soundings of this faith, in order to ascertain whether there was good holding-ground at the bottom. He was told that they abhorred pork, and would not eat it. " Very right too," said His Majesty; " your Sheen Gautama tried to eat it, and you know it killed him." " True, your Majesty," was the reply, " but our religion does not prevent our following his example if we like, whereas with them it is a matter of their faith,—they would die rather than pollute themselves with it." The cunning thought now passed through the Monarch's mind, that if they would rather die than taste a bit of pork, there must be some virtue at the root of their faith. "We will try."

Now there were many Mahomedans residing in Ava, some of them foreigners, others native-born subjects of the King. Of these he commanded several of the most considerable to assemble at his Palace, where, to their consternation, the flesh of the hated animal was placed ready-cooked before them, and they were commanded, without further ceremony, to fall-to at once. What a study for Lavater! What a subject for Leech! I feel it is wrong to make tyranny, in its most detestable form, an occasion for amusement; but who can control the imagination in such a case? Who does not picture to himself the countenance of a solemn Moulvie, with his hand on his flowing beard, cursing the savoury sparerib, as, with a retching, sea-sick stomach, he gapes to receive the unholy morsel! The look of despair—the ill-concealed rage—the mutual, recognizing glances of the chief actors, as much as to say, "We are all in the same boat—don't tell of me, and I won't tell of you." The scene must have been unique of its kind.

But was there no one, with the spirit of a martyr, to step forth from the throng, and, with the quiet firmness of the three devoted Children before the Babylonish Monarch, exclaim, "O king! we are not careful to answer thee in this matter"? No one, whose natural indignation urged him to beard the Tyrant, and refuse? None. Sad

F

to say they did all partake of the abominable pig, and his Majesty's doubt remained unsatisfied.

"Would Christian missionaries have done differently if put to a similar test?" asked Mr. Rodgers. Who can answer that question? We *hope* they would.

The whole affair looks like a practical joke of a character which, fortunately for the interest of the human race, few men in the world possess the power to play off. This arbitrary Monarch, however, must have been a humourist on a grand scale. Take another story. I wish I could tell it with the simple humour, the amplification and detail of the narrator, in whose hands the anecdote was irresistibly ludicrous. Let the reader take the facts, and exercise his imagination on them.

An eclipse of the sun was expected. When such a phenomenon was to happen, it was the custom of this whimsical Court, that the Cassay Brahmins, of whom there were many residing in Amerapoorah, should notify the same to the King, he being himself addicted to astrological studies. Whether these predictions were given from calculations made by themselves, or whether they acquired their knowledge elsewhere, I forget, but the time at which the eclipse was to take place was always presented from some source or other. These Brahmins, from the influence they had acquired over the King's mind by their proficiency in his favourite study, had become objects of general envy, and it broke out fiercely at this time, the malcontents taking their stand incautiously on very slippery ground. They aspired to a short-lived victory by denying the correctness of their opponents' prediction. Many of the chief courtiers joined the cabal from mere hatred to the Brahmins, without the slightest knowledge of the question, or dread of the consequences. The cunning old King maintained a vexatious silence until the chief men about his Court were committed to one side or the other; then, when he had drawn a sufficient number into his net, he threatened to punish the losing party, whichever it might be, for attempting to deceive him.

A pool of water lay invitingly near, and perhaps suggested the thought. "The Brahmins, or their accusers, shall stand up to the neck in that pond," said the King; then turning to Mr. Rodgers, "What do you say, Yadza? Are the Brahmins right or wrong?" "Now," said Mr. Rodgers, "if I had only had the wisdom to say that I was an unlearned man, and knew nothing of these matters, all would have been right; but, fired with the ambition of being thought a learned man, I replied, 'I have not made the calculation, your Majesty.' 'Oh! then you can calculate eclipses?' 'Yes, your Majesty, after a fashion.' 'Then go home instantly, and let me know what you say to-morrow.'

"I went home, not to study the deep things of Newton, you may be sure, but a book of far greater value to my weak comprehension, the *Bengal Almanack*, a copy of which had been sent me for that year. All I had to do was the schoolboy task of correcting for the longitude, and as bold as brass I gave the result to His Majesty. The heads of many a man of rank, and of many an ill-starred astronomer, did I behold, waving as thick as lilies, on the surface of that pond! But I had acquired a character that taxed all my ingenuity to support, and from that time, as long as the old fox lived, I took especial care, with the fear of the horse-pond ever present, never to be without a copy of the *Bengal Annual Almanack*."

The vagaries and eccentricities of the old King were not allowed, by him, to embroil or imperil his Empire.

They were controlled by so much of natural shrewdness and penetration, that it continued to flourish during his long reign, and at his death it descended to his grandson in the very height of its prosperity. As the crown rarely descends without a fight, two of the young King's uncles, the Princes of Prome and Toungoo, so often mentioned in the work of Colonel Symes, were accused of attempts at usurpation, and suffered cruel deaths. The fact is that, in such a crisis, suspicion and guilt are synonymous terms,— at least they meet the same fate; and those of the Royal blood who possess power, at the demise of the sovereign, knowing they cannot escape the imputation of the former, fly to open rebellion as affording the best chance of safety. Mr. Rodgers was himself a partisan, and nearly suffered in this rebellion. He was hidden some months, and when the young King was firmly established on the Throne, he saved his life by liberal bribery among the Queen's party, and once more ventured to appear at Court. No questions were asked, but he was ever after regarded with suspicion, and had never been able to regain his appointment of Akoupwoon.

It would appear that, when he was a younger man, the energetic character of Mr. Rodgers was appreciated by the old King, his master. There was a time, he told me, when the Irrawaddi was so infested by gang-robbers throughout its course from Amerapoorah to Rangoon, that the native trade was entirely stopped, and the Capital suffered for want of its usual supplies of grain from the low countries. The Governors of some districts declared their inability to put down these daring bands, whose atrocities became the terror even of populous towns, when the King, having great faith in the bold character of his English subject, constituted him Admiral of the

River, with unlimited powers. "I picked out," said the old gentleman, "a little army of the bravest men I could find, and let them loose upon the robbers wherever we came upon them, and, as the inhabitants were inclined to help me with information, I was pretty successful. We gave no quarter. Those who were taken alive we tied up to trees, and *used to paint a bull's-eye on their bodies for my men to fire at to improve their practice!*" How soon may a man forget the usages of civilized countries and descend towards those of the savage! He could not see any impropriety in the manner of the executions, nor in combining capital punishment with holiday pastime. The result, he said, was quite satisfactory; after a few months he succeeded in re-opening the navigation of the river.

CHAPTER X.

First indications of war.—Causes assigned for it.—Opinions of Tharawadi.
—Popular feeling in favour of war.- Bundoola crosses the river with
an army.—War-boats.—Magnificent regattas.—Dr. Judson arrives.—
Bundoola's army marched for the British frontier.—Accusation about
Mr. Stockdale's property.—I accompany the King to the Shwai-dyke.—
Tempting exhibition of silver.—Attempt to walk off with it.—My
failure therein.—Growing dislike and suspicions.—I confine myself
much to my house.

It was not until the year 1823 had nearly closed, when I had been two or three months at Ava, that the first indications of an unfriendly feeling towards the British Government became apparent. Up to that time the horizon was unclouded, success attended me, and in looking forward I saw nothing to check the sanguine anticipations my imagination had formed. The ease with which youth assimilates itself with the habits and ideas of the people of foreign countries, aided by the liberality my immense profits enabled me to dispense, had ingratiated me into the favour of all classes. Having no ambitious views of power, my favour at Court did not make me an object of envy to the nobles, and the commercial advantages I sought interfered with no interests of a people who had, in reality, no commerce to sustain. I was therefore a general favourite.

From this happy state of things I was aroused in the

month of December by the alarming recurrence to warlike topics whenever I went among the leading Chiefs, all pointing to a rupture with the British Government. The immediate subject of dispute was the alleged protection afforded by the British to four or five men who had incurred the displeasure of the King, and who had sought an asylum on British ground. It may appear a slight pretext for war, but I knew too well the value my countrymen attach, as a point of honour, to their territory being the sanctuary of the unfortunate, to suppose, for a moment, that they would consent to give up political offenders against an arbitrary Despotism, and this knowledge gave alarming importance to the rumour. In England, the mean surrender of a political refugee to a foreign Despot would cause more excitement than the breaking out of a sanguinary war. From such a nation there was no hope of concession.

Another cause of dispute was an insignificant boundary question about a worthless island in the river which divides our territory from the Burmese province of Arracan. This rumour gave me less trouble, for I was equally convinced that a trumpery question of this nature would never induce our Government to enter into a war.

But as time advanced these questions became the topics of general conversation—the constant talk of war in the ears of a people who had been accustomed to a long course of victory and usurpation, inflamed their ambition, and rendered it popular. The reports they heard of the unbounded wealth of Calcutta; the unwarlike character of such of the borderers as they had met on the frontier; the interested reports of those foreigners who hated our rule; the general forbearance of our

Government for a long course of years,—interpreted into timidity,—all conspired to lead them to the idea that Bengal would fall an easy prey,—that, like the great Roman, they had only to go, to inspect, and to conquer. It was easy to see that the question of the Refugees was fast becoming a mere pretext, as was also that of the island (called by the Burmese *Shemapyoo*), and that if both were ceded another would assuredly be found to suit their warlike propensities.

These alarming rumours met me wherever I went, but among the most open and violent instigators of the war was my impulsive friend the Prince of Tharawudi, who at once rushed into the debate whenever I went to see him.

"You know nothing," he would say, "of the bravery of our people in war. We have never yet found any nation to withstand us. They say your soldiers, when they fight, march up exposing their whole bodies. They use music, to let us know when they are coming. They do not know our skill and cunning. They will all be killed if they attack us in this way. Besides, you have taken our territory. When we conquered Arracan we acquired a right to Bengal as far as Moorshedabad, which formerly belonged to Arracan. You will have to give it up again. We shall go to Calcutta and take it. There is plenty of gold and silver there. The English are rich, but they are not so brave as we are. They pay Sepoys to fight for them. They are now frightened, lest we should make war upon them," &c.

It will be seen from these remarks, which fairly represent the general feeling, that the Court had no appreciation of the Power it was defying. How could it have any? None of their own leading men had ever been in

Bengal, and those from whom they derived the little information they possessed, were of classes whose hatred to the British name was bitter, and who used all their influence to precipitate the country into hostilities. I allude to the Brahmins of Cassay, and the Mahomedans, both of India and of native origin. The only persons who could give honest and sound advice were the two or three Europeans in Ava; but our counsels were despised as timid and interested.

To the Prince of Tharawudi I could reply more freely than to most of the Chiefs. I told him of the great power wielded by the Governor-General—the immense army at his command—their splendid arms, courage, and discipline—the conquests they had made—the long friendship that had existed between the two countries—the misery the war would cause—and urged all the usual arguments in favour of Peace. My representations to him and to the Woongees were as honest and straightforward as I dared to make them; in fact, I did everything but tell them, in plain terms, that if they went to war, they would be signally and disgracefully beaten.

On reading the despatches since published, I was surprised to find that this claim to the territory in Bengal, as a dependency of Arracan, alluded to by the Prince of Tharawudi, was not new. It had been made, in an irregular manner, so far back as 1818, but was allowed to lie dormant by the Burmese, as they had other wars of aggression on hand with nearer neighbours, which it was necessary first to bring to a successful issue. They had made several attempts on Siam, but finding her a tough customer, they were now turning their attentions to the Honourable East India Company.

On the first of January, 1824, the new year was ushered in by a splendid pageant, but one boding no good for the tranquillity of the country.

The Burmese General, Mengee Maha Bundoola, the Wellington of the army, so well known to the British in the subsequent war, having been recalled from his career of conquest in Assam, had levied a picked force of 6000 men, who had been assembled at the Capital, and were now to cross the river to Tsagain on the right bank, in the presence of the King and Court. My house commanded the river view, which gave me an opportunity of witnessing this brilliant spectacle to great advantage. A fleet of magnificent war-boats, many of them richly gilded, were in readiness to receive the troops at mid-day, who embarked in perfect order; each man was attired in a comfortable campaigning jacket of black cloth, thickly wadded and quilted with cotton, and was armed with a musket or spear and shield, as suited the corps to which he belonged. A profusion of flags, with gay devices, were unfurled to the breeze, martial music resounded, the Chiefs took their seats at the prows of their boats (the post of honour, as the stern is with us), and in the middle of each boat, a soldier, selected for his skill, danced a kind of hornpipe. When all was ready, the whole fleet, lining the bank for a considerable distance, dashed all at once across the river, nearly a mile wide; the loud song bursting from 6000 lusty throats, while the stroke from thousands of oars and paddles kept time to their music. It was an exciting spectacle, one which, but for certain misgivings of its purport, I should have looked on with delight.

No one seemed to know for certain what was the destination of this army. I had called on the Bundoola, in the hope of ascertaining, if possible, but the great man maintained a haughty silence. He was not of a communicative disposition, and was beside himself with pride.

In the management of these war-boats, the Burmese are wonderfully dexterous. A finer sight than their Regattas, when the King is present, can hardly be conceived; and perhaps no nation in the world was possessed of the means to get one up on so grand and imposing a scale. The boats are all of the light elegant canoe build, the bottom scooped from the trunk of a single gigantic teak tree, having very little beam, varying in length from sixty to eighty or even one hundred feet, and rowed by crews of nearly those numbers. They are not all designed for warlike purposes,—many are fancy-boats owned by the chief Nobles, who, knowing the devotion of the King to that pastime, and following his example, expend large sums in gilding and decorating their favourite craft. It is quite a national amusement, into which they enter with as much enthusiasm as the English do into the sports of the field or the turf, and a Burmese Noble will place as high a value on his favourite boat and crew, as any of our nobility would on an unrivalled racehorse.

At these Regattas, the wide river is covered with hundreds of such beautiful boats, rowing in every direction before the King, who is seated in his Water Palace enjoying the sport. It is astonishing how they avoid collision, rowing hither and thither, and crossing each other's bows at the top of their speed; now taking a wide majestic sweep in turning, which seems to monopolize one-half of the river's breadth, now performing the same evolution in an almost fixed position, as though turning on a pivot,

The whole has the appearance of being done on a programme, as much as a review in one of our parks, or accidents must ensue.

When this intricate manœuvring is finished, fresh boats and crews appear for the race. You may see them stretching to their oars here and there for short distances, just to impart life and energy to the men, as I have seen the experienced jockey canter his racehorse along the course before starting, to stretch his muscles and get him into wind. Then off they go like lightning. The distance is too short to admit any jockeyship—there is no holding back—the whole force is put out at once, and a speed attained that would astonish our Champions of the Thames. The velocity is such, that the contending boats have to shoot down the river a great distance, after passing the goal, before they can be rounded with safety, as horses at a race often pass the judge's stand nearly a quarter of a mile before their speed can be safely arrested. On returning, one of the victorious crew may be seen in the middle of his boat, dancing the favourite hornpipe to the music of the song, in exultation over his crestfallen adversaries.

Besides racing, many skilful feats of water-craft are performed, such as propelling a boat against the stream by merely beating the air with the paddles. This is done by the crew standing, with lengthened paddles for the purpose, and favourable circumstances are taken advantage of, such as a sluggish part of the stream, calm weather, &c. But the most beautiful thing I saw was a boat with a powerful crew, which passed the Water Palace at the top of its speed, and, before proceeding many hundred yards, hid herself in a shower of sparkling spray thrown up by the practised skill of the rowers. She seemed to be entering an atmosphere of glittering mist, and the spray she left behind which hid her from view, was like that caused by the water of a cataract falling on the rocks below. These truly Royal festivals must have suffered a sad eclipse since the Monarchy has been shorn of the best half of its dominions. Before that time, every town or river district had to provide its own boat, the Chiefs emulating each other to produce one with the highest qualifications.

About the beginning of February, Dr. Judson, another American missionary, arrived in Ava, to join his coadjutor, Dr. Price. He reported that on his passage up the river, he had seen the Bundoola's army encamped at Senpyoo-ghewn, a district assigned to support the establishment of the King's favourite white Elephant, who had his Ministers and retinue like one of the magnates of the land. From this spot, a road (if a mountain pass deserves the name) communicates with Arracan, and from the information Dr. Judson acquired, there was no doubt the army was bound for the frontier, to support their arrogant claim to a portion of Bengal. But had more frequent communication with India been possible, all doubts would long since have been removed; for it appears that so long back as October, fighting had begun, and several of our sepoys had been slain in an attempt of the Burmese to establish themselves in our territory. I had not yet had leisure to organize post-boats for my own use, and a month or two elapsed without any opportunity of passing a letter to my friends in Bengal. They, on their part, found equal difficulty; I was therefore left wholly to rumour and conjecture as to the complications of political affairs.

Meanwhile, as the proverb says, "a feather will show

how the wind blows," and a significant event happened about this time, clearly indicating that the current was setting adverse to my interests.

I have already mentioned the name of Mr. Stockdale. This gentleman, when he died, had some trifling property in his boat, which, as usual, fell to the rapacity of the Court. It was too little in value to make any great effort about, or I might possibly, while in favour, have succeeded in getting it restored to me for his heirs, though even then the attempt would have been attended with danger, as the money went into the coffers of the grasping and vindictive Queen. A story was invented that I owed Mr. Stockdale a large sum of money, and I was summoned to the Shwai-dyke, or Royal Treasury, where the demand was enforced. As no evidence was adduced to substantiate the claim, all I could do was to deny the fact. On the contrary, Mr. Stockdale had borrowed a little money from me, for which I held his written engagement. But explanation and assertion were useless. I was detained in custody at the Treasurer's house, and was not allowed to return home until I gained my freedom by a considerable bribe. After this not a word further was said about the alleged debt: the bribe was the *ultima ratio*, it was all that was wanted. As this was the first instance of extortion or personal disrespect, it was no dubious indication that the feelings of the Court towards me were undergoing a change.

I was now anxious to ascertain how far the King shared in this feeling, but as I had reason to believe my bribe had gone into the pocket of his abominable spouse, I could not muster the courage for a formal complaint. I absented myself from the Palace for a week or two, waiting to see whether I should be sent for as formerly.

My doubt on this point had not been cleared up, when, in riding through one of the wide streets of the town, I saw the Royal guard approaching in the distance, and knew by their manner that His Majesty was in the rear. According to etiquette, every one seats himself on the ground with clasped hands and downcast eyes while Royalty passes, for here the proverb does not hold good, that " a cat may look at a king." If an unfortunate puss were so inquisitive from an eminence above His Majesty, she would assuredly be brought down by the pellet-bows of the guard, a few of whom carry them for such purposes, and use them with great dexterity. As I always tried to avoid this humiliation of squatting on the ground, I sought the friendly screen of the trunk of a huge tamarind tree, behind which I hid myself, holding my pony by the bridle, and I thought he was hidden as well as myself. His Majesty, however, caught sight of the European saddle, and ordered me out of my hiding-place. He was taking his ride in a richly-ornamented English buggy, no doubt the present of one of our former Embassies. Between the shafts were a number of the loo-byo-dau, highly-honoured bipeds, proud to act as horses in the service of their Monarch. I was invited to become one of the team, an offer willingly accepted, as I rather enjoyed the fun. When the buggy stopped at the foot of the flight of the Palace stairs, I followed at his desire with the retinue, His Majesty now and then addressing a question to me.

He took his walk to the Shwai-dyke, the scene of my late dishonour, in front of which, exposed in the open air, were ranged some hundreds of logs of pure silver, shaped like pieces of ship's kentledge, but, unfortunately for me, wanting the handle with which kentledge is furnished for the convenience of lifting. The King made some remark about them. "Your Majesty," said I, "must have honest subjects: in my country they would be stolen."

"They are too heavy," he rejoined, "they cannot be lifted; each piece weighs 100 viss."

"My countrymen are very strong—they would walk away with them on their shoulders. I could almost do it myself, your Majesty."

"Try!" said the King; "if you can lift one I will give it you."

The calculation ran through my head in an instant—365 lbs. avoirdupois of pure silver! It is worth trying for at all events. I stepped forward. Oh! for the muscles of Hercules! I was young, and not deficient in strength. Up went one foot of the log in an instant, and I believe the Golden Foot was, for the moment, terrified lest I should run away with it. Had there been a handle, I should certainly have accomplished the feat of lifting it; but the sharp edge of the block cut my hands like a knife, and I was obliged to give it up, amid the bantering laughter of the King and his Courtiers. Little did they dream how soon the glittering treasure was to change its ownership, under the more expert practice of my countrymen!

The King afterwards took me into the Palace, and carried me to the Queen's apartments; nor could I discover from his manner that I was in any degree less a favourite than formerly. So long as this Royal patronage lasted I was safe; but how long could it be maintained, when the growing dislike and suspicion of all by whom he was surrounded, which was now but ill concealed, should burst forth into open attacks? Every day, as this war-fever gained strength, these suspicions increased. I could not go anywhere without being compelled to listen to arrogant boasting, sometimes accompanied by a word of commiseration for me, but oftener by scowling looks and menacing expressions. By degrees I withdrew from intercourse with the Chiefs, deeming it prudent to avoid these irritating conversations on a topic fraught with danger, if honest opinions were to be expressed. I began to stay more in my house, leaving the "Red Rat" to do my work, and seldom stirred abroad for fear of open insult.

CHAPTER XI.

Perplexities.—Departure of Mr. Richardson, who escapes in safety.—Taking a wild elephant.—Mode of taming him.—Royal pugilists.—My last interview with the King.—Scheme for escape with the Sakkya-Woongee.—Defeated by delays.—Might have been worse.

I was now involved in no slight perplexity. Had I been merely a traveller, or residing for my own pleasure alone, my course would have been plain. I should have attempted my escape against all hazards, while escape was yet possible. But such not being the case, it became a struggle between inclination and duty. I was left with a very large amount of property, which would unquestionably be lost if left unprotected. This did not entirely belong to me, and how should I reflect upon myself, and how would my character stand, if I deserted the interests confided to me? I might be wrong, too, in my estimation of the danger. If war were imminent, surely my friends in India would have found means to warn me—it was even the duty of the Government to do so. Then why submit to a certain sacrifice on such doubtful grounds? Besides, would not my flight be arrested? Would permission be granted? An abortive attempt to leave the country would make matters worse, and excite and increase the ill-feeling against me.

In this state of doubt and hesitation I consulted the

"Red Rat." He was a man of considerable penetration; but he could give me little comfort. He knew the feelings and practices of the Burmans in time of war, and admitted that to remain in their power at such a time was to perish; but he was equally sure that permission would not be granted for my departure, and secret flight was perilous, not to say impossible, without detection. The result of my reasoning was a determination to remain at my post, while the fact of my doing so would facilitate the departure of Mr. Richardson, whose fate there was no necessity to link with mine.

After coming to this decision I advised Mr. Richardson not to lose a single day, and if questioned on his voyage down the river he was merely to say he was going on my business. The "Rat" fully approved of this. The departure of *one*, he said, *to bring up fresh goods* might pass unnoticed, if the other remained with the property.

When this considerate scheme for his own safety was unfolded to the party who was to benefit by it, what was my surprise at meeting a flat refusal! He dreaded the dangers of the river—knew not the language—feared being seized and sent back a prisoner! He had acquired a blind confidence in me, and thought that where I was he should be safe. No argument could turn him from his resolution. At last, a little vexed at his obstinate folly, I reversed the proposition. As he would not go, would he be content to remain, and allow me the opportunity of running for my life? I said I was quite ready for either course, but felt it my duty to give him the option. This brought him to his senses. I dared not ask permission for him to leave, fearing it might be refused; but embarked him privately on a small fast boat, in which he happily arrived in safety at Rangoon.

I was rejoiced to hear of the poor fellow's escape, though it will be seen, as the story proceeds, that it well-nigh proved my destruction. Thinking it probable that my countrymen at Rangoon, not being aware of the state of feeling at the Capital, might be living in fancied security, I wrote a few lines to one of them by the hand of Mr. Richardson, warning him of their danger. The letter was delivered, but the caution was disregarded. Their negligence proved nearly fatal to themselves, for within a fortnight after they received my letter the British fleet appeared before Rangoon, and their lives were wonderfully rescued when in the extremest peril.

When our fleet anchored abreast of the town, their fate seemed inevitable. They were led to immediate execution. The executioners stood with their knives ready, the floor was strewed with sand to receive their blood, and nothing was wanting but the final order from the Governor, when, before this arrived, a broadside from H.M.S. *Liffey* providentially saved them. A 32-pound shot tore through the building, and so alarmed the gang that they instantly decamped, carrying their prisoners with them. Not knowing in the confusion what to do with them, the Governor having fled, they hid them in a house near the Great Pagoda, where they were found the next morning, heavily ironed, by a party of our soldiers and released. As for Richardson himself, the terror-stricken young man had wisely made good his retreat in the first vessel sailing from the port.

Although I had resolved not to show myself again at any of their public festivals, curiosity, on one occasion, overcame my prudence. Sitting at my window, I saw a huge, wild male Elephant escorted through the street by about a dozen tame females without riders, except one or two,—who, sometimes hustling, sometimes coaxing him, most ingeniously contrived to curb his vicious propensity to mischief in his passage through the town. More than once he manifested a disposition to unroof a house, when it was curious to see how the females interfered to prevent it by guiding away his uplifted trunk, and shouldering him into the midst of the herd, out of the way of committing damage.

I soon learned that the King and his whole Court were to be present at the entrapping of this beast. The temptation was too strong to resist. It was but a short distance from my house, so I sallied forth with the thousands of holiday-makers, hoping to relieve, for a time, the weight which oppressed my spirits, by joining in the amusement of the day. The scene has been described by travellers to Ava.

It is the duty of the female decoys to seduce the wild animal into an enclosure from 80 to 100 yards square. The brick walls of this enclosure are twenty or thirty feet thick, affording ample space at the top for the crowd of spectators out of harm's way. Within the walls, at a convenient distance from them, strong posts are fixed near to each other, as a refuge for the band of tormentors when pursued by the enraged animal. There is an entrance-gate in the centre of one wall, and a sally-port in the opposite one, through which the decoys escape, one by one, as they find opportunity. Each of these ports is opened or closed with great facility by means of a swinging post, so contrived and of such strength as to resist any effort to break through it.

When the herd reached the entrance-gate of this Quadrangle, the Hero of the day became suspicious that mischief was intended. The decoys went in and came out again, uttering a shrill note of pleasure, as if to convince their captive that his fears were groundless; but even this did not seem to satisfy him. Several times he went close, looked in at the gate, and then, as if he had made up his mind that all was not straightforward, turned round, and rapidly retreated with a loud cry. After a little while, finding him unreasonably suspicious, the decoys proceeded to encircle him, using a little gentle coercion and much coaxing. At length his scruples were overcome, and the reluctant victim entered with the rest, all together in a crowd.

Now came the difficult manœuvre for exit, and it was wonderful to see the tact with which some of these artful decoys amused their dupe on one side of the square, while their companions in deceit were making good their retreat on the other. It seemed as if each knew the exact part she had to perform, and the whole was done so quietly and cleverly, that the confiding male was not at all aware how fast his seraglio was diminishing in number. At length, when he came to his senses, only one unfortunate female was left within. There was something terrible in the deliberate survey the savage took when for the first time he missed his herd. He stood as though astonished at the treachery,—then, at the first impulse, he made a ferocious attack on the poor solitary female, burying one of his immense tusks in her side. The wound was mortal; the gush of blood might, without exaggeration, be compared to the stream of water pouring out from an ordinary house-pump. She, nevertheless, lived to effect her escape at the well-known spot, while her destroyer, who did not repeat the attack, was furiously ranging the enclosure, chasing the runners, who now made their appearance, endeavouring to irritate him with shouts of defiance. After an hour or two of teasing, he was entrapped in the sally-port, which he seemed all along to recognize as the spot of his desertion, and assaulted from time to time with great fury. Here the walls were so close together, as to prevent his turning round; once in, he was safe.

All the time the men were engaged in tormenting the poor beast, a goat, introduced probably to attract his attention occasionally from them, was quietly browsing, in a most unconcerned manner, on the grass growing in the quadrangle. Several times the Elephant made a furious rush at it, but without the least chance of success; the goat never fled before him, but eluded his attacks merely by dodging nimbly through his legs, and when the Elephant had passed, he continued provokingly to nibble the grass, as though the onslaught had not in the least discomposed his nerves.

My house was so close that I went daily to watch the manner of taming him. His cage was just large enough to hold him. Above it, was a ponderous beam embedded into the walls, and to this he was suspended by ropes, dexterously passed under his belly and over the beam, drawn tight enough to prevent his lying down, but sufficiently slack to permit him to stand without pain. His fore feet were then fastened together with fetters—a very taming process, as the writer can testify, as was also the craving of hunger to which he was subjected. In this solitary confinement he was left two or three days, and when he next saw the human form, it was not in the character of a tormentor, but in that of a benefactor, bringing dainty food and using every art of conciliation. He thus became accustomed to the sight, and voice, and handling of his keeper; the severities were gradually relaxed; in a fortnight he was suffered to shuffle out in his shackles to a shed, where he was again introduced to the civilizing society of his female betrayers, and became willing to forego his birthright of liberty for a mess of pottage. I had not his acquaintance long enough to see the end, but I was told that in two or three months he might be used with safety.

After the Elephant was secured, a band of Royal pugilists had a set-to. These combats would have appeared ludicrous to one of the Fancy in our prize-rings. The left arm was extended at full length, as though for the purpose of seizing or clutching an antagonist, and was quite useless for offence or defence, while the right fist was poised high in the air, watching an opportunity to come down like a sledge-hammer on the head of the opponent when he attempted to close. After closing, the elbows and knees were used with great dexterity as well as the fist. There was nothing of the brutal fighting, *à l'outrance*, which disgraces our English ring; the first blood shown usually decides the combat. The Prince of Tharawudi, a great patron of the ring, asked my opinion of the fights, and was incredulous when I told him we had a hero in England named Thomas Cribb, who would think it mere child's play to dispose of a dozen such champions one after another, and as to those produced at the festival, I thought I could beat them myself. The remark put his blood up, and he kindly invited me to enter the arena against some of his own boxers. I thought it prudent to decline the honour, not, however, from any distrust of my own prowess.

This was the last time I ever gained access to the King. He recognized me among the crowd of spectators, from an open Pavilion erected on the walls, where his Court was assembled to witness the sport, and assigned me a convenient place among them; but it was easy to see, from the bearing of the nobles, that his favour alone protected me from insult. The amenities of a state of war had commenced.

Dr. Judson thought it unbecoming a teacher of religion to appear at such an entertainment, but his less scrupulous coadjutor was there, tempted either by the sport itself, or more likely by the desire to attract the notice of Royalty, for my friend, Jonathan David Price, though an excellent person, set a higher value on the smile of Royalty, than might have been expected from a sturdy son of the States. If such were his motive, poor Price was doomed to a bitter disappointment. He had been, from some cause or other, out of favour at the Court for some time, but seeing me in a place of honour, he ventured to intrude, uncalled, into the Presence, when the silence and averted face of His Majesty gave him a hint that he had better retire, which he did, in great despondency.

On returning home from the Elephant-catching, I found a vanquished pugilist, who had been brought to my house for aid. His skull was laid bare by a terrific hammer-like blow such as I have described.

About this time a gleam of sunshine shot across my path. A chance arose, which, if cleverly improved, might even yet open the net and bring deliverance.

My old acquaintance, Meeadai Mengee, late Viceroy of Rangoon, had died, and a pacific old Woongee (Sakkya-mengee) had been ordered to Rangoon, to assume the Government of the Province. It was strangely inconsistent that, in the present excited state of the Court, they should have selected almost the only reasonable man among them, and one decidedly averse to the war.

When his boats were ready, and he was on the eve of taking his departure for his province, my "Red Rat" (for I dared not go myself) sought an interview by way of suggesting that if he took me to Rangoon with him I might, by my influence, open a negotiation between himself, as Viceroy, and the Governor-General, which would result in the British giving up whatever the King wanted, and so maintain peace between the two countries! He took upon himself to say that I was quite a Burman at heart, and would be sure to use my best energies in the King's interest. The old Minister was already in his boat (though he would not leave for two or three days), when he sent for me to discuss the subject. I waited on him late at night, and of course was loud in praise of Peace, as usual, and promised, if he thought fit to take me in his retinue to Rangoon, to undertake a voyage to Calcutta in the character of his Envoy to the Governor-General. I represented that a great portion of my property was already in gold and silver, ready to remove, that I would leave the "Red Rat" at Ava, under his authority, to collect and bring down the remainder, and that I was quite prepared to accompany him at a moment's notice.

I knew the folly of the whole affair, and that my proposed intervention was an utter absurdity; still it did not appear in this light to him, and as it might be the means of saving my life, together with the chief part of my property, and could do no harm to any one, I thought myself quite justified in allowing the old Woongee to remain under the delusion. It was not my duty, as it certainly was not my interest, to undeceive him. The suggestion pleased the kind-hearted old man, and his conversation with me inspired his confidence. The affair was to be left in his hands. He was to obtain an order that I should accompany him, without compromising himself with the *hlut-dau* by divulging his object.

Had time sufficed, this ridiculous compact would have been carried out. The wayward course of events would have conferred on me the character of a local Envoy to the Governor-General, on a mission about as promising as if I had to propose a union of the two Kingdoms. The impossibility of bringing it to a successful issue did not, however, render it the less welcome to me as a means of safety.

How well do I remember the state of nervous excitement in which I spent the few days following that night's interview!—the irritation created by delays of State, or the predictions of astrologers. Existence seemed to depend on rapidity of movement, yet day by day some new whim, some idle fancy, intervened to detain the Woongee's fleet, until at last it was too late—the time had gone by. The next chapter will show that I was inextricably caught in the toils; my diplomatic aspirations were dismissed, and the *quasi* ambassador had to succumb to circumstances which he could not guide.

And how happy it is for him that he had not the power to guide them! How much more to his advantage were they directed by the unseen and too often unacknowledged hand of Infinite Goodness, which is always at work in averting danger from our path! Had my wishes been gratified, there would have been little chance of my being alive at this moment to acknowledge, as I now do with a thankful heart, the failure of schemes laid with such apparent foresight and prudence.

CHAPTER XII.

Rangoon bombarded.—Effect of the news.—Hopes and plans of the Americans.—Mr. Rodgers.—Lanciego.—I confine myself to the house.—State of the city.—Message from Tharawudi.—Cure for cholera.—I am shunned by every one.—Summoned to the Bya-dyke.—Arrival of Mr. Laird.—I am accused of being a British spy.—Examinations.—I am committed to the custody of the Taing-dau, and remanded.

ONE Sunday morning, I think it was the 23rd of May, I got into a canoe and paddled across the Irrawuddi to the opposite bank of Tsagain, where Dr. Price lived, for the purpose of uniting in worship, as we had been in the habit of doing when opportunity permitted. Our little congregation consisted only of our worthy host and Dr. and Mrs. Judson, who met us by appointment. There was something in the retirement and beauty of the spot, the broad river, seen through the foliage of magnificent trees, rolling at our feet, the smallness of our number, assembled in a heathen, and it may be said by this time almost a hostile country, and especially the perilous circumstances under which we met, which combined to throw into our devotions on that day a peculiar impressiveness. We all knew full well that a dark storm was gathering around us, but from what quarter or in what manner it would burst we could only form vague conjectures, and never did bewildered mortals feel more in need of the aid of that Wisdom which cometh from above, to calm and fortify their minds, and to guide them aright through the intricacies of their difficult path. At that moment, however, we were not aware how soon the evil which we feared was to come upon us.

While thus occupied, our devotions were rudely disturbed by a man rushing into the apartment in breathless haste, with the appalling tidings that a British fleet had arrived at Rangoon, that the town had been bombarded, that the population had fled, and that the place was in the possession of the assailants;—in other words, that a sanguinary war had at last broken out between the two nations, in which the British took the initiative.

A short time was now spent in anxious deliberation, as to the course each party ought to pursue. A war between civilized nations is waged in a very different manner, and with very different feelings, to one maintained against a semi-barbarous people. All their history told us, and what we now saw and heard tended to confirm it, that the extermination or slavery of their enemies was the usual practice of the Burmese in time of war. The latter might be expedient when adjacent nations or tribes were to be subjugated, but the case was different when it respected a handful of Europeans, of race and colour so totally distinct; and there was reason to fear that the former course, with all its barbarities, would immediately be resorted to, as most consonant with their savage ideas and antipathies.

Impressed with this fear, the Americans very reasonably argued that, as their safety entirely depended on their being able to prove their distinct nationality, their aim should be to avoid, in their future conduct, anything which might tend to create a doubt or suspicion of its truth. With this view they besought me to discontinue my visits, thinking that too close an intimacy or alliance with a rebel Englishman might have the appearance of complicity. Much as it grieved me to lose the society of my friends at a time when it would have been most consolatory, I could not but subscribe to the prudence of the movement on their part, and henceforth we saw little of each other, until our fate involved us in one common calamity.

With respect to Mr. Rodgers, the wily old gentleman knew his interest too well to wish to exchange a word with any of us. He depended on his life-long services, his complete naturalization as a Burman subject, and hoped to save himself from shipwreck by steering with the art and skill acquired in his long experience. As to the Spaniard, Lanciego, his court alliance would protect him, but, strong as that was, he felt a nervous dislike at my entering his house, though close by, and this he told me in the plainest terms. Thus every one had his own peculiar plans to secure his life, all agreeing in this one fact, that I was a mightily dangerous person, a most undesirable acquaintance, and I found myself as strictly *tabooed* as if I had been a leper.

Leaving my American friends, I now paddled back to my own house, where I found the "Red Rat" awaiting my return, in a state of great consternation. The negotiation with the Sakkya-Woongee was of course at an end,—he set sail without me, not to take possession of his Province, but to find it in the iron grasp of the British commander. The "Rat" did not attempt to disguise the danger. He recommended me to shut myself up in my house, there to wait the course of events, and to avoid exasperating the people by showing myself in the streets. He did not think I should be molested for the present if I remained unseen, and, promising to come daily to report the state of affairs outside, he left me to my reflections.

These were far from agreeable. I have heard it said that there is a just line of limit between imprudent rashness, a wanton exposure of ourselves to danger, and a cowardly timidity or shrinking from it when a sense of duty calls us to endure the risk. This line of demarcation must be thin as a hair and hardly ascertainable, for all my logic failed to convince me whether I had been acting the part of a reasonable man or that of a simpleton, in allowing myself to be caught in this trap. It certainly did no great credit to my penetration, for nothing had happened that might not have been foreseen; but the growth of this feverish ardour for war had been so gradual, so insidiously creeping from mere rumour to acknowledged facts, that by the time I was aware of my real danger it could hardly be said there was a choice left me. As for the American missionaries, there was no excuse: they were positively to be blamed. They had no money to protect or to take away, and, allowing a strong missionary spirit to operate, it is not easy to see what good they could expect to arise out of their teaching, even if they were allowed to live at large, in the midst of such a scene of anarchy as must ensue. Their resolution to remain was little else than courting martyrdom, which they were likely enough to find, unless the Burmese were further advanced in geography and history than they had any right to look for.

The day and night passed away without molestation. My house was in a remote suburb, so that the noise and clamour prevailing in the town and around the Palace was too distant to disturb me.

On the following day Kewet-nee brought me the news. The whole city was convulsed with rage, as may be supposed, at the loss of their great sea-port, but there was an element in the popular excitement which was working in my favour, and to it I attribute my preservation on the first ebullition of their fury. It was a feeling of satisfaction and exultation that the white foreigners had entered into a trap from which they could not escape, and would inevitably be destroyed like vermin. Such a hold had this delusion taken, that the only fear now expressed was that their enemies would plunder the town and escape, before the Royal army had time to arrive and give them battle. Their expressions of confidence were as unbounded as their indignation; indeed, this buoyancy of feeling gave the town the resemblance of a joyous festival, intermingled with fits of frantic rage. Many songs were extemporized, teeming with ridicule and defiance. The burden of one of them was singularly refined and elegant. It contemplated nothing less than hunting the British General for the sake of his hide; he was to be caught, flayed, and his skin tanned into leather to make shoes for the Heir apparent! Little did the innocent poets know of the vigour Englishmen manifest in defence of their hides! His Majesty at the same time issued a merciful command. He did not wish the white men to be involved in indiscriminate slaughter, but desired that a certain number should be caught alive to serve him as slaves, and especially that their arms should be preserved with great care, to be ready for his next attack on his neighbours, the Siamese. My reporter could not hear that any inquiry had been made about me.

The following day a polite message came from the Prince of Tharawudi, which may be fairly rendered into plain English, as follows:—

"The Prince of Tharawudi presents his compliments to Mr. Gouger, and, having formed a partiality for him, would be sorry to see his throat cut, and recommends him to come quickly to his Palace, where the Prince would like to see the man who dares to touch him. —P.S. Mr. Gouger had better bring his wine and beer, gold and silver, for safety."

This was very kind, and, in truth, something of the sort had passed through my mind more than once; but before accepting this all-powerful protection, I thought I would consult the "Red Rat," to whose guiding genius I had committed myself. Common sense told me that I could not well be in a worse plight than at present, and dictated compliance; but common sense also suggested that it might be as well first to take counsel from one much better versed in the intricacies of Burmese diplomacy than myself. It was well for me that I used so much caution.

When the "Rat" made his appearance, and saw how elated I was with the idea, he looked a kind of contemptuous pity, as much as to say, "You have made but little progress in the knowledge of Burmese character under my teaching." "Sahib," said he, "if the Prince were to know what I am going to tell you, my life would not be worth a day's purchase. This offer is only made that he may get you and your property in his power, and you would then soon find a grave in his garden, as many persons have done before, when it suited his purpose. He knows you have a great deal of gold and silver, and thinks he may as well get it as any one else. When you came to be demanded by the *hlut-dau*, as you would be, the only answer he could give would be that you had died, and there the matter might end. You will stand a better chance by remaining quiet, and allowing yourself to be apprehended by the Woongees, and disposed of according to their pleasure."

So spoke my Ahithophel. His counsel was as an oracle, and experience proved its wisdom. A few years later, when in troublous times this truculent tyrant usurped the Throne of his brother, no fewer than 3000 of his subjects were sacrificed to his jealousy, and that of his hopeful son who succeeded him—not slain in war, but victims of private assassination. His palace-yard was spoken of as teeming with bodies foully disposed of. This was probably an exaggeration, but it is certain that I had no reason to be proud of my acquaintance. A polite answer was returned to His Royal Highness, couched in terms of equal dissimulation. "With a thousand thanks for his benevolent intentions, I had such perfect confidence in the promise of protection, given me by His Majesty, that I reposed without fear, knowing he would not permit any violence to be done to a stranger, who lived under his favour."

For two or three days I was allowed to brood in silence over my hapless fate. Shunned by all my fellow-creatures, the mind constantly reverting, in spite of every effort, to the same harassing train of thought, I became at last a distressing burden to myself; books could not solace me in this nervous state of depression, and I began to think a change to positive suffering, if it only brought activity, would be a relief. My faithful reporter came daily with his budget of local news; but I could hear nothing about myself, nor could he collect any authentic tidings of the fate of the few of my fellow-countrymen, who were living in fancied security at Rangoon when the British fleet made its unwelcome appearance. It was much to be feared they were all massacred, and such was the report.

One night, while sitting in my house, in this disconsolate mood, pondering as usual on the strange vicissitudes of my fate, the voices of a multitude of people outside aroused me from my reverie, and presently commenced such a furious attack, with sticks, on the framework of the house fronting the street, that I thought, at last, the vindictive mob had found me out, and was about to turn its fury on me. Soon it extended along the whole length of the street, while the yelling and shouting became louder and fiercer, mixed with horrid imprecations and threats of vengeance. What could it mean? The house stood firm, and no one attempted to force open the door. I listened with bewildered astonishment. fter five minutes of screaming, and yelling, and thumping, as if Bedlam had been let loose, the tumult suddenly ceased, and the silence of the night was restored. I believe the faculty has long been searching out a specific for the cholera. Here was the Burmese mode of treating it. The demon had been making havoc in our neighbourhood, and the parishioners had united to frighten and hunt him out. If the evil spirit loved to pursue his work of destruction in silence, there was no doubt he would decamp to seek a more quiet field for his labours elsewhere.

On the 28th of May, a body of men made their way into my house and carried me off to a court of justice, called the Bya-dyke, held in the palace-yard, presided over by the Attwenwoons; and the first examination there convinced me that I was caught in a net, from which there was about as much chance of my disentangling myself, as there is for an unfortunate fly to free itself from the web of a spider. The ostensible cause of this examination was simple enough.

An unlucky Scotchman, named John Laird, who had recently commanded a ship in the country trade, had aspired to be the agent to the Prince of Tharawadi, in Rangoon, for the sale of teak timber, with which the Prince's forests abounded. It did not enter into the ambitious Captain's calculations that the honour he courted was a perilous one. The Prince, his master, foreseeing the course affairs were likely to take, and wishing to have his slave in his power, despatched a boat to Rangoon, with instructions to the crew to return with Mr. Laird to Ava. There was no "*habeas corpus*" to save him. When safely on board, he was astonished at the exhibition of a pair of fetters, but from this indignity he freed himself by a bribe. Fortunately for himself he had not brought with him property sufficient to tempt his master to violence. He had just arrived in Ava, bringing with him a Calcutta newspaper, of late date, containing a paragraph indicating, in no doubtful terms, that a hostile expedition to Rangoon was meditated by the British Government. This newspaper he had shown to me; but at the same time he had been imprudent enough to have it explained to his Royal master also. It was to answer for my complicity in this transaction,—knowing the intention to invade the country and not revealing it,—that I was now brought to justice. The accusation was unpleasant, but standing alone it might have been explained. In the course of the examination, however, I found that it only formed a link in a chain of evidence to bring on me the fate of a spy.

I was accused of having made maps of the country, by means of instruments, and of having forwarded them to the enemy; of having sent away my emissary, Mr. Richardson, with intelligence, and of furnishing him with money for his journey; of retaining the Missionaries in my pay, giving them constantly money for their subsistence; of having written to Bengal about affairs of State; of being lavish in my gifts and expenses, and of keeping a retinue of servants inconsistent with a private station, and only such as a man in office could support. The worst of it was that all these accusations were more or less true, while the explanations of them, though simple, were not understood, or, if understood, were not credited; but had they been both understood and believed, they would not have saved me from the consequences.

The history of the maps was this. Before leaving Bengal, a friend (the late Captain Thomas Prinsep, of the Bengal Engineers) expressed to me a wish to get some sketches of temples, monasteries, and scenes near Ava, and, as I was unpractised in the art, he made me a present of instruments to assist me;—I had used these without secresy, often for the amusement of the Burmese themselves. The application of this to my case is evident, and certainly it looked ugly enough. As to Mr. Richardson, his flight and the cause of it have been already described,—it had, nevertheless, a suspicious appearance. The sums given to the Missionaries were of course repaid to me by the agent to the Board in India; still it proved a troublesome charge, especially against the Americans, who were now regarded as my accomplices in Treason. The extent of my gifts or bribes, and the number of my native servants, were no doubt excessive and unaccountable, *in their estimation;* and as to writing the news to Bengal, I could not deny it. It will therefore be seen, that to none of these accusations could I oppose a flat denial, and their total ignorance of our customs prevented their believing such explanations as I could offer. The result was—and I must do them the justice to say that I do believe it was the honest opinion of my judges—that I stood before them a convicted Spy. It was in vain I urged that my countrymen, being anxious to avert a war, had no need of *spies* to give information; the invasion of the country, though the aggression was entirely on the part of the Burmese, was regarded as undeniable proof to the contrary.

Among the various reports flying about to my prejudice, Kewet-nee told me of one, singularly sagacious,—that I was brother-in-law to the East India Company (Goombanee Meng) in disguise,—that the East India Company had married my sister! No doubt my lavish expenditure had been the means of procuring me this undesirable honour, as they found it difficult to reconcile the show of wealth I had displayed with any other than a high station.

A lengthened examination was taken, which was the more alarming as it was conducted with an affectation of unimpassioned calmness, while in its progress every word I uttered was tortured and twisted into evidence against myself. At its close I was not permitted to return home, but was detained under what in England would be called a *remand.* I was committed to the custody of a body of men designated the *Taingdau* (the Royal Shield), a figurative and pretty expression, indicating that they were the personal Guard of the King. These troops had a long line of sheds in the Palace-yard, serving as barracks. Two of them, who were appointed my sentinels, lodged me in their own small apartment, for the present, without any further restraint than close confinement to the cell, receiving me in charge, with strict injunctions to keep me safely and ready to be produced, for further examination, when it might please the Attwenwoons to summon me again for the purpose.

CHAPTER XIII.

Changed prospects.—My Guards accompany me home.—Our flight discovered.—I am taken back to prison at midnight.—Another examination lasts all night.—I am again committed to the Taing-dau, and consigned to the stocks.—Punishment of my keepers.—Corruptibility of the Taing-dau.—I am stripped and carried to the Death-Prison.—Some account of that Establishment.—Let-ma-yoon.—Terror of its name.—I am loaded with three pairs of fetters.

THE events of this day gave a new current to my thoughts. It was clear that the immediate danger I dreaded was averted, only to give birth to another, which seemed more certain and more revolting in its character. Instead of becoming the victim of an enraged mob, I had now to look forward to undergoing the judgment of a vindictive Government for a crime it never forgives. Death always is the penalty of disloyalty, and what they chose to think disloyalty in this instance, was aggravated by feelings of revenge for their humiliation in the attack on their seaport.

It is a misfortune to a man, when he is thrown into circumstances of distress of which he cannot see the end, to have his perceptions too acute for the occasion,—to try to trace and to reason them through various uncertain phases, to a result either favourable or disastrous to himself, as his temperament inclines to be hopeful or melancholic: in the one case, he renders himself liable to the pangs of disappointed hope; in the other, to harrowing anxiety and fear of evils which are never to happen. How much better is it, instead of this, to repose on the truly philosophic as well as Christian maxim, that the evil of each day is sufficient for a person to endure, without encouraging thoughts of a perplexing or disturbing nature beyond it! What an amount of heart-misery should I have avoided in the two years of wretchedness and of marvellous preservation on which I am now entering, had I only learned to adopt this simple but difficult lesson, the hardest that the active mind of man can be brought to submit to, and never achieved but under the influence of strong Christian faith! In the absence of this frame of mind, which might have brought me repose, I now began to speculate on the probabilities of the fate I had to endure. I knew the common practice of the Burmese to resort to barbarous *tortures* when they wished to extract evidence or confession,—the crime imputed to me was one peculiarly within its province; the remembrance of the calm, determined manner of my judges, placid and cruel as priestly Inquisitors, was ever present; the threatened renewal of my examination, the varied charges, the trouble and care it must have cost to get them up,—these and many other topics were contemplated, until my imagination, in spite of a naturally hopeful disposition, pictured to me racks and horrid tortures consummated by an agonizing death. Now it cannot be denied, that all these were likely enough to happen, but it is equally certain that the Christian maxim heartily adopted would have drawn the venom from the sting, by leaving *realities* only to distress me. Truly does one of our poets say,—

"We die a thousand deaths in fearing *one!*"

My two guardsmen were not inclined to subject their prisoner to any severer treatment than his safe detention rendered necessary. This was fortunate, for the hottest season of the year, when the mercury rarely stands lower than 100° in the house, was barely over, and the front of the line of sheds exposed to the maddening glare of the western sun, would have been insupportable had the soldiers prevented me from adopting some protection from its intense glitter and heat. In a few hours we became excellent friends; they procured admission for my terror-stricken servants to pass the gates at all hours to bring me food and comforts, the more readily as I soon found the way to their hearts was no other than that which never fails to gain a *British* guardsman,—beer and brandy; and these were not to be got by excluding my people, or by ill-treating me. During the day, they had the prudence to keep me closely hidden in my crib of eight feet square, for fear the eyes of His Majesty, who often walked that way, should chance to light on the Traitor; but at night, when no one was stirring, the good-natured fellows allowed me to sally forth and take the air in front of the huts.

After two days and nights of wearisome anxiety had been passed in this ward, I began to feel an irresistible desire to see my home once more, and try to bury my sorrows for a short time by a good sound sleep in a comfortable bed. Seeing my Judges had not sent for me a second time, that my Guards were easy fellows, fond of a bribe, and owed me a good turn for liberal drink, I ventured to propose it to them. At first they were alarmed at the consequences of discovery to both parties, wondered what I wanted to go for (well they might!), feared the Attwenwoons would send again for me, and a hundred other things; but at last I overcame all their scruples, and they promised to accompany me home that night, on my assurance that I would not attempt to *make my escape* (a run of 500 miles through a strange country!), and that I would return with them to my prison before the day dawned. It was at best an insane thought, and it is not easy to say what prompted it, unless it were a desire to run away from myself,—to restore a wholesome state of mind by a long walk and a night's rest.

When night came, my confederates disguised me in a native dress, and away we went. My house was a mile and a half distant, the only difficulties to be encountered before reaching it, being the sentries at the two gates of the Palace walls. One of my conductors took the lead to answer questions, while I followed close behind with the remaining doughty guardsman. In this manner we safely passed the sentries, and no one but he who has suffered the weariness of close confinement can estimate the exhilaration I felt, when, emerging beyond the walls, we rapidly pursued our way through the streets of the half-deserted and silent town, with an assumed air of boldness that ill assorted with the nervous fear of detection lurking within. My servants, who never looked for such an apparition, were struck dumb with astonishment, but were sadly cast down when they heard that my stolen visit was to last only a few hours. The soldiers claimed their reward, and kept a watch at the gate while I sought what I so much needed—a good night's rest.

But, alas! the best-laid plans are often disconcerted. A little after midnight a posse of armed men aroused me from a deep sleep with loud clamour and vociferations, that told me at once my flight had been discovered. My trusty guards, terrified at the consequences of their breach of discipline, wisely took to their heels, leaving me in the hands of a dozen of their corps who had been sent in search of me. As ill luck would have it, the Attwenwoon on duty that night (for one of these ministers was always on watch through the night in his Court, guarding his Monarch's rest) bethought himself that he should like to beguile some hours of darkness by renewing my examination, perhaps at the same time thinking he might take me off my guard by the unseasonable hour he selected. Great was his consternation when it was reported that the Traitor, with his keepers, had made their escape. The hue-and-cry was instantly raised, and men were despatched in pursuit in all directions, with what success the reader is already aware.

My captors, who were not in a heavenly temper, would not give me a moment with my people, but hurried me back along the road I had so recently traversed, never resting until they had ushered me into the august presence of the old Minister, the Cerberus of the night. For hours did this wily old interrogator use every art and dissimulation to induce me to commit myself by a confession, coaxing and threatening by turns, but of course in vain. My refusal, or rather my inability to confess anything, was looked upon as obstinacy, and every moment I was expecting the introduction of the cord or the hammer, the usual instruments of persuasion in such cases; but from this terrible infliction the merciful providence of God, which so repeatedly succoured me in the perils of the two following years, now preserved me. When the morning dawned, the old rogue, growing tired, ordered me back to my old quarters, but to prevent a second attempt at flight, he directed that my feet should be made fast in the stocks night and day. Nature was exhausted by the events of the night, and I fell into a deep sleep in spite of the stocks and angry Taing-dau.

This was paying dearly for my frolic, but it fared even worse with my unfortunate confederates. When caught they were pegged down to the ground by the wrists and ankles, *in extenso*, with the face upwards exposed to the fierce rays of the vertical sun. Such an infliction would have killed a European in a very short time. Barbarous as this punishment may seem, and impolitic, as being likely to cripple a soldier for life, it is not long since we ourselves emerged from such folly. I have a lively recollection of seeing, when a boy, two soldiers, for a less crime, suspended by cords in such a manner as allowed the whole weight of their bodies to rest on a spike tipped with a button about the size of a penny. On this button the culprit stood with bared foot at the manifest risk of being lamed for life. This torture was called "*picketting.*"

When I awoke, a feeling of shame passed over me as I contemplated the result of my foolish *escapade*, the undignified attitude to which I had sunk being that of a disorderly rogue found drunk in a country village. Very degrading, certainly, but well merited by my folly. Two new men of the same corps had the charge of me, rather morose fellows, rendered more sulky, perhaps, by the scrape their comrades had fallen into through their kindness to me. But, alas! they were destined to fall away from their duty by the force of the same seduction; and I do believe, that, like true soldiers, there was hardly a man of the corps of the Royal Shield whom I could not have gained over by the promise of a glass of grog. As soon as the tempter became aware of his power, the stocks lay before him a useless piece of furniture. Our compact was that I was to be on the alert to secure them from danger by slipping my feet into the stocks on the approach of any stranger. So we got on together amicably enough.

Through the latticed bamboo walls I frequently saw the King pass by on his visits to his stables, so close that I was strongly tempted imprudently to raise my voice from within in supplication for liberty. Did he know how ignominiously I was treated?

Ten days of this melancholy life passed away, still no remand, no further examination. What could it mean? Had a sentence been arrived at, and what was it? The uncertainty was becoming insupportable; but nothing is more true than that every condition of life, bad as it may be, is capable of becoming worse.

This was bitterly exemplified on the eighth of June, when the face of affairs changed from bad to worse. On that day a gang of boisterous ruffians, carrying cords and long canes, rushed into my little room with some evil intent, as their manner and countenances indicated. My feet being released from the stocks into which I had thrust them, according to my compact, a furious battle commenced between the intruders and the Taing-dau soldiers for the few trifling articles of furniture the apartment contained. One might have supposed from the fierceness of the contention that something of value, at least, would reward the victorious party. No such thing. A knife and fork, some pieces of worthless glass and old crockery, and a not very clean pillow, were the only plunder within reach. After appropriating these, an attack was made upon me for the clothes I wore, and it really seemed as if I should be torn in pieces by the combatants for the possession of my jacket, shirt, and trousers.

"They will be of no use to you," urged the considerate guardsmen; "they are going to carry you to the *Let-ma-yoon toung*,"—the Death-Prison! Now, thought I, for the last scene of this trying drama; the fate of the spy comes at last. This was an appalling piece of intelligence, but wherever they were to take me, I did not wish to go naked, so I successfully resisted their attempts to denude me. My jacket and waistcoat were torn off, but the rest I succeeded in saving. In doing so I was not at the time aware, that I was merely acting as a partisan of the worst faction of the two, who knew they could plunder me more at leisure when they got me into their den, or I should not have thought it worth while to make so vigorous a defence. They now proceeded to bind my arms behind my back with a piece of cord, and to lead me away bare-footed and bare-headed to the *Young-dau*, or Criminal Hall of Justice, presided over by the Governor of the town. To ascend the steps of his Court-house was too great an honour for such an atrocious criminal. I was made to squat down in front of it in the street below, while my name and crime were entered in the Prison list, which being done, the procession moved onward, and halted at the gate of the *Let-ma-yoon*, nearly opposite.

There are four common prisons in Ava, but one of these only was appropriated to criminals likely to suffer death. It derives its remarkably well-selected name "*Let-ma-yoon*"—literally interpreted, "hand! shrink not"— from the revolting scenes of cruelty practised within its walls. This was the prison to which I was driven. To those acquainted with the Burmese language, the name conveys a peculiar impression of terror. It contemplates the extreme of human suffering, and when this has reached a point at which our nature recoils—when it is supposed that any one bearing the human form might well refuse to be the instrument to add to it, the *hand* of the executioner is apostrophized, and encouraged not to follow the dictates of the heart. "Thine eye shall not pity, nor thy hand spare."

My heart sank within me as I entered the gate of the prison-yard, which, as it closed behind me, seemed to shut me out for ever from all the interests and sympathies of the world beyond it. I was now delivered over to the wretches, seven or eight in number, who guarded this gaol. They were all condemned malefactors, whose lives had been spared on the condition of their becoming common Executioners; the more hideous the crime for which he had to suffer, the more hardened the criminal, the fitter instrument he was presumed to be for the profession he was henceforth doomed to follow. If a spark of human feeling remained, it could hardly be expected that any of these men would voluntarily adhere to their calling; therefore, to render escape without detection impossible, the shape of a ring was indelibly tattooed on each cheek, which gave rise to the name they were commonly known by, "*pah-quet*," or "ring-cheeked," a term detested even by themselves as one of reproach, and one we never dared to apply in addressing them. The nature of his qualification for the employment was written in a similar manner across the breast. The Chief of the gang was a lean, wiry, hard-featured old man, whose qualification for his office stared in unusually large characters, as though he were proud of

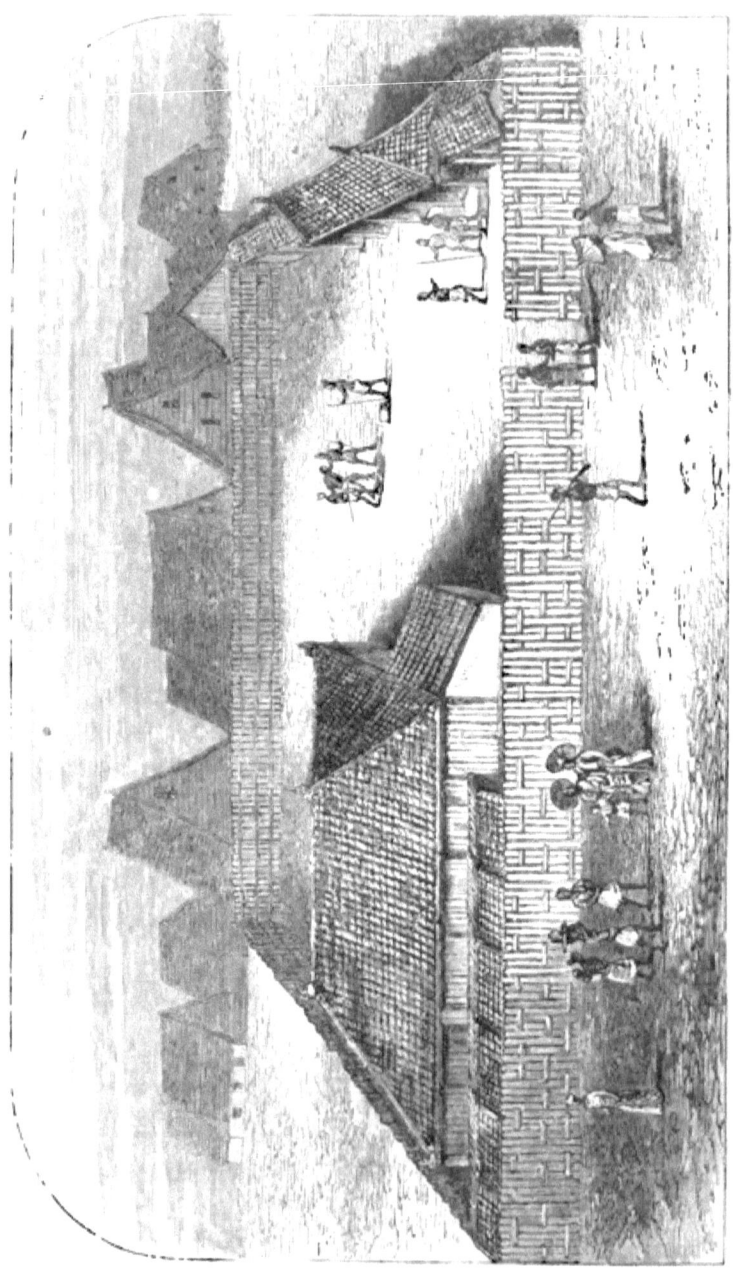

EXTERIOR OF PRISON ENCLOSURE.

To face page 141.

it, "Loo-that," *Anglicè* "murderer." On the principle that "a soft answer turneth away wrath," we taught ourselves to address this miscreant under the appellation "*aphe*," "father," as did all his subordinates. Another, bearing an appropriate motto, had murdered his brother, and had hidden his body piecemeal under his house. A third was branded "*thoo-kho*," "thief,"—another, who had a spice of the unnatural humour of Petit André, "*myeng-kho*," "horse-stealer."

This troop of wretches were held in such detestation, that the law prohibited their entering any person's house except in execution of their office. It happened, soon after I entered, that the exigencies of this brotherhood were great from an increase of business, and no brave malefactor (*inhumanity* was always styled *bravery* here) being ready to strengthen the force, a young man convicted of a petty offence was selected to fill the vacancy. I beheld this poor youth doomed to the most debasing ignominy for the rest of his life by these fatal rings, his piteous cries at the degradation he was undergoing being drowned by the jeers and ridicule of the confederates. They soon made him as much a child of the Devil as themselves. Such were my gaolers!

The "*father*" of this interesting family received me at the gate with a smile of welcome like the grin of a tiger, and, with the most disgusting imprecations, hurried me to a huge block of granite embedded in the ground in the centre of the yard. To his mortification I had been partially rifled before, so that little remained to be done in this way beyond the mere gleaning of my dress that was left. I was made to sit down and place my ankles on the block of stone, while three pairs of fetters were struck on with a maul, a false blow of which would have maimed me for ever. But they were too expert for this, and it was not a time to care for minor dangers. Thus shackled, I was told, as if in derision, to *walk* to the entrance of the prison-house, not many yards distant; but as the shortness of the chains barely permitted me to advance the heel of one foot to the toe of the other, it was only by shuffling a few inches at a time that the task was accomplished. Practice, however, soon made me more expert.

It is not easy to give a correct idea of the scene which the interior of that Prison-house disclosed, as the door shut behind me, and left me to survey it at leisure; yet, as it was destined to be my dwelling-place for the first year of my captivity, I must endeavour to describe it, impossible as the task may be to convey by words what the eye alone can appreciate.

Although it was between four and five o'clock on a bright, sunny afternoon, the rays of light only penetrated through the chinks and cracks of the walls sufficiently to disclose the utter wretchedness of all within. Some time elapsed before I could clearly distinguish the objects by which I was surrounded. As my eyes gradually adapted themselves to the dim light, I ascertained it to be a room about forty feet long by thirty feet wide, the floor and sides made of strong teak-wood planks, the former being raised two feet from the earth on posts, which, according to the usual style of Burmese architecture, ran through the body of the building, and supported the tiled roof as well as the rafters for the floor and the planking of the walls. The height of the walls from the floor was five or six feet, but the roof being a sloping one, the centre might be double that height. It had no window or aperture to admit light or air except a closely-woven bamboo wicket used as a door, and this was always kept closed. Fortunately the builders had not expended much labour on the walls, the planks of which here and there were not very closely united, affording through the chinks the only ventilation the apartment possessed, if we except a hole near the roof, where, either by accident or design, nearly a foot in length of decayed plank had been torn off. This formed a safety-valve for the escape of foul air to a certain extent; and, but for this fortuitous circumstance, it is difficult to see how life could have been long sustained.

The only articles of furniture the place contained were these:—First, and most prominent, was a gigantic row of stocks, similar in its construction to that formerly used in England, but now nearly extinct; though dilapidated specimens may still be seen in some of the market-places of our country towns. It was capable of accommodating more than a dozen occupants, and like a huge Alligator opened and shut its jaws with a loud snap upon its prey. Several smaller reptiles, interesting varieties of the same species, lay basking around this monster, each holding by the leg a pair of hapless victims consigned to its custody. These were heavy logs of timber bored with holes to admit the feet, and fitted with wooden pins to hold them fast. In the centre of the apartment was placed a tripod, holding a large earthen cup filled with earth oil, to be used as a lamp during the night-watches; and lastly, a simple but suspicious-looking piece of machinery whose painful uses it was my fate to test before many hours had elapsed. It was merely a long bamboo suspended from the roof by a rope at each end, and worked by blocks or pulleys, to raise or depress it at pleasure.

Before me, stretched on the floor, lay forty or fifty hapless wretches, whose crimes or misfortunes had brought them into this place of torment. They were all nearly naked, and the half-famished features and skeleton frames of many of them too plainly told the story of their protracted sufferings. Very few were without chains, and some had one or both feet in the stocks besides. A sight of such squalid wretchedness can hardly be imagined. Silence seemed to be the order of the day; perhaps the poor creatures were so engrossed with their own misery that they hardly cared to make many remarks on the intrusion of so unusual an inmate as myself.

If the *ensemble* be difficult to portray, the stench was absolutely indescribable, for it was not like anything which exists elsewhere in creation. I will, therefore, give the facts, and leave the reader's nose to understand them by a synthetic course of reasoning—if it can.

The prison had never been washed, nor even swept, since it was built. So I was told, and have no doubt it was true, for, besides the ocular proof from its present condition, it is certain no attempt was made to cleanse it during my subsequent tenancy of eleven months. This gave a kind of fixedness or permanency to the fetid odours, until the very floors and walls were saturated with them, and joined in emitting the pest. Putrid remains of castaway animal and vegetable stuff, which needed no broom to make it *move on*—the stale fumes from thousands of tobacco-pipes—the scattered ejections of the pulp and liquid from their everlasting betel, and other nameless abominations, still more disgusting, which strewed the floor—and if to this be added the exudation from the bodies of a crowd of never-washed convicts, encouraged by the thermometer at 100°, in a den almost without ventilation—is it possible to say what it *smelt* like?

As might have been expected from such a state of things, the place was teeming with creeping vermin to an extent that very soon reconciled me to the plunder of the greater portion of my dress.

I have done my best to give a faithful picture of the Burmese *Let-ma-yoon* on first impressions — but this was merely superficial—its hidden secrets had yet to be learned.

CHAPTER XIV.

I find Mr. Laird in irons before me.—Mr. Rodgers taken.—Apprehension of the American missionary, Dr. Judson.—His ill-treatment.—Dr. Price arrested.—The "Red Rat" entrapped.—We are prohibited the use of the English language.—We are put on the bamboo.—Prison discipline.—Our first night.—How passed.—Starvation of prisoners.—Alms-giving in the prison.—I am taken from my companions.—Torture of a man accused of robbery.—Its result.

MUCH time was not given me on entering to make these observations, for a young savage (himself a felon in chains) who had intrusted to him the safe keeping of his fellow-prisoners, came shuffling up to conduct me to the darkest and most loathsome corner of the dungeon. Here I was sorry to find my fellow-countryman, Mr. Laird, who had already gone through the same process as myself, and now lay weltering in the filthy sty allotted to him. I attempted to speak to him, but the first words had scarcely escaped my lips when the young savage, brandishing a formidable club, gave me to understand that he had received strict orders from our worthy "father" to brain any foreigner who attempted to speak, unless in the Burmese language. This put a stop to our conversation, as poor Laird did not understand a word of Burmese.

Stretched on the floor by the side of my countryman,

I waited to see what was next to happen. A short time brought Mr. Rodgers, already known to the reader. All the precautions his timidity suggested had been unavailing to shield him from suspicion, and his hope of safety from naturalization was as nothing when contrasted with his rebel origin. It was melancholy to see the poor old man, bending with age, tottering to join our company.

All the Englishmen were now collected. We three were the only true rebels in blood, and we had reason to hope, as no others had yet appeared, that our friends, the Americans, had made good their defence, and would escape the general destruction. We soon perceived our mistake.

Dr. Judson was next brought in. We had scarcely seen each other since the memorable Sunday when we were dispersed like a flock of sheep at Tsagain, by the news of the fatal invasion. Useless were all the politic and cautious steps they took to avoid suspicion—in vain did they plead their sacred profession as teachers of Religion—in vain that they were the subjects of a separate State, often at war with the English:—they spoke our language—they were supplied with money by the English spy—they had been his intimate friends—that was enough. As to their sacred character, it probably told against them, seeing they had been making unconcealed attempts to subvert the Buddhist faith. We all suffered the same treatment, though it is probable we were not all in the same danger of our lives. From one of Mrs. Judson's letters, written after the war, Dr. Judson's arrest appears to have been attended even with greater barbarity than my own. One cannot read it without a feeling of sympathy in the sufferings of a lady of refined and amiable manners.*

Dr. Judson had just taken his place by our side, when the tall, gaunt figure of Dr. Price came into view. Unable, at first, to distinguish our disconsolate group through the gloom and smoke, we watched him as he entered with an air of bewilderment and a soliloquy which, at any other time, would have made us all laugh, but it was quickly interrupted by a flourish of the club of

---

* "On the 8th of June, just as we were preparing for dinner, in rushed an officer, holding a black book, with a dozen Burmans, accompanied by one, whom, from his spotted face, we knew to be an executioner, and a 'son of the prison.' 'Where is the teacher?' was the first inquiry. Mr. Judson presented himself. 'You are called by the King,' said the officer; a form of speech always used in arresting a criminal. The spotted man instantly seized Mr. Judson, threw him on the floor, and produced the small cord, the instrument of torture. I caught hold of his arm; 'Stay!' said I, 'I will give you money.' 'Take her too,' said the officer; 'she also is a foreigner.' Mr. Judson, with an imploring look, begged they would let me remain until further orders. The scene was now shocking beyond description. The whole neighbourhood had collected. The masons, at work on the brick-house, threw down their tools, and ran—the little Burman children were screaming and crying—the Bengalee servants stood in amazement at the indignities offered their master—and the hardened executioner, with a kind of hellish joy, drew tight the cords, bound Mr. Judson fast, and dragged him off I knew not whither. In vain I entreated the spotted face to take the silver, and loosen the ropes; but he spurned my offers, and immediately departed. I gave the money, however, to Moung Ing to follow after, to make some further attempt to mitigate the torture of Mr. Judson; but instead of succeeding, when a few rods from the house, the unfeeling wretches again threw their prisoner on the ground, and drew the cords still tighter, so as almost to prevent respiration. The officer and his gang proceeded on to the courthouse, where the governor of the city and officers were collected, one of whom read the order of the King to commit Mr. Judson to the death-prison, into which he was soon hurled—the door closed, and Moung Ing saw him no more."—*Mrs. Judson's Published Letters.*

the young savage. Price seemed at first inclined to show fight, like a true free-born Yankee, at being thus arbitrarily deprived of the liberty of speech and the relief of uttering his lamentations aloud, but the upraised arm of power satisfied him that he had better quietly succumb to his fate. He was quite subdued, when at length he beheld his silent friends, by whose side he took his place.

With the exception of the Spaniard, there was not another white face in Ava, and, knowing he was secure, we now thought our number complete—but again we were mistaken in our conjecture.

To my consternation, as it was growing dark, I could distinguish the diminutive forms of the "Red Rat" (caught at length in the trap) and his friend the "Red Gold," glimmering in the portal. If any confirmation were needed of the conviction of the Government of my treasonable practices, it was now furnished in the fact that these two men, native born, never having left the country, conversant with all the convolutions of Burmese diplomacy, had not been able, with all their cunning, to keep their necks out of the halter. Their presumed complicity with the arch-Traitor was the crime they were charged with.

When night came on, the "father" of the establishment, entering, stalked towards our corner. The meaning of the bamboo now became apparent. It was passed between the legs of each individual, and when it had threaded our number, seven in all, a man at each end hoisted it up by the blocks to a height which allowed our shoulders to rest on the ground while our feet depended from the iron rings of the fetters. The adjustment of the height was left to the judgment of our kind-hearted parent, who stood by to see that it was not high enough to endanger life, nor low enough to exempt from pain. Having settled this point to his satisfaction, the venerable chief proceeded, with a staff, to count the number of the captives, bestowing a smart rap on the head to those he disliked, whom he made over to the savage, with a significant hint of what he might expect if the agreed tally were not forthcoming when the wicket opened the next morning. He then took his leave, kindly wishing us a good night's rest—for the old wretch could be facetious—the young savage trimmed his lamp, lighted his pipe, did the same act of courtesy to all who wished to smoke, and the anxious community, one by one, sought a short oblivion to their griefs in sleep.

In vain, however, did our little party court that blessing; passing by the torment of thought, the sufferings of the body alone were enough to prevent it. I had youth on my side, and my slender frame enabled me to bear the suspension better than my fellow-sufferers. The tobacco-smoke was a mercy, for it robbed the infliction of half its torment. A year afterwards, when we had to undergo a punishment somewhat similar, though in a purer atmosphere, we found the sting of the musquitos, on the soles of our undefended feet, "without the power to scare away" these venomous little insects, was intolerable; whereas in this well-smoked apartment a musquito could not live. We were not aware at the time what a happy exemption this was.

What a night was that on which we now entered! Death, in its most appalling form—perhaps attended with the agony of unknown tortures—was thought by all to be our certain lot. Kewet-nee, who occupied the next place on the bamboo, excited a horrible interest by the

INTERIOR OF THE LI-I-MA-YOON PRISON.

relation of a variety of exquisite tortures which he had known to be perpetrated under that roof. It chilled us to the heart to think on them, but the very abjects around us confirmed their truth by giving utterance to their opinions on our case, spoken *sotto voce*, as between themselves, though too well understood by those they chiefly concerned.

But all sank into insignificance before the awful thought that soon—perhaps in a few hours—all affinity with this world's cares and troubles would cease, and we should be summoned into Eternity. I must make my honest confession that it was then I felt the force and value of those sacred truths which I had so often heard, but so little regarded. A thoughtless, careless life, absorbed in the pursuits of this world, to the utter neglect of a future one, is a sad position from which to contemplate the sudden change to Eternity. I felt it truly to be so. No one can enter completely into the thoughts, and feelings, and imagination of a person in this fearful position—it is useless to attempt to describe them, for words cannot convey an idea of the intensity of the struggle between doubt, and hope, and fear, which by turns flit across the unprepared soul in the prospect of its immediate change. For a long time I lay, as Jeremy Taylor quaintly expresses it, "like a fox caught in a trap," aware of my danger, and racking my imagination for the means to break through it. But the more I thought, the more confused and misty my thoughts became. Regrets in parting with the world hardly found a place. The gloom of the prison, and the mass of misery strewed about it, brought dimly into view by the melancholy light of the single lamp, were in harmony with the diseased tone of my mind, and led me to acknowledge that this is not a world one ought to grieve at parting with. Just look on the scene before me, and think of what the coming day will disclose, and then judge. No! it was not the giving up *this* world, for I felt in my irritable mood it was not worth keeping; but the doubt of attaining the *future one* in safety, the leap in the dark, was the alarming thought. The sufferings of the body, severe as they were, disappeared before the all-important question, which was worse to endure than the fetters of the Monarch, or the sword of the Executioner. I could reason myself without much difficulty into contempt of bodily pain, were I but satisfied with my title as it stood to future happiness. It is probable that a large majority of my fellow-creatures, even of my own faith, would undergo similar perplexities and misgivings, if suddenly hurried into a like state of peril. Our religion, intended to fortify us against the terrors of death, must be wofully misused when it becomes the means of exciting alarms, which even heathens do not feel to the same extent. The deficiency does not lie in our creed, but in our habitual neglect of its provisions, as I could not but acknowledge and lament in this, my hour of trial.

After some hours of painful confusion of intellect, my mind became more calm. The hope which our Faith alone holds out to sustain those who sincerely believe its sacred truths, dawned on my mind. I was not ignorant of the foundation of the Christian's hope, and began to reason, that if the gift of Eternal life, through our Saviour, was promised, not to those who laid claim to it in virtue of a strictly moral and holy life, but to those who were convinced of their inability to attain it by such means, why should I hesitate to appropriate the promise to myself? Could I doubt the sincerity with which I embraced its provisions at this awful moment? The theology of learned schoolmen was as nothing to me now. It was not a time to reflect on their subtle reasonings and nice doctrinal distinctions; but I felt that my Religion was nothing if it failed to afford consolation at such a time as this. God does not demand impossibilities, nor does He consign any human being to despair. The usual proof of sincerity held out—that of a blameless life—it is impossible for me to acquire, if I have only a few hours to live; but I can, at all events, show it by sustaining the trial allotted to me with fortitude, and resignation, and hope. I recalled to memory the various promises which, in the plainest and most forcible language, are to be found mercifully scattered in profusion throughout the Holy Scriptures, to give light and comfort to the troubled spirit, and I found, with gratitude, that those promises did most amply meet the emergency. With the mind once in the right direction, and with earnest prayer to the Almighty that He would succour us in our utmost need, such as those alone can utter who are on the verge of Eternity, composure of mind was restored, and the natural horror in the contemplation of torture and death was so far overcome that I could at least regard them in their true light, as things of transitory trouble only, and the appointed gate of entrance to a happier state of existence. The cruel prohibition to use our own language prevented our uniting our prayers; but my companions passed the night in training their minds in a similar manner to the events which they expected would befall them on the morrow.

The rays of the morning sun now began to struggle through the chinks of the prison walls, and told us that day had dawned, bringing life and happiness to the world outside, but only the consciousness of misery to all within. As it slowly emerged from the darkness, one could not help thinking the scene more cheerless than when the night concealed the half of its horrors. The sleeping convicts awoke one by one with a yawn, clanking their chains and shaking the swarms of loathsome vermin from their rags, only to scatter the plague upon their neighbours. All that offends the eye became more visible. The melancholy but musical intoning over and over again some words in the Pali language, the meaning of which the singers themselves did not understand, formed the matins of some of our fellow-captives more attentive to the claims of their rubric than the rest. At another time I could have listened to these plaintive airs with pleasure, but now they disturbed my thoughts and were annoying. How indelibly are they engraven on my memory! Every note of their monotonous chaunt, which each succeeding morning gave notice of the first streaks of light as regularly as the crow of the cock, is so vividly imprinted on my memory, that even after this lapse of years I should have no difficulty in setting it to music.

The prisoners being counted, and found to tally correctly with the reckoning of the overnight, symptoms of the routine of the day began to attract attention. Our considerate parent made his appearance, and, with his customary grin, lowered down the bamboo to within a foot of the floor, to the great relief of our benumbed limbs, in which the blood slowly began again to circulate. At eight o'clock the inmates were driven out in gangs of ten or twelve at a time, to take the air and for other purposes, for five minutes, when they were huddled in again, to make way for others; but no entreaty could secure a repetition of the same favour that day, though a bribe, which few could promise, might effect it. Fresh air, the cheapest of all the gifts of Providence, was a close monopoly in the hands of the Sons of the Prison, who sold it at the highest price, and with a niggard hand.

At nine o'clock one of my servants ventured to come with some breakfast for me, tied up in a towel. The packet was taken from him at the outside gate, and, after being opened for inspection, was handed to me within by one of the *pahquets*; but I was not permitted to hold any communication with him.

The only chance any of the prisoners had of getting their daily food was by the kind offices of their relatives or friends at large. If they were so unfortunate as to be friendless, they had only to depend on the fortuitous charity of strangers; in other words, it was slow starvation. One of the most meritorious forms of almsgiving—and a very useful form of charity it was, for many lives were saved by it—was held to be the feeding of the prisoners. It was a common thing, especially on their festivals at the change and full of the moon, to see large baskets brought into the place, containing as much boiled rice and *ngapwee* as would afford a hearty meal to every prisoner; but often a week or two would pass without such bounty, and during that time the destitute portion had to depend on the uncertain remnants of those who had the heart to leave a trifle of their scanty meal. This accounts for the famished look of many of the prisoners. An abundant supply of the broad leaves of the plantain-tree always accompanied these offerings, serving, when torn, as platters for the feast. Their thickness, and glossy surface, admirably adapted them for this use, and imparted a rather picturesque appearance to the dinner. When the famished creatures had satisfied their cravings, if any remained, they were seen carefully to roll it up in the leaf, fasten it with a little bamboo skewer, and carry it inside the prison for the next day's use; the heaps of these rotten leaves inside formed one of our standing pests. It was said, indeed, that a basket of rice was allowed by the King to each man by the month; but if such was the case, it must have gone to enrich the brotherhood of the spotted men, for we never saw any sign of rations during our long incarceration.

We noticed that the most frequent benefactors were women, whose hearts here, as everywhere, are most open to acts of charity. The donors, dressed out in their finest clothes, prudently accompanied their offerings in person to ensure their being properly applied, as well as to receive the pleasing gratitude of the starving recipients of their bounty.*

Just as I had finished my breakfast, I was singled out from among my companions, and conducted into the prison-yard by one of the ringed men, shuddering as I felt the villain's fingers on my shoulder. "Now," thought I, "for some indication of my fate;" and so thought those I left behind, who took farewell by a word, while their distressed countenances indicated their fears that we should never meet again. A *Myo-serai* (assistant to the Governor of the city) was seated in the opposite shed, but had an unpleasant investigation on hand at the moment, which I

---

* When a man is imprisoned for any State crime, especially if it takes the form of treason, few people have the courage to supply him with food, lest it might bring on them a charge of complicity or commiseration for the prisoner. A curious instance of this is related by Colonel Burney. When Tharawudi became King he sent our present enemy, Men-thagee, to the Let-ma-yoon, where he would certainly have starved had not the British Envoy sent him his daily mess of boiled rice. No other person had the courage to do it.—*Manuscript of the late Colonel Burney.*

had to witness with very disagreeable anticipations. The fresh air was reviving, and how my ill-used lungs did leap to inhale it! So let the Myo-serai take his time.

Seated on the ground opposite to the Judge was a young man, accused of being concerned in the robbery of the house of a person of rank. Whether the accusation was well founded or not I had no means of judging except by the result; but certainly the man had not the appearance of a robber. As a matter of course he denied the crime; but denial was assumed to be obstinacy, and the usual mode of overcoming obstinacy was by some manner of torture. By order of the Myo-serai, therefore, he was made to sit upon a low stool, his legs were bound together by a cord above the knees, and two poles inserted between them by the executioners, one of whom took the command of each pole, the ground forming the fulcrum. With these the legs were forced upwards and downwards and asunder, and underwent a peculiar kind of grinding, inflicting more or less pain as the Judge gave direction. Every moment I expected to hear the thigh-bone snap. The poor fellow sustained this torture with loud cries, but still with firmness, until the agony became so intense that he fainted. "The tender mercies of the wicked are cruel." To restore animation they resorted to cold water and shampooing. Thus revived, he was again thrust back into his den with menaces of fresh torture on the morrow, as no confession had yet been wrung from him. I may as well finish the revolting story at once.

True to his word, the Myo-serai returned the next day to renew his diabolical practices. This time the culprit was tied by the wrists behind his back, the rope which bound them being drawn up by a pulley just high enough to allow his toes to touch the ground, and in this manner he was left until he should become more reasonable. At length, under the pressure of agonizing pain, just in time to save the dislocation of the shoulder, the criminal made his *confession*, and criminated two respectable persons as accomplices. From what followed I presume this was all that was wanted. The man of justice had now two men in his toils who were able to pay. The unfortunate man, who, when relieved from the pain of the torture, acknowledged he had accused innocent people, was returned to gaol fearfully mangled and maimed; but instead of meeting a felon's fate, when time had been given to fleece the two victims, he was *released!*

CHAPTER XV.

I am examined about my property.—Hour of execution in the prison.—A Greek and an Armenian arrested.—Arrakeel's escape from Tharawudi.—Our second night in prison.—Dr. Judson examined about his property.—The "Rat" and Mirza released.—Mrs. Judson visits her husband in prison.—She gains us some comforts.—We are lodged in an outside shed.—Examinations by torture.—How practised.—Our growing apathy at beholding these scenes.

HAVING disposed of this every-day affair with as much unconcern as a London magistrate would get rid of one of his trifling night-charges before proceeding to more serious business, the Myo-serai next turned his attention to me. The Governor of the city, his immediate superior, very rarely showed his face within the prison compound. Besides being considered rather *infra dignitatem* to descend from his court in the Yoong-dau, for the purpose of prison examinations, he was a man of a naturally mild, benevolent temper, and these disgusting scenes of cruelty were better suited to the shark-like character of his Deputy, who had no feelings of pity or delicacy to disturb him in the prosecution of his hateful office. As my story proceeds, it will be seen that we more than once owed our lives to the Governor's kind interference.

As his Deputy turned his meagre visage and unpitying eye on me, I saw in a moment there was nothing to hope from his commiseration or clemency. Notwithstanding the scene I had witnessed, my mind was remarkably calm and composed; the meditations of the past night had not been without their influence, and I felt in some measure prepared to meet the worst that could happen. I was aware that if this sort of questioning was to be applied to me, it could not be to extort money, for all I had was already at their disposal; but for the more legitimate, though impossible, object of ascertaining my complicity with the Indian Government in the invasion of the country. I think the fellow saw through my suspicions, and my mind was relieved from a sore burden when he told me such were not his intentions. His orders were simply to take a schedule of my property, together with a list of all persons indebted to me. No doubt they were pretty closely fleeced, but that was no business of mine. I rendered a faithful and, apparently, a satisfactory account of property to a large amount.

It was ominous of evil that no questions were asked with reference to the crime imputed to me, nor was it even alluded to in the most distant manner. I therefore concluded that affair to be finally settled against me, and that the account now taken was a prelude to the closing scene; a kind of last settlement of all worldly affairs which need no longer disturb the mind of the passing criminal, and so thought my companions, to whom I found means to whisper all that had passed on my return to join them in the prison. During my absence their feet had been released from the torturing bamboo.

Within the walls, nothing worthy of notice occurred until the hour of three in the afternoon. As this hour approached, we noticed that the talking and jesting of the community gradually died away. All seemed to be under the influence of some powerful restraint, until that fatal hour was announced by the deep tones of a powerful gong suspended in the Palace-yard, and a death-like silence prevailed. If a word was spoken, it was in a whisper. It seemed as though even breathing were suspended under the control of a panic terror, too deep for expression, which pervaded every bosom. We did not long remain in ignorance of the cause. If any of the prisoners were to suffer death that day, the hour of three was that at which they were taken out for execution. The very manner of it was the acme of cold-blooded cruelty. The hour was scarcely told by the gong, when the wicket opened, and the hideous figure of a spotted man appeared, who, without uttering a word, walked straight to his victim, now for the first time probably made acquainted with his doom. As many of these unfortunate people knew no more than ourselves the fate that awaited them, this mystery was terrible and agonizing; each one fearing, up to the last moment, that the stride of the Spot might be directed his way. When the culprit disappeared with his conductor, and the prison-door closed behind them, those who remained began again to breathe more freely; for another day, at least, their lives were safe.

I have described this process just as I saw it practised. On this first day, two men were thus led away in total silence; not a useless question was asked by the one party, nor explanation given by the other; all was too well understood. After this inhuman custom was made known to us, we could not but participate with the rest in their diurnal misgivings, and shudder at the sound of the gong and the apparition of the *pahquet*. It was a solemn daily lesson of an impressive character, "Be ye also ready."

This day our party was increased by two fresh arrivals; a Greek of Constantinople named Constantine, and Arrakeel, a young Armenian merchant, who had some property in Ava, were the gleanings of the class the Burmese call *Kula-pyoo* (white foreigners). We did not know, until now, even of the existence of these two persons. Of the black Kulas, natives of British India, they appeared to take very little notice; their colour, and the numbers always spread through the country, probably protected them. To this, and to their having nothing to be plundered of, may be attributed the escape of my native servants from arrest.

The Prince of Tharawadi had tried the experiment on Mr. Arrakeel which had been attempted and failed with me. The young man had been seduced into his Palace by promises of protection, only to be committed to the stocks the moment of his arrival there, and it is more than probable, that the instant demand which followed for his surrender by the Hlut-dau,—to which, in spite of his boasting, the Prince thought it wise to succumb,—was the means of saving him from assassination.

As night drew near, the old scene was reproduced. The "father" again entered with his staff to take an account of the number of his children; superintended the adjustment of our limbs on the dreaded bamboo, and saw it hoisted to its proper height; gave his renewed orders to the young savage to use his club effectually if we attempted to speak; and took his leave. The savage trimmed his lamp, advised us to be quiet, lighted sundry pipes, and then all who could take advantage of the blessing, sought repose.

Wearied nature now asserted her merciful prerogative, and in spite of horrors, past, present, and to come, we slept. But what a sleep! O ye who with untroubled minds stretch yourselves on beds of down, look on this scene and be thankful! Picture in your imagination the filthy planks for a pillow, the benumbed bloodless extremities, the creeping vermin, the clank of the chains, the pestiferous atmosphere, and beyond all the tortured mind, which raised visions as horrid as the waking realities, and denied us the welcome companion of sleep to the wretched —forgetfulness. It was rather a state which our Noble poet happily distinguishes from it:—

> "My slumbers—if I slumber—are not sleep,
> But a continuance of enduring thought
> Which then I can resist not: in my heart
> There is a vigil, and these eyes but close
> To look within."

The "vigil" was too painful for description. It might be compared to that of a condemned person the night before his execution, who was conscious of his innocence of the crime for which he was to suffer, though in other respects indifferently prepared for the coming change.

Unrefreshed by such broken and uneasy returns of partial oblivion, the hours of the night wore away, and again we beheld the streaks of light force their way through the prison-walls. The religious Buddhist sang his intellectual matins, the "father" counted his sons and daughters (for there were some women among us in chains), and the prison woke again to life.

On this day, the third of our captivity, the Myo-serai paid us another visit. This time it was Dr. Judson's turn to make over his temporalities, a movement which he justly considered as a very sinister one, placing him, as it did, in the same category as myself, so far as the event foreboded evil. In rendering his account, he was again compelled to admit that he had been supplied by me with money. On this fact they seemed to found ridiculous assumptions of his guilt; perhaps because they could find no other. I may here remark, that each morning the Myo-serai returned to take information of the prisoners' goods and chattels, until all in their turn had been questioned.

My two *employés*, Kewet-nee and Mirza, were removed from us this day, and we saw them no more. We surmised that these two men were arrested, and allowed to remain a short time with us, as spies on our secret conversation, and if such were the case, as is very likely, it was consolatory to reflect that not one word which we uttered could in any way tend to compromise us. My mind was at all events relieved from one source of discomfort by their release, seeing I was the innocent cause of their arrest.

As the day advanced, the ominous gong in the Palace gave out the hour of three. I had lain all the morning, in the expectation of the approach of the *pahquet* at that fatal hour; but I might have saved myself those harrowing thoughts, for the time passed, and I was still in existence. A faint hope now arose, that as the third day had gone I might be mistaken, and the course of events in the afternoon tended to confirm the hope that, at least for the present, my life was not in such imminent danger as my fears led me to believe; and if so, who could say that some favourable but unforeseen turn might not yet save me?

Mrs. Judson, who had been closely guarded in her house during these two eventful days, had managed to convey a bribe to the Myowoon. He desired that she might be brought into his presence, and, once there, being well versed in the language and the management of Burmese officials, she pleaded for mitigation of the sufferings of the Missionaries in such eloquent terms, that the old man could not refuse her permission to see and converse with her husband in the prison. The meeting was most affecting, for though she had been informed of his being in fetters, she was quite unprepared for such a scene as she was now about to witness. It so happened, that at the moment of their interview outside the wicket-door, I had to hobble to the spot to receive my daily bundle of provisions, and the heart-rending scene which I there beheld was one that it is impossible to forget.

Poor Judson was fastidiously neat and cleanly in his person and apparel, just the man to depict the metamorphosis he had undergone in these two wretched days in its strongest contrast. When Mrs. Judson had parted from him he was in the enjoyment of these personal comforts, whereas now none but an artist could describe his appearance. Two nights of restless torture of body and anxiety of mind had imparted to his countenance a haggard and death-like expression, while it would be hardly decent to advert in more than general terms to his begrimed and impure exterior. No wonder his wretched wife, shocked at the change, hid her face in her hands, overwhelmed with grief, hardly daring to trust herself to look upon him. Perhaps the part I myself sustained in the picture may have helped to rivet it on my memory, for though more than thirty-five years have since passed away, it reverts to me with all the freshness of a scene of yesterday. Chains and Felons are so inseparably connected in the imagination of an Englishman that he cannot look upon a man whose limbs are bound with the one without investing him with the character of the other. When first under restraint and in the stocks in the barracks of the Taing-dau, my mind ran on something like roguery or petty larceny, but now my chains had raised me, in my own imagination, to the infamous dignity of Felony. At this distance of time it causes a smile when I call to mind the shame I felt at first at being seen even among my abandoned associates wearing a badge so degrading, and the foolish arts I used when let out in the morning to hide my chains from the inquisitive gaze of the passer-by as he stood to watch us through the bars of the outer gate.

When I saw what a loathsome figure my friend Judson presented, and looked at myself, I made my recognition of his wife as short as possible for very shame's sake, and shuffled back to my den. Had a stranger seen the group, his pity would hardly have restrained his laughter for the moment.

But Mrs. Judson was not a person to waste her energies in useless grief. In addition to amiable manners and a benevolent disposition, this excellent lady was endowed with unwearied activity in ministering to the wants of those who needed her aid, and before night came on with its attendant horrors, the soothing effects of her diplomacy were felt by us all. The Governor and the Spotted brotherhood had been bribed to gain some relief for her husband, and a promise had been given that we should all follow her example according to our means, a promise which, as yet, we had the power to fulfil, as the flight of harpies had not yet alighted on our dwellings, nor swept away our subsistence. The effect of this was perceived in an instant. Our quarters were changed from the filthy corner to an open shed opposite to the prison-door, where the Inquisitor sat when questioning his culprits. This was a boon indeed which called forth our gratitude to our amiable negotiator. Irrespective of the freedom from the bamboo, the filth, and the vermin, we regarded it as an indication of our lives being safe for the moment, assuming that if we were doomed to immediate execution, this favour would not have been extended to us. In this we were mistaken, as we afterwards found it was a fertile source of the standing revenue of the gaol establishment, who sold this sort of favour to all who could pay for it; but, at all events, we had the consolation of thinking so. Heavily ironed as we were, a *pahquet* guard stationed at the entrance was considered sufficient for our security, and this arrangement gave us the unspeakable comfort of communing with each other on our sorrows for the first time without the fear of the Savage and his club. We had also the luxury of water to cleanse our begrimed persons, which had been hitherto denied us.

The next morning, however, disclosed to us that the alleviation we had purchased was not without its alloy. The horrors of the inner prison were of a different character, but barely less endurable than those of the yard outside. There, we heard the cries of agony, and saw the results; here, we had to witness their perpetration. What we gained in comfort to the body, we lost in the constant disturbance of our peace, and the violence done to our feelings.

It is not my intention to make this narrative a chronicle of all the diabolical cruelties inflicted in this den of abominations, but the first specimen which greeted our eyes on the morrow may serve as a fair sample of the practices which it was our fate to behold almost daily. The routine was generally this:—

The Magistrate takes his seat in the front of the shed in which we occupy the back-ground, as though the spot had been selected for our convenience, as spectators to behold an amusing exhibition. A criminal is now summoned from the interior. He hobbles out and squats down in terror before the Judge—the crime of which he is accused is stated to him—he denies it—he is urged by various motives to confess his guilt—perhaps he knows that confession is only another word for execution—therefore he still denies—the magistrate assumes an air of indignation at his obstinacy—and now begins the work of his tormentor, the man with the ringed cheek, who has hitherto stood by waiting the word of command. He has many means at his disposal, but the one selected for the present instance was a short iron maul. It would simply excite disgust were I to enter into detail. Suffice it to say that after writhing and rolling on the ground and screaming with agony for nearly half an hour, the unfortunate wretch was assisted to his den, a mass of wounds and bruises pitiable to behold, leaving his Judge not a whit the wiser.

Shall I be credited when I say that, in process of time, such spectacles as these passed unheeded and almost unfelt,—that the sufferings of our fellow-creatures, which at first we shuddered at, and almost fainted to behold, we lived to regard with unconcern? Strange and unnatural as it may at first appear, such, nevertheless, was the fact; and what makes this apathy more surprising is, that we knew at the time the extreme probability of our being ourselves subjected to similar treatment. It is terrible to think on the force of habit.

I do not mean to say that our *reason* was perverted, or that we looked with complacency on such doings,—reason and Religion taught us to hate and abhor them;—but the finer feelings and sympathies of our nature were so continually and violently outraged, that in time they became, in a great degree, unimpressible and callous. This force of habit appears to be a law of nature, often even making that attractive which was at first repulsive; but happily it is powerful for good as well as for evil, or I fear we ran the risk of becoming very unsympathizing members of society during the rest of our lives. At any rate, it was a merciful law for us, for had our sensibilities remained acute, we must have been driven mad.

CHAPTER XVI.

Some account of our prison party.—Dr. Judson.—Remarks on the Baptist mission to Burmah.—Missionary misrepresentations.—Some account of Dr. Price.—And of Mr. Rodgers.—His superstition.—Some account of Mr. Laird.—Constantine, the Greek.—Arrakeel, the Armenian.

As our society was now made up for nearly two years to come, it may not be irrelevant to my subject to say a few words on each of its component members, for fate had thrown us inseparably into one common calamity, and much of our comfort (if such a term be admissible where that quality is absolutely excluded) depended on our good-fellowship.

We were seven in number. Dr. Judson has been already introduced to the reader. He was then about 35 years old, generally cheerful in disposition, but subject to intervals of depression, well read in literature, of a strong discerning mind and agreeable conversation, not unmixed with a keen sense of the ridiculous, often extorting from us a hearty laugh, even in the midst of our afflictions. I have before remarked that he was imbued with deep religious feeling, which referred every trial and suffering to the will of God, and in exercising a perfect resignation to His dispensations he had a resource, similar I hope in character, but far greater in degree, than the rest of his companions. Dr. Judson was a great admirer of Madame Guyon, and seemed to aim at the calm and placid spirit, and at acquiring the heavenly temper, of that rather enthusiastic lady, the more, perhaps, as he knew his *own* naturally to point another way. Often have I heard him repeat some of her simple verses, as translated by our poet Cowper, and long to attain the spirit of them:—

> "No bliss I seek, but to fulfil
>   In life, in death, Thy lovely will;
> No succour in my woes I want,
>   Except what Thou art pleased to grant.
> Our days are number'd—let us spare
>   Our anxious hearts a needless care;
> 'Tis Thine to number out our days,
>   And ours to give them to Thy praise."

At the same time he had thorns peculiarly his own. He had an amiable and beloved wife involved in his troubles, whose unprotected state gave him great alarm, and what made the matter worse, she was in a condition which would peculiarly need his aid, and add to his anxieties. His temper was quick and hasty, too apt to take offence, and his painful sensitiveness to anything gross or uncleanly, amounting almost to folly, was an unfortunate virtue to possess, and made him live a life of constant martyrdom.

I cannot refrain, while speaking of Judson, from making a few remarks about the Burmese mission, with which he was connected, gleaned partly from conversations with him, and partly from my own observations. As is well known, Dr. Judson was the first missionary sent out by the American Board of Baptist Missions. His landing on the coast of Burmah, in 1813, was purely accidental. It was not his original destination when he left America, but was the result of the needless alarm of the East India Company, who were at that period sensitively jealous of interference with the superstitions of the natives, and tyrannically chased him from their territories, one after another, until an asylum was found in the independent kingdom of Burmah. Here was a field suited to the ardent missionary aspirations of Dr. Judson. With a vigour and perseverance for which he was remarkable, he spent some years in mastering the language, and in translating and printing the New Testament. He then set about his work of conversion, by preaching to the natives, with but very limited success, for some years, due more to the intolerance of the Government, than to a disinclination on the part of the people. Up to the time when we met in Ava, he could barely number twenty converts, and these were compelled to hold their meetings in secret places, like the early Christians, for fear of punishment.

After various unsuccessful attempts to obtain toleration for his proselytes, hearing that his coadjutor, Dr. Price, had succeeded in establishing a reputation at Court by his medical cures, he proceeded thither to make another attempt, founded on the favour Dr. Price had acquired, which ended, as is seen, by his arrest and imprisonment.

Although the number of Judson's converts was not great, they were earnest and sincere, and under a tolerating Government would have proved the nucleus of a flourishing church. Unlike the sweeping conversions of the Roman Catholics, every one who was admitted to baptism had undergone a long probation, and had received careful religious instruction. Two or three of these converts had accompanied him to Ava, where I had the opportunity of becoming acquainted with them.

I sometimes spent my evenings at Dr. Judson's house, where they were present at the family devotions, which were held in the Burmese language, and it was impossible not to be struck with the reverence of demeanour, the propriety of language, and above all the knowledge of the New Testament and its saving doctrines, which some of them manifested in their extempore prayer. No one who heard could doubt their sincerity. One man I especially remember. He had been a fisherman, and as a disciple of Boodh had been troubled in conscience by the guilt he was incurring from the wholesale destruction of lives he caused in the prosecution of his calling. He was no longer ignorant, but entered into the spirit of the Gospels with surprising intelligence and delight.

My ideas of missions, for I was much inclined at the time to consider them useless, were changed by what I saw, and although there may be, and I know there are, many disgraceful exaggerations in journals devoted to the subject, yet I know also that churches of sincere believers have been founded in Burmah, and that, as a large tract of the country is now under British rule, they may be indefinitely extended. If those who take an interest in missions were aware of the mischief these misrepresentations do to the cause, we should never see them resorted to. I will give an instance, one which, at the time, shook the little faith I had in the whole undertaking.

When Dr. Price first arrived in Ava, the King was desirous that a few youths should be instructed in the English language, merely to qualify them as interpreters when their services were needed. Price undertook the task, though, like most whims of the King, it was never followed out; and thinking it might be a good opportunity to insinuate the English Bible, he wrote to Calcutta an indent for a few Bibles, merely as school-books. What was our astonishment, shortly after, to read in a periodical the announcement that the King of Ava was favourable to the Christian religion; that there was every prospect of his immediate conversion to Christianity; that he had sent to Calcutta for a number of Bibles; and that we might hope as the result, that *the whole of this mighty nation would become shortly evangelized!* Judson knew so well this tendency in America, and had seen his own letters so garbled, that he wrote a peremptory prohibition to print his letters, unless they were given entire. No one who knew him could doubt his truthfulness.

I have lately read, with great pleasure, that this Mission, so faithfully and ably begun by Dr. Judson, has rapidly extended, and that its churches are numerous and flourishing. The American Baptists were the pioneers in Burmah, and have done their work well. I had also the pleasure to know several of the missionaries who afterwards joined Dr. Judson in the work, all of whom had imbibed the same spirit.

Having been an eye-witness of their zealous and self-denying efforts, and the actual good they have accomplished, I cannot allow any minor differences in our respective creeds to interfere with the honour and esteem in which I hold them, but most heartily wish them continued success.

A life of Dr. Judson has been published in America. Although in the main it is a faithful biography, I was rather amused in reading the following paragraph:—
" He had not been long in New York, before he contrived to attach himself to a theatrical company, not with the design of entering upon the stage, but partly for the

purpose of familiarizing himself with its regulations, in case he should enter upon his literary projects, and partly from curiosity and love of adventure."

Now this is german to the pious frauds on the religious public, which I have just complained of. Why not tell the truth at once? It is not one that will not bear the light. I will give the story as I heard it from the actor's own mouth, and, as nearly as I can recollect them, in his words:—" In my early days of wildness, I joined a band of strolling players. We lived a reckless, vagabond life, finding lodgings where we could, and bilking the landlord where we found opportunity—in other words, running up a score, and then decamping without paying the reckoning. Before leaving America, when the enormity of this vicious course rested with a depressing weight on my mind, I made a second tour over the same ground, carefully making amends to all whom I had injured."

Judson's coadjutor, Dr. Jonathan David Price, was a very different character,—a tall, gaunt, rawboned, sallow-complexioned Yankee, singularly uncouth in appearance, his light hair bristling towards all points of the compass, and his nose of the kind termed, by those who have classified this feature, "celestial," I suppose from its tendency to point upwards. Price had acquired a smattering of the medical science, by attending some hospitals in America, and possessed a decided turn for mechanics, both of these accomplishments affording him amusement in his after prison life. He was a sincerely religious man, and, in his way, was no doubt a very useful missionary, but his eccentricities were at times not a little troublesome to his brethren. His wife, who came out with him from America, having died, he had married a blind native woman, of Siamese extraction, who had a little sight left when she submitted to an operation by the doctor, and he, through his want of skill having deprived her of that little, married her by way of compensation. I venture to hazard this conjecture, as her plainness of person, irrespective of her blindness, was repulsive, nor was there any other conceivable motive. At first Judson, who saw the folly, refused to perform the ceremony, but a threat of a peculiar nature by the eccentric doctor, rendered it expedient that he should comply with his request. "Brother Judson, *the law of America and of nature provides for cases where a minister is not to be found!*"

I once had the little wit to place myself in his hands to get rid of a headache with fever. I very soon found my head shaven, several snake-like leeches pendant from its bald surface, bleeding at the arm, and a dose of opium which sent me to sleep for a night and a day—from which last I awoke just in time to save my skull from being trepanned. The worthy doctor, who was somewhat absent in mind, and had forgotten what an *ad-libitum* dose he had administered, had been shaking me and using other means to awake me without success; when, at last, to use his own expression, thinking I "was sleeping the sleep of death," he prepared to experimentalize with his trepanning instruments. He was a very simple-hearted, good fellow, notwithstanding; and no one could quarrel with him, even though he put their lives in jeopardy. As may be supposed, such a character was utterly careless of dress and cleanliness, taking to a prison life and its impurities with better grace than any of us, as though it were not altogether uncongenial to his habits and feelings.

Mr. John Laird, the thoughtless wight who got me into trouble about his newspaper, was a hardy Scot. He had commanded a ship in the country trade before he settled at Rangoon, and told us, for our comfort, that he had been twice shipwrecked in his earlier days,—once in the *United Kingdom*, off the Cape of Good Hope, and once in a transport on the coast of France, on both which occasions he was one of twenty-two persons saved from a watery grave, while several hundreds on board perished. On the strength of these fortunate escapes, he foretold that, however present appearances might be against him, he should be saved from death now. The inference we drew from the premises was not quite so bold, but merely extended to the conjecture that he was *not born to be drowned*. Mr. Laird's religious opinions were very much those of a fatalist, and he cherished, what appeared to him at the time a consolatory belief, that there was no such thing as *hell*, except in the punishment of a man's own evil conscience in the life that now is. How he came to entertain such an absurd fancy I now forget, but I should think the doctrine could not have been taught him by the good minister of Forfar, his native town. Whenever any sudden or unexpected cause of disquietude befel us, he did not appear to derive much consolation, either from his bearing a charmed life, or from this strange conceit; and, from an article in a public journal, which I have since read, it was with pleasure I observed, that before his death, which happened many years ago, such fantasies and heterodox opinions had vanished, under the faithful guidance and teaching of the missionaries. He was a very kind-hearted, inoffensive person, and lived on excellent terms with us; but he had the misfortune to possess a countenance so frightfully seamed, and indented, and discoloured by the small-pox, that when presented to the King as a Scotchman, His Majesty, struck with his matchless visage, innocently inquired whether all Scotchmen were as ugly as he was. The manner of life he had led rendered him hardy, and well fitted to endure the buffets of fortune.

Mr. Rodgers, the old gentleman who surprised me at my first audience of His Majesty, was as much a native as it is possible for an Englishman to become. His forty years of experience had taught him to form a just appreciation of our present perilous position, and it was far from encouraging to us to witness the utter despair to which he was reduced. To avoid the pains of torture which he looked upon as certain to follow, he resolved to commit suicide by poison. He had found means to disclose his intention to his wife, and to desire her to provide him with the fatal dose; but the good woman had a more hopeful disposition than her husband, and refused. Knowing what he was bent on doing, it was with a feeling of horror I saw him ransacking the bundle of boiled rice brought him for dinner, in the hope of finding this last resource of a soul without hope. His despondency was great when he could not obtain his desire.

Mr. Rodgers was as superstitious as the people among whom he had passed his life. One would hardly credit the follies he was driven to by the total subjugation of his mind to such influence. Once he had to go a journey of several days, on horseback, from Amerapoorah, and after accomplishing nearly a whole day's march, he was encountered by a hornet, which disputed his passage, repeatedly attacking him in front whenever he attempted to move forward. "It desired me to go back, as clearly as if it spoke my language; so, thinking there was some fatal mischief ahead, I took the hint, and rode back again." He was satisfied it was a preternatural intimation.

He had once suffered the wreck of his boat, on the Irrawaddi, through the indignation of a Nat, or evil Spirit, who rules a reach of the river near Thelai, and has a temple erected to his honour, where voyagers make votive offerings to avert his wrath. This temple he had impiously passed without allowing his crew time to make their propitiatory offering of rice and fruit, and in revenge for this the Evil Spirit wrecked his boat; but he adds, "I took good care never again to incur his displeasure, as I was often passing that way from Prome." Mr. Rodgers was bending under sixty-five years of an anxious life, but had an iron constitution, and was found afterwards to be as well able to endure privation as his younger companions.

Our two remaining comrades could not speak a word of English, and but little Burmese; we therefore held but little communication with them. The Greek was a poor diseased creature, advanced in years. The Burmese had no hesitation in pronouncing him a leper, *kula-noo*— the "leprous foreigner"— and it cannot be denied he had very much that appearance. His colour indicated it, as did several suspicious-looking sores upon his limbs. He seemed to be aware of the fact himself, growing sullen because, from motives of prudence, we did not court his propinquity. He was a thorough hater of the English nation, and was not blessed with an amiable temper.

The Armenian was a quiet, good young man, who took to his fate without repining.

These were my companions for the next two years. Considering we were thrown together by accident, and not drawn by any mutual sympathy or choice on our own part, we could not be called unfortunate in our society. The only one on our list, whose malady made him an unenviable comrade, was destined to be taken from our company when we had travelled but half of our journey through this dreary wilderness, by an inhuman death; but I must not anticipate the events of my story.

CHAPTER XVII.

We are shut up in the inner prison again.—Our property is seized.—Impure state of the inner prison.—How to change our dress.—We are released from the bamboo.—News from Rangoon.—Signal-guns.—Prison thoughts.—Thanba Woongee made General.—Prison disclosures.—Superstition.—Execution of a native for stepping over the King's image.—Strange treatment of a man who fancied he could fly.—Arrival of an Irish soldier.—His treatment.—News brought by him.

On the evening of the third day of our incarceration we were removed to the more comfortable shed I have alluded to. Here we were allowed to remain three or four days without further molestation than that described, waiting, in torturing suspense, the first news of the war from Rangoon. As so many days had rolled on, and our lives were still preserved, it was clear we had passed through one crisis in safety—the one we had most dreaded—and that our fate now depended on the course events might take at Rangoon. We knew better than our tormentors what that course must be when civilized man was matched against the barbarian; discipline and steady bravery against a tumultuary army and the fitful ebullition of savage fury. What we now feared was the anger of the King on the overthrow of all his sanguine hopes of conquest. We could but wait the result in patience, and encourage ourselves in the protection of the Almighty. There was only one man among us who doubted the success of our arms; this was Mr. Rodgers. He looked upon the advantages the Burmese possessed in their dense jungles and forests, their numbers, their hardy endurance, their skill in bush-fighting, the want of roads, the facility of cutting off supplies, as fully counterbalancing the superior discipline of the British army. It must be admitted that the Burmese did not make the best use of these advantages in the subsequent war, but committed the fatal error of meeting their foe in masses within their entrenchments and stockades, and even in the open field.

On the fourth day we were hastily thrown back, amidst the usual torrent of abuse, to our old quarters in the inner prison. What did this portend? Had the dreaded, but expected, disastrous intelligence reached the Court from Rangoon? Had our time come? As the usual mystery was preserved, and no reason assigned, we were left to conjecture until the following morning, when the truth came out.

The official plunderers had visited our houses, and, in carrying off our property, had come to the knowledge that large bribes had been given to the Myowoon and his gang, which they had now either to disgorge, or to share with others. Our ill-usage was the consequence of their rage at being detected. All the horrors and impurities within were renewed. Reader! did you ever take a voyage in a packet-boat?—the State-room overcrowded with passengers, the reeking viands removed, rain pouring down, thermometer at 100°, gratings and skylights down, seasick wretches filling every berth and strewing the floor? Ascend to the upper deck, breathe for a while the pure breezes of heaven, then try to re-enter the fetid cabin, and you will have some idea—a faint one, it is true, but the nearest approach I can call to mind—of the permanent atmosphere of the Let-ma-yoon.

While outside in the shed we each obtained the luxury of a pillow to rest our heads on, and we found it so comfortable, that, by an effort, we carried them inside with us; but, alas! no comfort there! we were obliged to rest contented with the planks of the floor, for the *living* reasons before assigned. Perhaps the most ridiculous sight in the prison was our little white pillows, glittering like so many stars in a firmament of unspeakable dinginess. The wretched criminals persisted in cherishing their long hair even in their desperate plight. It was an intolerable nuisance to their neighbours, and we set them a wholesome example by clipping ourselves quite bald with a pair of scissors lent us by "*papa*"—almost the only favour he ever did us—but the *ruse* did not take. They were not to be so easily entrapped into losing the glory of their crowns, and our attempt at salubrity only made us the laughing-stock of the whole community.

Hitherto we had not been able to effect a complete change of our raiment, much as we stood in need of it; there was a difficulty in the way which we knew not how to overcome. The shirt we did manage, but how were we to divest ourselves of our nether habiliments? The problem was this—with three rings on each ankle, and each pair of rings united by a short chain, how to take off a pair of trousers without tearing or cutting them. We thought it over, and gave it up in despair, and were about to tear the subject of the problem into shreds from our bodies, when a knowing *pahquet* solved the difficulty. The rogue must have had some trouser-wearing animal in his clutches before;—he showed us that it was not the impossibility we supposed, and the wonder is that we did not discover it without his assistance. As the discovery is not likely to be generally useful in this happy country, I leave the *modus operandi* as a riddle for the ingenuity of the reader.

While we were in the shed, the work of confiscation went forward at our houses. Everything of value was taken away except some wearing apparel, which the entreaties of our servants induced these plunderers to leave, and this was not much objected to, seeing it formed but an insignificant part of the general stock, and from its foreign fashion was useless to them. We had now no more the means of bribery beyond the value of a few pence now and then to avert the tyranny of our gaolers, supplied by our servants from what they had been able to hide before the plunderers visited the house.

I must not omit to state that when it was found we had really no more to give, we were released from the infliction of the bamboo, and were removed from the dark corner to *enjoy* our fair share of the *comforts* of the prison in common with the rest of the convicts; an exact spot was assigned to each person, from which we were not allowed to move. That dark corner, and that bamboo, constituted the inaugurative ordeal of those who were supposed to have money at command.

After passing a few days of suspense in the inner prison, the booming of a gun from the river-side announced that news had at length arrived from the seat of war. In order that no time might be lost in conveying the intelligence to the Palace, a Royal command had been issued, that whenever a battle had been fought, the war-boat which brought the news should fire a signal-gun—if a victory had been gained, two guns—if decisive, and the invading army had been driven back into the sea, three guns. This plan was so far useful to us as it gave us some vague idea of the news in the prison as soon as they had it in the Palace. On the present occasion but one gun was heard, and the rumour soon gained ground that the British troops, leaving their lines, had carried some stockades with the bayonet, killing several hundreds of their defenders within. The gloomy countenances of the ringed men silently confirmed the truth of the report.

It was now to be seen how the news of disaster would operate on our fate. The moment was an anxious one; but the crisis passed, and we had cause for thanksgiving. It was a cheering indication that the day went over without any further mischief than brutal abuse, which, in the face of more serious evils, we soon learned to disregard. Our condition, in all respects, remained unchanged.

As days rolled on, and our heads were still on our shoulders, we began to lose the sense of immediate danger in the more harassing and abiding feeling that we were living in the daily and hourly liability to it. This may be said to be the case with all mankind, and that ours was only the common lot exaggerated. This is true, and the reflection was not altogether without its value. The difference is, that in the one case the cruelty of man and the hand of violence are the instruments to bring it about, while, in the other, the skill and sympathies of man are exerted to avert it. In many respects death, when contemplated from the gloom of a dungeon, should be more desirable and welcome than when viewed from a bed of sickness, surrounded by sympathizing friends; yet, contrary to this admission, it is always most dreaded when our reason tells us it ought to be most welcome. The arguments which succeed in convincing our reason fail to overcome this natural horror of death by the hand of man. Nature revolts at the idea. It was this terrible uncertainty, with all the chances in human estimation against us, which, for nearly two years, weighed with such depressing force upon our spirits. Argue as we would, we could never admit any reasonable chance of our ultimate escape. It was the despairing feeling of a man condemned to death, but kept in constant ignorance of the day and manner in which he was to suffer. Although my case was admitted to be the most desperate of the party, hope never altogether deserted me, unless at moments, which too often happened, when my fate seemed so near and certain that to hope was almost presumptuous.

The historian Hume puts a just value on this sanguine and hopeful spirit when he says, "I was ever more disposed to see the favourable than the unfavourable side of things; a turn of mind which it is more happy to possess than to be born to an estate of ten thousand a year." I also had the happiness to possess the turn of mind the historian alludes to; it was a great help to me in my trouble, and, like him, I estimate the inheritance as more valuable than that of wealth.

Many weeks passed over our heads before the signal-gun announced fresh news. The first reverse they had experienced, though insignificant in itself, had taught our enemies that they had a more difficult task than was at first expected, and they did not hazard another attack until a larger force was concentrated before Rangoon. My old friend, the Sakkya Woongee, was found unequal to the command; he was superseded by another General, styled the Thunba Woongee, in whom greater confidence was placed.

In the mean time, we were settling down into the

habits of the prison, and were becoming familiar with such scenes as I have recounted. We began also to speculate on the length of time nature could hold out, if we were left to test it. How long could we live in such plight, without the use of water or other means of cleanliness? Would habit reconcile us to it, as it apparently had done many of our fellow-prisoners? Some of them had lived there for years.

We gradually became acquainted with them and with their crimes, real or imputed. There were many cases in the calendar that were almost incredible, and showed that accident, caprice, superstition, and even carelessness, occasioned their confinement. One grimy, half-starved old man, had been kept there three years, and neither knew why he was there nor who sent him! Our young friend with the club was an old inhabitant, and was probably kept there because he could be trusted as the guardian of the night—a good watchdog. The crime of another must have been that of a madman, or more probably it was a false accusation, preferred to gratify private revenge. He was said to have made an image of the King, and to have walked over it! The mere imputation of practising necromancy against the sacred person of the King was a fatal charge. The poor fellow was taken from among us at the hour of midnight, and despatched by breaking his spine. Why this singular method of slaughter was resorted to, as well as the manner of carrying it into execution, was as mysterious as the crime itself; but they were not at all particular as to the mode of depriving their victims of life, but seemed to be guided altogether by caprice.

But the most ridiculous instance of superstition, was that of a man brought into prison because *he said he could fly.* Why they should interfere to prevent his doing so, if he really possessed the power, no one could tell.

The case was a difficult one. "Father" Moung-lah was responsible for his safe custody, and was in terror lest the bird should take wing in the course of the night. The sagacious old man thought it was possible he might be able to fly out of one sort of fastening, but not out of another; so he wisely determined to take every kind of security his wits could invent.

The man was first put in three pairs of irons,—the jaws of the central Alligator then snapped upon his ankles, holding them tight,—his wrists were bound together with a long rope tied to one of the rafters of the roof of the building,—his long hair was twisted into braids, and each braid fastened separately to the floor,—another rope was tied round his waist and confined it to the floor also.

As he lay thus prostrate, Moung-lah stood over him in contemplation, apparently deliberating in his own mind what further means he could adopt to clip the wings of this subtle captive. At last he bethought himself of the holes pierced in the man's ears, which usually are large enough to save the trouble of carrying a cigar-case, and through these holes the ingenious Moung-lah contrived to pass strings, confining his ears also to the floor. One would have thought he had read Gulliver. Still the cautious "father" had his misgivings, and before leaving the prison, very strict injunctions were delivered to the Savage with the club, to watch the creature, and if it attempted to fly, he was to brain it as it rose. While all this was going on, the sufferer ceased not to ridicule all their precautions, and to assert his own ability to elude them, as he fully intended to do in due time. The confidence of his manner raised the credulity of Mr. Rodgers. "These people know more than you think they do," said he to me. I suggested our tying ourselves to him,—perhaps he might take us under his wing, and so we should escape when he took his flight. "Wait till you see, sir." We did wait, and to the joy of our Chief, next morning, the bird had not flown. The gaolers soon began to doubt his powers; day by day the lashings were relaxed, and when it clearly appeared that he was an Inhabitant of this Earth only, and that he had no power to soar above it, no further means were taken to confine him to it. The poor lunatic was permitted to participate in the usual privileges of the prison.

The next time the signal gun was fired from the riverside, while we were listening in breathless anxiety for some indication of the news it might announce, the silence was broken by the entrance of a new captive. We could hardly credit our senses. He was a rough, strongly-built Irishman, around whose body a thick iron ring was fastened with a fathom of chain appended to it, just as in olden time I have seen the dancing bear exhibited in England. By this he had been led, and by it he was now staked down to the floor, as if he were a wild animal that might do mischief if you went within the range of his chain. Poor Cassiday (for that was his name) was by no means so wild as his appearance indicated. When he discovered among the dense tobacco-smoke a row of faces which were intended by nature to be white, he gave way to an exclamation of joy, which was quickly repressed by the Savage, but was quite enough to disclose to us the isle of his birth. The English language was now more strictly forbidden than ever, and it was not until late at night that we

K

learnt his history, not from himself but in the following manner.

Late at night he was called out for examination by the Woongees, Mr. Rodgers attending in his chains as interpreter. After an hour's absence, they returned together to prison, when Mr. Rodgers related to us what he remembered of the colloquy. That portion of it which interested us most ran as follows. To elude the vigilance of the youth with the club, it was passed in a low whisper, a few words at a time, from one to another, as we lay extended in a line on the floor.

Woongees.—What do the Kulas want by coming to Rangoon?

Cassiday.—I believe they are going to march up to take the country (a loud laugh).

Woongees.—How many men have they brought with them?

Cassiday.—About 3000 British soldiers, besides a good many black troops.

Woongees.—What do you think will become of them, when they are attacked by 100,000 of our army?

Cassiday.—I think we should make very short work of your army, if they be no better than those we met in the stockades. My regiment has had great experience with the bayonet (great excitement).

Woongees.—What is the name of the *Kula-boh-kyop* (Commander-in-chief)?

Cassiday.—They call him Major-General Sir Archibald Campbell.

When the Woongees had done, it became the Irishman's turn to put a question that was near to his heart. "Will you be kind enough, sir, to ask these people what rations they allow their prisoners?" The question was

so simple that Pat had no idea what it was that caused
the burst of laughter which followed it. He was told he
should have some food, and was ordered back to his stake.

It is not likely that the ring and chain were made after
securing the prisoner; they had no doubt been manu-
factured wholesale, under the impression that they would
be worn by all the white men when paraded before His
Majesty in triumph. Mr. Rodgers told us the Woongees
were still in high spirits, and he attributed to this our
preservation up to the present time.

We had by this examination learned the force of the
invading army, and what to me individually was another
source of alarm, the name of the General commanding it.
I had known Sir Archibald Campbell in Calcutta, and I
now feared this acquaintance might become known to the
Burmese, by the inquiries the General would naturally
make about me. Any such inquiries, however kindly
meant, would only tend to revive and strengthen the
charges against me, already sufficiently numerous. Cassiday was a private in the Honourable Company's Madras
European regiment. He had been captured by the
enemy while absent from the camp, wandering about in
search of pine-apples, with which the country abounded:
in a day or two he was taken away from us, and we saw
him no more.

CHAPTER XVIII.

We are transferred to the cells.—Description of them.—Plan of the prison.— Plague of rats.— Murder in the prison.—Its cause. — Frailty of a Menthamee. —How punished.—My house being burnt down, I am accused of arson.—Narrow escape.—Fortunate destruction of my journal.—Providential interferences.—Anecdote of escape from a tiger.

It is not improbable that we should have sunk under the intense heats of the month of June, in such a place and under such circumstances as I have described, had not our guardian angel, Mrs. Judson, again contrived to soften the heart of the Governor, when his anger at being compelled to restore our bribes had a little subsided.

The plan I have given of the prison-yard shows that on two sides there were a number of small cells, used for many purposes by the ringed brotherhood, and the pleading of our amiable protectress secured for us the liberty to occupy them. It is true they were very small, the one I inhabited being about five feet wide, with just enough length to lie down in; it was also so low that I could not stand upright, except in the middle, where the roof was highest; but it was Elysium when compared with the suffocating choke of the inner prison. Nor could it be called altogether *solitary* confinement, for one of our gaolers had a pretty daughter, about sixteen years old, who took a wonderful fancy to me, and was a frequent

PLAN OF THE PRISON.

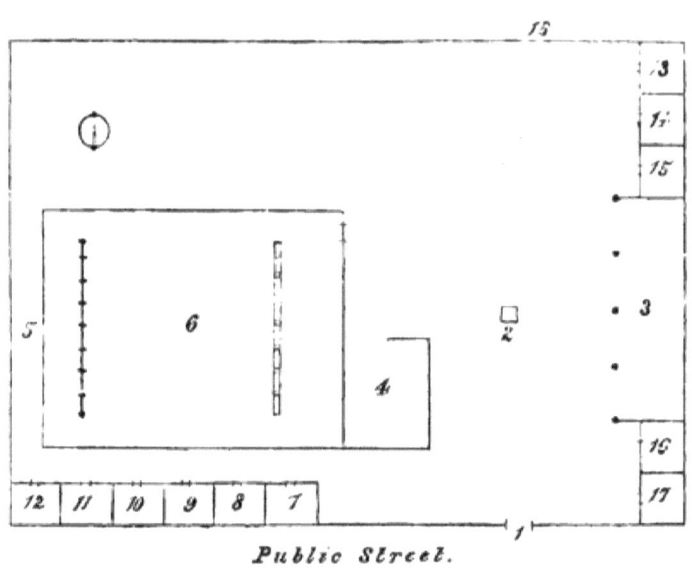

Scale of Feet.

1. Entrance gate.
2. Stone on which fetters were struck on.
3. Magistrate's shed.
4. The gaolers' guard-room.
5. A lane round the prison.
6. The inner prison.
7. The cell occupied by the author.

8 to 17. Cells occupied by various prisoners and the pahquets.

visiter in my cell. She supplied me, too, with an unspeakable luxury, water for ablution. Oh! who can appreciate the gift but those who have been long deprived of it. A scrap of rag, moistened with some of the water given us to drink, only served to smear the grime like a plaster over our bodies. Now, once again, I could call myself comparatively clean.

My cell had other advantages. My eyes escaped many scenes of revolting cruelty; my ears, many foul anathemas and gross abuse; my lungs and olfactories, all sorts of abominations. It abutted also on the main street, and through the chinks I could amuse myself by watching the passers-by. I once saw my old favourite "Dart," who, happier than his master, continued to enjoy the Royal favour, as was evinced by his ridiculous costume, while led on his constitutional airing. I was strongly tempted to whistle to him from my hiding-place, but dared not.

The chief loss was the society of my friends. The rats, too, were numerous and troublesome at first; but these, though a disgusting nuisance, I managed to turn to account by the fancy of the pahquets for their flesh. The Burmese hold rats in about the same estimation as we do hares, and sell them commonly in their markets for about their own weight in lead. My cell, therefore, might be regarded as a well-stocked preserve for game. The burrows ran in all directions, and hardly a day passed without my bagging a few heads of this novel kind of game, and handing them over to my pretty visiter's father, who willingly lent me his spear for the purpose of destroying them. The bait of a few grains of boiled rice at the entrance of the burrows brought them out in shoals, and gave me the opportunity of spearing them. "What do you expect will be your fate?" said this pious

A BURMESE GIRL—NOT UNLIKE MY JAILOR'S DAUGHTER.

From 'Yule.'

Buddhist, as he once took the struggling vermin from the spear, "when the time comes for me to serve you as you are serving that creature!" They all looked forward to the pleasure of decapitating us, and, when in a mild humour, would promise me, as a favour, to use their greatest skill so that I should scarcely feel it. What a consoling thought!

Shut up close in my little cell, I thought that, at all events, my feelings would no longer be harrowed with the sight of deeds of blood. To a certain extent it was so; but even here there was no abiding peace and quietness. One night, as I was vainly endeavouring to coax myself asleep, the screams of an unfortunate wretch in the inner prison fell upon my ear, and, the door of my cell being at the time unfastened and the prison wall not more than three feet off, curiosity prompted me to peep through a crack to see what fresh mischief was on foot. Never shall I forget the foul assassination I witnessed. The inmates were breathlessly silent, evidently expecting some evil.

The cries proceeded from a young man, who lay stretched on the floor, with his feet in the stocks. The lamp was burning dimly, giving just enough light to show the form of a grim pahquet striding towards his victim. Without a word he stamped several times on the mouth of the youth with his heavy wooden shoes, with a force which must have broken his teeth and jaws into fragments. From my hiding-place, where I stood trembling with terror, I heard the bones crack and crash. Still, the cries were not altogether silenced, when the monster seized the club of the Savage, and with repeated blows on the body and head, pounded the poor sufferer to death.

The corpse was then taken from the stocks and buried in the prison-yard. Chilled to the heart by what I had seen, I crept back into my cell unperceived, with a resolution never again to give way to unnecessary curiosity. "My soul, enter not thou into their secrets." What a gang of fiends was I living amongst!

I noticed that a deed of blood, whether in the way of a public execution or a private murder, invariably raised a hell of bad passions in the breasts of the brotherhood for some hours after it had been committed, and until these excited passions had subsided it was dangerous to speak to them; but the following day I ventured to inquire what was the cause of this butchery.

It turned out that the youth was a slave of the Prince Menthagee—a Cassayer by birth, who had made the acquaintance of a girl of the same nation, also a slave of the same master. A criminal intercourse followed, and was detected. What became of the female I did not hear, but the youth was consigned to the Let-ma-yoon by the Prince, with private orders that he should be assassinated. The spotted men thought the least troublesome way was to starve him to death, but the cries of the famished creature were heard by the passers-by in the street, and caused his sufferings to be ended more quickly, as we have seen. As some note of the transaction must be made on the prison register, as a matter of form, it was recorded that he was an opium-eater, and that he died for want of his favourite drug!

And this was the all-powerful Tyrant that governed the country!—in whose hands our destinies were held! A righteous retribution overtook the monster some years afterwards. After suffering prolonged and appropriate tortures,* he perished in the rebellion which placed his rival, Tharawudi, on the Throne.

Peccadilloes of this kind are not always so severely punished, even when they affect the sacred person of the King himself. A son of my old acquaintance, Meeadai Mengee, had been guilty of a folly of the kind, wherein a young lady in the Palace, of the class of Menthamee, was involved. The Sovereign was merciful. The lady's beauty was marred by the tattooing of her face, and Lothario was banished to Mogoung, to work as a charcoal-burner in the forests, with a heavy timber-frill strongly clamped round his neck. I saw him take his departure, looking very foolish; but I heard afterwards that he succeeded in captivating the heart of the daughter of the Governor of Mogoung, through whose influence he was eventually pardoned.

One would think, from the course of events which I have endeavoured to describe, that it was not easy to add to the weight of our troubles; nor from the circumscribed intercourse which it was possible for us to hold with the outer world did there seem much reason to fear that any fresh crime could be imputed to us. I have before remarked, however, that there is no lot which man has to sustain in this life so wretched that it is incapable of becoming worse. In our discontented imaginations we may think we have reached the bottom of the pit, and be disposed to defy Fate to make us more completely miserable; but in this we are mistaken. Some unlooked-for mischance sends us still lower, and shows us that no line can sound the depths of the calamities to which human

---

* Colonel Burney relates that his ill-gotten wealth was extracted from him by bringing him face to face with alligators, and threats to throw him among them.

life is liable. After I had been two months in the Letma-yoon a misfortune happened which left me still more destitute, and at the same time—the reader will stare with astonishment—well nigh cost me my life for the crime of *arson!* "Did I then, in a fit of despair, set fire to the prison," he will ask, "and try to make an end of all our miserable lives in one general conflagration?" Not much to be wondered at if I did. But no such thing.

One morning, about ten o'clock, while I was seated in my cell, hungry, and wondering what could have prevented my man from bringing the daily bundle of boiled rice, as usual, a cry of "fire!" arose in the street, and people were running in great excitement to the quarter whence the danger proceeded. In a city built of combustible materials, like Ava, a fire is a terrible thing to contemplate. A division of the spotted men rushed away with the crowd, like so many vultures to their prey, exulting in the hope that some of their craft would be in request; nor were they mistaken in their conjecture.

After a short time they returned, bringing with them as a prisoner, to my consternation, the very man who ought to have brought my breakfast—one of my Bengalee servants. The whole affair was now plain enough without further explanation. He had accidentally set the house on fire while boiling my rice, and was paying the penalty of his carelessness. The fellow would have turned pale with fright (for a Bengalee *can* turn pale), had not his countenance been liberally smeared with charcoal by the spotted men when they took him into custody, while round his neck they had suspended a firebrand, to indicate his crime. His hands were bound behind him, and in this guise he was turned into the inner prison, there to wait until the morrow, when the usual punishment of flogging round the town would be administered; for, a man who may be ruined by his house taking fire, instead of meeting assistance and sympathy as in England, is here unmercifully flogged for his misfortune, unless he can buy himself off. Doubts were expressed whether I should not have to participate in the punishment, as the house was considered my dwelling.

When the news of the fire reached the Palace, and it was known that it originated at my house, enemies were not wanting to throw the crime on me. The King was made to believe that the traitorous Spy had, by his emissaries, attempted to burn the town; and it was not to be wondered at, blackened as my character already was, if the excitable nature of the King led him to credit it. While the question was being debated, and while the King was working himself up into one of his insane fits, and on the point of issuing the *ultima ratio* of Despots, one of those trifling but decisive incidents happened which so often intervened opportunely to save my life. Mr. Lanciego entered the Palace, and gave the King a correct version of the affair. When, at a later period, this gentleman fell into the same condemnation as ourselves, and joined our party, he told me that his opportune arrival saved me—that His Majesty was fast rising into his accustomed frenzy at the instigation of those around him, and that a delay of a few minutes would most likely have sealed my fate.

Nor did this providential escape stand alone. Another, still more marvellous, stands connected with that fire, and deserves to be recorded.

In happier times it was my custom to keep a journal, for in a country so little known scarcely a day passed without some interesting matter occurring to commit to my diary. As politics became complicated, and dangers began to appear, it may be supposed that remarks on passing affairs, and on the Government, would creep into it, even if I had used greater precautions than I was wont to do. Common sense told me that it was a dangerous book to possess in troublous times like the present, so, not without some regret, I ordered its destruction, while I was a prisoner in the barracks of the Taing-dau.* The man to whom this duty was committed, knowing the value I put upon the book, instead of obeying my instructions, dug a hole in the ground under the house, and hid it there in a small box, hoping, that if happier times came, I should be pleased at recovering it. Now comes the marvellous part of the story. What could have influenced me to inquire, a few days before the fire broke out, whether the book had been destroyed as I had desired? What but the guiding hand of God's Providence, which in a thousand different ways, unseen and unnoticed by us, is constantly maintaining man's life by averting hidden perils? His Will was that I should not perish, and this being so, little did it matter whether we "dwelt in the midst of alarms," or whether we were living in seeming security in a peaceful home. The fact is, we are so completely influenced by outward circumstances and appearances, that we are apt to forget this, and to lose our confidence, until the truth is again brought home to our minds by some such incident as the one I am narrating. Influenced by a higher Power, I *did* make the inquiry about this book, and finding my order had not been obeyed, I repeated

* Mrs. Judson also kept a diary of the same kind, which, she tells us, she felt it prudent to destroy on the first indication of approaching hostilities.—*Life of Judson.*

it, and the journal was dug up and destroyed just in time.

It is common with the Burmese, when a house is destroyed by fire, to dig up its site to search for valuables, and in this case, where booty was probable, the plunderers did not fail to follow out the practice with more than usual care. Now, suppose for a moment the diggers had discovered a small box concealed underground—the box to contain a book written in the English language—which book, on being translated, is found to be full of strictures on the characters of the King and his nobles, and on the acts of their Government! Yet all this must have happened but for the inquiry being made just at the time it was. I did, indeed, tremble when I heard of the search that had been made, and thought of what must have followed. The loss of this journal was a misfortune to me. Had it been preserved, the book which I am writing would have been better worth the reader's perusal.

I have heard men, whose opinions on most subjects I should willingly adopt, object to our appropriating to ourselves, as special interferences of God's Providence in our favour, what they look upon as the ordinary accidents and occurrences of life. Instead of dogmatizing on a subject which is from its nature incomprehensible to us, we ought, they say, to rest satisfied in the general conviction that the Judge of all the earth must do right. Besides, if we are justified in appropriating these special interferences with gratitude, by a parity of reasoning, adverse dispensations would tend to encourage feelings of an opposite character, which we all acknowledge to be sinful and repulsive, not only to our ideas of virtue and morality, but to our very nature. Perhaps the best reply to such objectors is, that facts are against them, for it is invariably found that those persons who, acknowledging a particular Providence, feel the deepest gratitude for special benefits, are the very last to impugn the beneficence of their Creator when afflictive dispensations befall them. For my own part, I feel that in such instances as I have narrated, and many that will follow, there is no reason why my heart should not be as grateful as if I beheld with my own eyes the Hand that delivered me.

I was once relating to a friend, who held such uncomfortable opinions, an anecdote which, although it has nothing to do with the subject of this book, I feel a desire to introduce;—its truth may be relied on, as I had it from the mouth of the gentleman who so dexterously slipped out of the scrape.

Sometime about the year 1830, an old friend of mine, in the Indian Navy, commanded the Honourable East India Company's surveying vessel *Investigator*. He was sent on service, in company with his senior, Captain Ross, to survey the sea entrances of the river Hooghly, and the duties of this service included the coast of the well-known tiger-tenanted island of Saugor. On this low island of jungle, neither building nor hill, nor any natural object, presented itself to assist the surveyor with a good landmark for his operations, and my friend was obliged to content himself with the indifferent object of the dead stump of a solitary tree, some 200 or 300 yards from the shore, which, to render more conspicuous, he proposed to daub over with white paint.

"I landed," said he, "with one lascar, to whom I gave my sextant and a pot of white paint, leaving the rest of the crew to take care of the boat. We reached the tree in safety, washed it with the paint, and prepared to return. The path, apparently the track of wild animals, was among patches of long grass and tangled jungle. I walked first, the lascar following a few feet behind me, carrying, as before said, my sextant and the paint-pot. When about halfway between the tree and the boat, our passage was disputed by a tiger of enormous size, who had *actually taken* his fatal spring at me when I first caught sight of him. There was a moment only for me to evade it. I had just time to make *one step* aside, when the impetus of the spring brought the animal, with its full force, directly upon my follower, whom it carried off into the jungle with as much ease as I would carry a hare. The tiger and his prey had disappeared almost before I could turn round."

"Surely," said my friend, "you do not mean to say that the Captain had a right to claim *this* as a special interference to save his life! What would the man who carried the paint-pot say about it if he could speak!"

CHAPTER XIX.

My utter destitution.—My servants abscond.—Fidelity of my Mahomedan baker.—Defeat and death of Thunba Woongee.—We are thrust into the inner prison again.—A prisoner brought in with smallpox.—We escape infection by tobacco.—Its universal use.—Prison recreations of Dr. Price.—I play chess with Dr. Judson.—Chess in the Palace.—Amusements of Mr. Rodgers and of Mr. Laird.—Laxity of prison regulations.—My dangerous illness.—Barbarity of the gaolers.—I recover unexpectedly.

My life was thus saved, but how was it to be sustained? Hitherto my people had been able to pay the expense of supporting me from what they had managed to secrete before the confiscators visited my house. All they had was now gone, as well as the few clothes which enabled them now and then to give me a clean shirt. Nothing was left but the clothing I then wore. After the shirt and trousers had rotted off in shreds, a native waist-cloth constituted the whole of my wardrobe.

Seeing the state of utter destitution that had befallen me, all my servants forsook me and fled, except my Mahomedan baker, a bright example of attachment and fidelity, who, at this time, seeing his master deserted, and in danger of starvation, set to work industriously at his calling, and supported me from the profits of his labour. He baked hard biscuits, a sort of food much sought after by the Burmese troops departing for the war from its keeping quality, and from its requiring no cooking; for these he had a ready sale, with sufficient profit to support us both. For more than a year-and-a-half this faithful fellow never allowed me to pass more than a single day without food of some sort, and that exception of one day arose from an impossibility to convey it, nor did he cease to minister to my wants until we both together rejoiced in our freedom. For fear I should forget it, let me here record, that when my friends in Calcutta heard the story from me, knowing that having lost everything, it was out of my power to reward these faithful services, they made up for him a purse of 1000 rupees as an acknowledgment of his devotion, on the strength of which the foolish fellow got married, and spent every farthing of it in the usual extravagance on such occasions.

Time rolled on, with little more than the ordinary disgusting detail of the prison, such as I have attempted to describe, until the middle of July, when the report of the signal-gun again aroused our curiosity and alarm. Still it was but *one* gun, announcing a battle, but no more. Within an hour, the lowering countenances of our keepers told that some disaster had befallen the Burmese arms.

This time the defeat was more severe and decisive. The Thunba-Woongee had been attacked in his stockades, his whole force dispersed, with the loss of 1000 men killed, among whom was the Woongee himself, who was slain, bravely defending his position to the last.

The Governor wreaked his vengeance on us. We were all hustled again from our cells into the inner prison, to await any fresh orders that might be issued from the Palace. A merciful Providence again averted the danger. For a few days, probably a week, we were kept in the old den of corruption, when time, as before, softened down asperities, the rage of the Governor and of our keepers began to evaporate, and a little renewed coaxing, backed by such insignificant bribes as our people could yet afford to pay, regained for us the favour of the cells, in which we were once more installed, and my war of extermination against the rats recommenced.

While we were passing this week in the inner prison, a frightful event took place, which threatened the immediate destruction of the whole community; indeed, it is wonderful that the instinct of self-preservation did not deter our parent of the prison from executing his order.

A woman was brought in covered with the pustules of the smallpox! Our doctor looked aghast, and so did we all, as well we might. It was a case quite beyond his treatment, though it is strange the versatile doctor did not undertake the cure. Even the Burmese prisoners themselves expressed their astonishment, but remonstrance was useless. The gaolers, however, showed a little common sense by placing the unfortunate creature in a clear spot by herself to avoid contact with the other inmates of the prison, with delicate threats of punishment if she moved from it. We never heard what induced this barbarity, but she was most likely suffering for the misconduct of some relative in the war, and the authority who sent her there could not have been aware of the disease, for she had not been among us more than twenty-four hours when she was again taken away.

But by what means was infection averted? Inoculation or vaccination was unknown. Here were about fifty persons living in the same confined room, without ventilation, and yet not one of them took the disease.

The fact seems almost miraculous, and I should have doubted the nature of the malady had it not been acknowledged and dreaded by every one, the natives as well as ourselves. I can only account for our immunity by the free use of tobacco.

What a luxury as well as safeguard in this pest-house was tobacco! Every one smoked it. It was so cheap as to be within the reach of all; for if any one was so absolutely destitute as to be unable to procure it, he was liberally supplied by his neighbours. There is hardly a person in the kingdom who does not smoke. I observe, in reading an account of a recent mission to the Court of Ava, by Captain Yule, that the King and Queen both smoked cigars while seated on the Throne, even at a state-reception, and that it is no breach of etiquette, either in a stranger or a subject, to smoke a cheroot during an audience, though I never saw this attempted.* Our prison imitated the example of the Palace—the atmosphere was often so beclouded that it had the appearance of the densest fog,—it overpowered all hurtful miasma, that of smallpox not excepted; and such was our faith in its purifying properties, that we did certainly smoke with increased vigour while the infected person was in our company. Irrespective of infective disease, the effluvium from so many bodies in a confined space might have created deadly evils, but for the counteracting force of tobacco-smoke. We all acknowledged that we were indebted to it for the preservation of our lives.

As each scrap of intelligence arrived from the seat of war, or as any change or caprice influenced the mind of

* Yule's Embassy, page 85.

the Court, we were now bandied about from the prison to the cells, or from the cells to the prison, sometimes enjoying the seclusion of the one for weeks, then hurried again, without knowing why, into the seething-pot of the other. In the absence of books we sought to beguile our gloomy thoughts by such occupations as were yet within our reach.

Our worthy but eccentric Doctor had crept up the sleeve of the Chief of the prison so far as to draw from him the gift of a bamboo and a lump of clay, which he promised to convert into a clock, that should go well enough to keep the prison time. How he expected to succeed with such materials I know not, and began to think he had taken leave of his senses. After much labour and thought bestowed upon it he began to see his folly, and gave it up in despair; but unwilling to part with his playthings, the versatile doctor made use of the clay to model a human head with phrenological compartments, on which he discoursed to an auditory of wondering convicts, endeavouring to instil scientific knowledge with about as much success as attended his experiment on the clock.

One of the spotted men was afflicted with a large troublesome wen, or swelling, on one of his eye-lids. The doctor had often cast a longing eye on this wen; his fingers itched to be at it, but his case of instruments had been taken by the plunderers. At last he summoned the resolution to beg the rascal to submit to have it extracted with the stump of a common penknife. We became alarmed. We were all, to a certain extent, in this man's power, and fearing a result as disastrous as followed the experiment on his wife's eye, without such ample means of making peace in the event of failure, we remonstrated. The undaunted Doctor, however, persisted; the opportunity for practice was irresistible.

Never did I see such a hacking! Such a mopping! I could not have wished my worst enemy in more ruthless hands. After many ejaculations and contortions on the part of the patient, the operator succeeded in whittling out a something which very much resembled in appearance two or three inches of a large dew-worm; when, I suppose, not knowing what more to do with it, or unable to extend his discoveries further, the disgusting string was snipped off. The result was a little better than was anticipated. After some days, when the wound healed, it was found that although the inconvenient swelling had been removed, the muscular power had by some means been destroyed, and the lid fell helplessly over the eye like a curtain, leaving the sight uninjured. The Doctor cared little for this, and tried to console his patient by telling him how much better off he was than before. He had an eye always ready in reserve. "Never mind," said he, "the eye will keep all the better. When you want it, all you have to do is to lift the lid, and when you have done with it let it drop again—it will be always at hand, you know." Such were the prison recreations of Jonathan Price.

Judson and I hit upon a much better resource; a game at chess. What! a game at chess in the Let-mayoon! Yes, it certainly has a sound of civilized life; but let not the imagination of my reader carry him to two comfortable arm-chairs placed opposite to each other, while between them stands a table spread with curiously-carved pieces of red and white ivory. Our surroundings could not boast that elegant character. We set our wits to work with more success than our friend Jonathan David, whose knife and discarded bamboo very soon produced such a set of pieces as answered our purpose, though they bore but a faint and ludicrous resemblance to their established forms. Still we had no difficulty in assigning their respective powers to these nondescript whittlings, nor in distinguishing them readily enough after a few games. The board would have been a serious difficulty if the earth oil cup had not befriended us, in yielding a good supply of lamp-black, which we smeared into chequers on an old remnant of buffalo hide, discovered in the abandoned corner of the prison. Cross-legged, or stretched at length on the greasy floor, how many hours did we beguile with this absorbing game, which must otherwise have been passed in deep dejection, or in unprofitable speculation on the course of a destiny which we could neither alter nor improve!

Our gaolers, when in a *good humour*, allowed us this privilege. Chess was a game well known; there was no suspicion of necromancy. It was commonly played in the Palace, where two or three large boards are kept in the outer Hall for the amusement of the Courtiers. The game differs in several essentials from ours, especially in the arrangement of the pieces, which are disposed on three lines instead of two as with us. As I have seen it played in the Palace, it differs still more in the manner of conducting it. Instead of being a silent, contemplative game, it is a very noisy, boisterous one. The players make their moves rapidly, with an abundance of chattering and bullying, and when one of the combatants has driven his adversary into the necessity of thought for his next move, a burst of ridicule is sure to follow at the expense of the hesitating party, the spectators thinking it by no means indecorous to join in it. The charm of the game is thus quite destroyed.

Mr. Rodgers, who, as I have already said, was as much native as English in his thoughts and habits, passed most of his idle hours in chatting with the convicts—learning their several histories, with all which he soon became familiar—and in discussing with them the fashionable news of the day; even the ringed men themselves now and then honoured him with their company, talking kindly and jesting with him with about as much feeling as a butcher might be expected to manifest when he caresses a lamb one day which he expects to be called on to slaughter the next. His list of acquaintance was certainly not very inviting, but anything was welcome which could, for the moment, occupy the mind. After we had been relieved from the bamboo, and when the savage passions of the brotherhood were not under any peculiar excitement, the old gentleman was allowed to hobble about the room in his irons, and to pay a gossiping visit to each of his friends in turn.

Poor Laird was most at a loss for something to do. Smoking and meditating he did not form a pleasing picture, but time brought some alleviation even to him. There is nothing permanent or abiding in a Burmese prison except dirt and cruelty. Any new order or regulation, especially if it be one to inflict pain, is energetically and furiously acted on at first, but by slow and imperceptible degrees, when it is no longer new, it is suffered to fall into neglect by the simple lapse of time. Thus it was with the prohibition to speak in our native tongue. So long as our faces were new to the gaolers, they regarded us as dangerous prodigies, in whose mysterious consultations Treason or Witchcraft might lurk. Gradually, as we became better known to them, the stringency of the order relaxed, though it was not rescinded. So, also, with the order for our rigid confinement to the exact six feet by three on the prison floor, which had been allotted to us. As these died away, our friend Laird had, once more, the consolation of holding intercourse with his fellow-creatures.

Oh, that we could have had the unspeakable relief of a few books, but above all, the Book of books, where consolation might be found for suffering humanity! I concluded that my Bible had gone with the rest of my effects, but as I should not, under any circumstances, have been allowed, at this time, to read it, inquiries after it were useless.

Down to the month of September, in spite of all privations, my health had not given way. Time had brought me through the rough handling of Jonathan Price, and the harassed mind seemed to insist on the body supporting it under its trials. After some months, however, when the changes and chances of the prison had brought me again into one of the cells, the damps of the night in the rainy season penetrating its latticed walls, aided perhaps by the want of sufficient clothing, brought on an attack of acute dysentery, which, in the absence of medicines and proper treatment, made rapid progress. The poverty of diet, too, might have assisted, for rice boiled in water and flavoured with *ngapwee*, and a cup of water to drink, was but a sorry substitute for the more generous diet to which I had been accustomed. Whatever the cause, the disease, unchecked in its course, soon brought me to a piteous state of helplessness that threatened to carry me, in a short time, beyond the reach of human cruelty.

When brought to such a state of weakness that I could scarcely stand, one of the spotted men came to my cell as night was closing in, and ordered me forthwith to follow him into the inner prison. Remonstrance was useless. Even the rascal's pretty daughter, who I believe felt for me, and was the only being who ever uttered a kind word, could not prevail. With the man's aid I got inside, but the slight exertion was too much for me, and I sank on the floor at the spot pointed out, quite exhausted. We had been so often bandied backwards and forwards from cell to prison, and from prison to cell, that the movement ceased to cause surprise, but on this occasion I could not understand why my fellow-prisoners were not subjected to the same treatment. Up to this time we had all shared the same fate. Why were they now absent? Why was I the only sufferer? What could it mean? I concluded that at last the Government had made the distinction between my guilt and that of my companions, and that I had to die a felon's death. They must be quick, however, or the last Enemy would snatch the prey from their grasp.

Again I was wrong. I did not owe it to this; nor is it likely that any human being—not a pahquet—could guess the true reason. I did not myself learn it until some time after. It was this:—If a prisoner dies within *the walls of the prison*, his funeral obsequies are performed at the expense of the Government. His body is rolled up in a mat, slung on a bamboo, and deposited in the adjoining grave-yard. If he dies *within the cells*, his corpse is disposed of in a similar manner, the only difference being, that in the one case the cost of the mat is paid by the Government, in the other it falls on the keepers. These men, judging from appearance that I might die that night, had an eye to saving the expense of the mat,— a few pence at most,—probably none at all, as an old one serves for the purpose.

Again I say, how often are we wrong in the conclusions we come to when appearances are against us. How often an event, which comes in the guise of an enemy, proves to be our best friend. In this instance the very act, which, in human reasoning, ought to have deprived me of life, was overruled to be the one which preserved it. It so happened that the inner prison was unusually full that night. The heat brought on a profuse perspiration. I fell asleep and awoke better the next morning. The equal temperature of the inner prison, and the exclusion of the night damps that penetrated the cell, gradually restored me to health in spite of all the abominations of the place. Let none despair.

While health was returning I made no effort to return to the cell, preferring to put up with the living foulness until I could venture with safety to return to my solitary abode, where at length, seeing they were not likely to incur the expense of the mat, the gaolers made no objection to restore me.

CHAPTER XX.

Bundoola is recalled from Arracan to command the army.—Runaway soldiers.—Their superstitious reports.—Captured sepoys arrive and are imprisoned with us.—We escape suffocation.—I am chained to a leper.—Native officers starved to death.—Their want of endurance.—One man saved.—News of Mr. Richardson.—Accusations revived.—A gang breaks out of prison.—Oppressions in prison.—Father Ngalah's system.—Uncomfortable dispute between the missionaries.—A mother and daughters in irons.

During this time the whole strength of the country was put forth in the prosecution of the war. After the defeat of the Thunba Woongee, the Court began to see the wrong estimate it had formed of the enemy it had to encounter. No success had yet cheered them. On the contrary, their outlying provinces on the sea-coast, Arracan, Martaban, and others, had, one after another, fallen into the hands of the invaders, and the eyes of the nation were now turned on the hitherto successful Chief Bundoola, as the only man to whose skill and bravery they could confide the conduct of the war. He was recalled from the British frontier of Chittagong, where he had gained some trifling advantages, and was now organizing a considerable force to attack us in Rangoon.

The confidence of the nation was far from being destroyed, though the reports of those who had seen the attacks of the British troops might well have inspired terror. Some of these men, who had fled from the war, were thrown into our prison, and gave us marvellous accounts of the skill and prowess of the English troops, exaggerated by their own superstitious fancies. They firmly believed in our using enchantments. One of these convicts affirmed, that even our missiles were charmed before they were fired off, and knew what they had to do. He was standing, he said, near his *Tsek-kai*, an officer of rank, when a huge ball of iron came singing " tsek, tsek," which he distinctly heard in its flight, when, true to its mission, it burst upon the very man it was calling out for, the unfortunate *Tsek-kai!* Those who have seen shell practice know the peculiar hissing noise made by the fuse in its course through the air, and can enter into the mistake of the wonder-stricken soldier. Our surgical operations too had come to his knowledge, but, with the ignorance of a savage, he concluded our surgeons amputated injured limbs, only to repair and fit them on again. He could not conceive any other motive for cutting them off.

Bundoola left Ava in October. I saw through the crannies of the wall the march of his troops in parade. It was melancholy to see thousands of fine athletic fellows, ill-armed, and without discipline, marching with exulting confidence to certain destruction. Spears, swords, with shields, and muskets, were intermixed in admirable confusion.

While this redoubted Commander was in Ava, the fruits of his victory, on the frontier, arrived. He had succeeded in overpowering a body of native troops at Ramoo, under the command of Captain Noton. Most of the British officers were slain in the defence of their entrenchment, the rest made their escape, but several hundreds of the detachment now arrived as prisoners to grace the triumph of the victorious General. When these men were drawn up in line, those who bore the rank of officers were desired to step forward. It is clear there must have been a difference of opinion among them, some thinking that their rank would secure to them better treatment, others, with more acuteness, arguing that it would only place them in greater jeopardy. Eight men only stepped out from the ranks. These, together with as many of the sepoys as the building would contain, were committed, for the night, to our prison, merely as a matter of temporary convenience, the intention being to march them on the morrow to a considerable distance in the interior of the country.

Unfortunately, it so happened, that one of the freaks, already noticed as common to the gaolers, had at this time consigned all our party to the inner prison, and we beheld, with horror, about a hundred of these men step one after another through the wicket into our already well-filled prison, one of the ringed fraternity remaining inside to see that they were packed as close as possible. The floor was literally paved with human beings, one touching and almost overlapping the other on every side.

It soon became evident what must follow. Difficulty in breathing, profuse perspiration, and other disagreeables, overcame the natural terror of their tormentors, and the suffering multitude began to cry aloud for air and water. The horrors of the notorious *black-hole* must have been re-enacted had the building been of brick, but the manner of its construction, before explained, fortunately prevented it. At length the clamour of the captives, working probably on the fears of the gaolers themselves, induced them to open the wicket door for the night, some of their number keeping ward outside as sentinels. By this means a general disaster was avoided.

This temporary influx of prisoners was the cause of greater anxiety to me than to my companions from a peculiar circumstance. The stock of fetters, in the establishment, ran short, for it was thought necessary to invest the eight heroic native officers with these decorations, as well as others, whose dispositions were suspected. To provide for this unexpected demand, our three pairs of fetters were taken off for the night, one ring only being left on the ancle, and by this we were chained one to another, two by two, like hounds in couples, only by the leg instead of the neck.

Perhaps the reader may think this was, at all events, a slight respite, for which we ought to have been thankful. So it was, to all except myself, for the luxury of being able once more to stretch the legs apart, was, no doubt, a most grateful refreshment. But—my flesh creeps when I think of it—*I was chained to a leper.* My companion was the unfortunate Greek, whose ancles had, by this time, broken out into unmistakable open leprous sores, with which a few inches of chain alone prevented contact, while at the same time it kept me in terrible proximity. The chain was kept at its full length all night, as may be supposed, and sundry nervous jerkings from time to time, on my part, to assure myself that it was so, indicated the nature of my alarm to the poor man, who was not unconscious of his malady, though he would not openly admit it. He grew irritated at my studied avoidance of him, and raised the question himself only to deny it. This voluntary allusion to it by himself, notwithstanding his denial, only tended to confirm the fact.

With what joy did I submit myself the next day to the hands of my worthy parent, while he again invested me with my wonted complement of irons! With what anxiety, too, did I watch for weeks, searching diligently my ancles for the first symptoms of the contagion, fearing I might, unwittingly, have rubbed against the infected man, and become inoculated with his loathsome disease! I had passed a good many nights of wretchedness, but this was the worst.

The next day the place was cleared of all the sepoys, the eight native officers only remaining with us. Being unbefriended, they were starved to death in a few weeks, one man alone escaping. Not that the Government deliberately intended to starve them. It simply neglected to take the trouble to see that they were fed. When thrown on the bounty of the charitable persons, whose benevolence I have elsewhere described, they one day devoured a ravenous meal: another, or for several days together, they endured starvation. Their line of confinement was just behind ours, but crosswise, at right angles, touching our heads. As we did not possess the means effectually to relieve their necessities, we had to endure the distress of seeing the emaciated creatures, day by day, sinking under the cravings of hunger, or the quick ravages of disease, until seven of the eight miserably perished. One man who died was not removed until the following day, and I had to pass the night in contact with the stiffened corpse.

I was rather surprised at the want of endurance manifested by these men, as I had always believed the natives of India, from their constitutional apathy, could hold out with less food, and live under greater hardships and privations than the European. They certainly might have made a better struggle for existence, if they had only had the prudence to husband their resources, but they appeared to lose heart and sink into despondency from the beginning, and did not exhibit any sign of the fortitude in trouble that I had looked for.

These seven men who died were Mahomedans. The survivor, Davy Sing, a Brahmin, who told me that he held the rank of Jemmadar in the 45th N. I., owed his life to the strict maintenance of his caste. He steadfastly refused to eat rice cooked by the Burmese. When alms were distributed, he begged that his portion might be given in uncooked grain, and this he carefully bound in a strip of cloth round his waist, eating a little now and then, as hunger impelled him. Strange to say, on this meagre fare the man lived through the war, and at its close was surrendered to the British army alive—but stone-blind. I have since been told that this is a common consequence of subsisting on raw rice alone for any length of time without change.

The old story about my being a Spy, which I hoped the lapse of five months had sent into oblivion, was revived about this time in a singular manner. This reproduction of so dangerous an accusation was alarming, as the Burmese Government is more apt to forget a crime than to forgive it. However, it could not be helped.

It has been related how my assistant, Mr. Richardson, had taken his timely flight, and had reached the port of Rangoon in safety. After warning his countrymen of their danger, he fled from the country in the first vessel leaving the port, which happened to be a small schooner bound for Bengal. After beating about the coast for some days with contrary winds, they became in want of water, and put into a harbour on the coast o Arracan to replenish their stock. The anchor was cast at night, and it was proposed to lower a boat at early dawn with some empty casks, Mr. Richardson desiring the mate to wake him betimes that he might accompany the watering party. Morning came: Mr. Richardson was called — but on what trifles does a man's destiny often depend!—he felt drowsy, preferred his bed, and declined.

Mr. Sutherland (the mate) and some Lascars, ignorant that war had broken out, proceeded on shore without him. They were surprised by the natives, taken prisoners, and sent to Ava. It soon got wind that it was the vessel on which the Spy had made his escape. The first intelligence I got of this unpleasant *contre-temps* was the arrival of Mr. Sutherland in the prison-yard, where, to my consternation, I could hear from within that in his examination they got upon the dreaded topic. After his examination he was carried away to another place, nor was I ever allowed to see him, but I had heard enough to make me very uneasy, and I passed many days in alarm, lest this revival of the subject should direct their attention afresh to me. More urgent business at the moment most likely prevented it. My emissary may be thankful for his drowsiness; had he been captured in the boat, we should both, most likely, have undergone the *question*.

Before we changed the prison for the cells this time, a daring plot, partially successful, raised the fury of our "father" and his assistants almost to madness.

Among the select society we were associated with, there was not wanting a liberal proportion of "roughs," desperate fellows, ripe for any mischief. A gang of the boldest of them had concocted a plan to make their escape. It was carried into effect at midnight, by their quietly assisting each other to take off their fetters, and then, dexterously loosening a plank of the floor, they crept out from below, unperceived by the drowsy pahquet sentinel outside. Fortunately for his own throat he was asleep, but the rush to break down the outer gate, when the gang found themselves at liberty, aroused the brotherhood just in time to see the enterprising rogues take to their heels and disperse in all directions. The punishment fell on the timorous ones who were left, for it was a wise precaution of Father Ngalah to hold his captives jointly and severally responsible for the safe keeping of the community. But where was the man to be found bold enough to give the alarm, with the prospect before him of being shut up in the same apartment with a gang of irritated and disappointed ruffians? Well might such an one tremble for his officious fidelity! Terrible, however, were the penalties inflicted for some days on the faithless securities inside—especially on the Savage with the club, who, albeit we owed him no debt of gratitude, was an object of pity—until the fury of the tempest abated, and time, as usual, restored the old order of things. On the whole, we were the gainers, by getting rid of some of the most unruly and least *amiable* of our friends.

We had now become old gaol-birds ourselves. We knew how to conduct ourselves—and understood the method of warding off many of the minor asperities of the earlier months. When any petty privation was put in force, we knew that it was time our people outside should provide the means for a *refresher*. I had no money nor effects, but a few of my good baker's biscuits answered the purpose where nothing better could be got. There were many methods of giving a hint before resorting to severer measures; such as stopping for a time our food or water—the spot assigned to each in the prison—the stocks—the weight of the fetters —preventing the communication with friends—the working on the fears of the timid—and innumerable screws which they well knew how to work to the greatest advantage. Our keepers never showed mercy even to the destitute. Nor can it be wondered at—they must either oppress or starve. Judson has preserved a pithy remark of Father Ngalah that exactly depicts the principle they acted on. An under-gaoler was complaining to him that he could get no more out of a poor fellow, whom they had been tormenting for several days, his wife and house being completely stripped. "My son," said the venerable old man, "be sure you have never wrung a rag so dry but that another twist will bring another drop." They knew, almost by instinct, whether a drop of water did remain in the rag, but, after the fire, I stood on vantage ground, and, except for a biscuit or two, they were quite aware it was labour in vain to give my rag another twist. Not so was it with my comrades, who had no such incontestable proof of destitution to produce.

We might almost have thought that Ngalah had discovered a new and refined mode of putting on the screw, by the classification of his prisoners; *certes*, if another drop remained in Judson's rag, he might have wrung it out by keeping him next in proximity to Brother Price. Though he aimed at *quietism*, he had not altogether attained it. The dangers and discomforts common to all did not prevent an occasional burst of impatience, sometimes from the most ridiculous causes. A feud arose between these two excellent men, which had been gradually gaining ground, and broke out on a certain midnight with such violence and recrimination, that I was fain to come between the contending parties to preserve the peace. Every one who has had the patience to read this book so far, cannot fail to appreciate the value to us of sound sleep, when it could be got, and will admit that it ought not to be lightly disturbed.

The prison was crowded—the time was midnight. Judson in a sound sleep—Brother Price the same, being next to each other on the row. But Jonathan Price, though a good companion when he was awake, was a wretchedly bad one when he was asleep. I have already said that he was a gaunt, angular, raw-boned Yankee, who could never compose himself to sleep, until he had brought his knees to touch his nose, a custom of long standing, acquired in times of yore—when freedom sanctioned his occupying as much space as he pleased. Now, it is not to be wondered at, under present circumstances, if during the night Jonathan was often disturbed by evil dreams, and, when such occurred, he had the ugly habit of launching his terrible knees, well weighted with iron, with fearful force at the back of his unoffending neighbour, till he made the fetters of both parties rattle again. Judson bore these concussions with becoming fortitude for some time, until one of these poundings became more severe than human nature could endure. "Brother Price! you are a public nuisance. I insist on your sleeping as other people do." Brother Price assured him it was unintentional, but failed to convince him that it was unavoidable. Some threats of retaliation passed, in which poor Judson would have had no chance. To restore harmony, I offered to sleep between them, and when the battering-ram assaulted my back, I would awaken the sleepy Doctor from his night-mare, and challenge him to a pipe of tobacco, which we smoked at all hours of the night in good-humour. Besides, I could get him to fall asleep sometimes on the other side, and so bestow a fair share of his attentions on the sturdy frame of old Mr. Rodgers, whose ill-luck brought him to occupy the next place on the line.

But, notwithstanding little unavoidable disturbances of this nature, we might be fairly called a "*united*," if not a "*happy* family," and did our best to cheer each other in the endurance of our afflictions. The politics of the prison, as well as those of the nation, tended to divert our thoughts, and to keep us from despondency. The society was as continually changing as that at a fashionable watering-place, and every new arrival was an object of interest. Nor were they always of the baser sort. A very nice family, consisting of a respectable matron and several pretty daughters, were barbarously sent among us, ironed like the rest—the head of the family having misbehaved himself in the wars. It was painful to see their terror, and sickening to witness the indelicacies they were subjected to. But if I were to single out individual cases, my volume would be filled with them.

CHAPTER XXI.

Our fetters are increased to five pairs each.—Increased severities.—Orders given for our assassination.—Why not executed.—We are not allowed to be seen.—The Governor's communication to Mrs. Judson.—Bundoola's victory.—His defeat and death.—The King's Horse in prison.—Advance of the British army.—The crowing hen.—Superstitions.—Nostrum to ensure longevity.—Prison museum.—Pacahm-woon in irons.—He is appointed Generalissimo.—His hatred of the English.—Mr. Lanciego arrested and put to the torture.—Our wretched condition.

THE old year closed, and the new one set in with fresh disasters to the Burmese arms, and without throwing a ray of hope across our desolate path. While our friends and relatives at home were holding their family gatherings, and enjoying the festivities of Christmas, our minds were fast sinking into gloomy despondency, and our bodies so changed by the long endurance of trouble, that we should hardly have been recognized at those happy meetings, and so vile that the dogs would have hunted us from the door. Every few days tidings reached us of fresh defeats, sustained even by their great Chief, Bundoola, and these were always followed by a renewal of some practice of malice and revenge against us. It would be most agreeable if I could vary this monotonous history by recounting some act of grace, some relief to suffering, some symptom of commiseration, but we were in a place where the accents of sympathy were never heard, and where the light of hope is almost excluded.

I pass over the time to the 1st March, one of those days, riveted on my memory with bolts of iron, never to pass into oblivion. We had now endured this horrible captivity nine weary months, daily expecting to be relieved by the hand of the executioner, and trying to sustain our fortitude by such little arts as we could invent to drive away thoughts which, unchecked, would have led us to insanity. In our condition it may be thought "laughter is madness," and indeed so it appeared to me oftentimes; yet the sound of laughter would at times be heard even in our chains. But let me speak of this day of despair, the 1st of March.

It found us in our separate cells so often described. Towards evening a pahquet went to each cell and brought out his man, assembling the whole party around the well-known granite block. No noise—no abuse—no questions. Not a word was spoken. Hatred and revenge were too deep for words; besides, it was clear there was *business* to be done, and of a nature which needed not the usual garnish of execrations. We looked each other in the face, and there read our several opinions of what was going forward. We dared not break the silence by a word, surrounded as we were by a band of dumb demons. One by one we were motioned to the block, where our already heavily-laden limbs received two additional pairs of fetters, making five pairs in all. This done, we were directed to the inner prison, into which we staggered with great difficulty, and where we were all huddled together in a knot by ourselves.

When night set in, we ventured, in whispers, to commune with each other. There was no disguising the truth that we were left for death, not openly by the hand of the executioner, but by secret assassination, most likely on the spot where we lay. Those of us who understood the Burmese language gathered this from the conversation of our fellow-prisoners, who most likely had heard it from some of the pahquets. A night followed, so much resembling the first of our incarceration, that to describe it would be mere repetition. Our meditations, I trust, were all directed to the Throne of Grace, in preparation for the great change that appeared so near at hand. It was with an indescribable feeling of satisfaction that I heard the spotted men outside sharpening their knives for action, as it was an indication that our exit from this world would be by the steel, and not by the cord, and I had an instinctive terror of strangulation beyond most other forms of death. Every moment of that awful night, when the slightest noise disturbed the silence, I looked for the entrance of the pahquet with his instrument of slaughter. I believe the expectation of it kept many of the native prisoners awake also. This constant habit of listening to conversation going on outside the building, to gain information, had a lasting and singular effect on my nervous system. For years after I gained my freedom I could never hear people talking in another room, or out of my sight, without a sensation of fear.

The morning returned, and with it fresh signs of our condemnation, although the rumours of the night had not been verified. We could not yet comprehend to what we were indebted for our preservation during the night. When the convicts were allowed their short breathing time in the morning we were deprived of it. When our people brought us our daily rice we were carefully kept from seeing them; and I could not help noticing that, when strangers came to the prison, we were studiously concealed from their view. Whenever I approached the wicket for a breath of fresh air, as I sometimes ventured to do, I was instantly driven back to my recess; though, strange to say, we were allowed our few minutes' grace in the darkness of the night, when no one was moving, instead of the morning, as had hitherto been the custom. Our condition was altogether inexplicable.

Some days elapsed before the mystery was solved. Our inveterate enemy, the Prince Menthagee, had desired the Governor to dispatch us in secret. As this wretch was all powerful at the Court, it may be asked why he preferred thus satisfying his revenge in darkness, when he might have brought about our public execution. Perhaps he already foresaw the possibility of retribution being taken for our blood;—perhaps he thought it might not be agreeable to the King, who had shown favour to some of us in former times. Be the cause what it may, it is certain the Governor had received these diabolical instructions; but he, too, had his misgivings. He had no public order to show;—if any mischief ensued, or if he should at any future time be called to account for the deed, his superior might disavow the part he had in the affair, and leave him to bear the consequences. He therefore took the middle course of keeping us effectually out of sight to afford some plausible excuse for his daring to *disoblige* the Prince; and thus it would appear that the increased severity of our confinement was intended as an act of kindness, and became the means of our escaping a worse fate. It is probable the Governor wavered in the difficult choice he had to make, and only came to the resolution to save us in the early part of the night—just in time.

Mrs. Judson, when she heard of her husband's intense sufferings, made her way to the Governor, as usual, entreating for relief, when the terrible communication was made by him, as recorded in the memoirs of that amiable lady. She had, by repeated visits, gained the old man's sympathy. "He wept," she says, "like a child. I pity you, Tsaya-Kadau, but believe me I do not wish to increase the sufferings of the prisoners. When I am ordered to execute them, the least I can do is to put them out of sight. I will now tell you what I have not told you before. Three times I have received intimations from the Queen's brother to assassinate all the white prisoners privately, but I would not do it,—and I now repeat it, though I execute all the others, I will never execute your husband, but I cannot release him from his present confinement, and you must not ask it."

The missionary was worthy such a wife. Though sometimes giving way to despondency, he would generally comfort himself, in a true missionary spirit, by thinking of the advantages the war must bring to the cause of the mission. Often has he expressed to me such sentiments as these:—"Think what the consequences of this invasion must be. Here have I been ten years preaching the Gospel to timid listeners who wish to embrace the truth, but dare not,—beseeching the Emperor to grant liberty of conscience to his people, but without success,—and now, when all human means seem at an end, God opens the way by leading a Christian nation to subdue the country. It is possible that my life may be spared;—if so, with what ardour and gratitude shall I pursue my work,—and if not, His will be done,—the door will be opened for others who will do the work better."

It became now more difficult than ever to gain intelligence of the state of affairs outside, as the people who brought our rice were not allowed to see us. For some time Mrs. Judson* managed to convey news to her husband by a slip of paper hidden in his dish, but this did not long escape the inquisitive search of the father of the institution, and on its detection she narrowly escaped becoming one of our party.

After the lapse of a week, news reached us through the arrival of a notable prisoner, known among us by the title of the "King's Horse." It was the duty of this Hercules to attend His Majesty in his perambulations, and to carry him like a child when he was tired. He was a huge man, chosen to this post of honour for his size, symmetry, and immense power; also, perhaps, for the comfortable saddle his broad shoulders, well covered with flesh, presented to his rider. It was altogether a very ludicrous exhibition. At a given signal the *Horse* kneels down, and His Majesty jumps astride his brawny shoulders, maintaining his equilibrium with apparent ease, while the "*animal*" below him proceeds at a rapid trot or amble. The revenues of the town of Tharowah had been given him for provender, an unfortunate gift, as it lay exactly in the line of march of the British army, when it debouched from the jungles of the Delta on the main river, and was consequently one of the first towns that fell. This brought the Chief into trouble, though it is difficult to see how he could have prevented it, while his

---

* The author of the "Second Burmese War," when speaking of the release of the European prisoners at *Rangoon* at the opening of the first war, says, "Major Sale, afterwards the hero of Jellalabad, found Mrs. Judson, of missionary celebrity, tied to a tree, and immediately released her." Where could he have picked up such an idle tale?

duties kept him at the Court. However this may be, His Majesty soon found that his favourite animal was indispensable to his comfort, so he wisely ordered his release, before his paces were injured by his fetters, or his constitution undermined by the impurity of his stable.

By this incident we learned that our army had safely accomplished a most difficult part of its march through the dense jungles which intervene between Rangoon and Tharowah; that the army of Bundoola had been totally routed; and that the Chief had fled to his stronghold of Denoobew, where he intended to make a stand, while the victorious British were in full march towards the Capital.

The only living creature to be seen within the prison-yard (rats and pahquets excepted) was a bird of ill omen, but a great favourite with the gaolers on that account—a hen that crowed. It was a nasty, ill-favoured bird, of no describable colour, the head and neck covered with ugly warts or excrescences, the feathers on its body growing in tufts here and there, and staring to every point of the compass. It was, in truth, a frightfully-disgusting piece of poultry; but was caressed by the ringed men especially for its gift of prophecy. When this unnatural beast croaked—for it could not be called a crow—it was an indication of good luck to the Establishment, in giving notice of the advent of some prisoner of eminence worth the bleeding. True it was they arrived so often in these troublous times, that, crow when it would, the prophetic hen could scarcely be mistaken. One morning it took to crowing vigorously, when, to the joy of the eager pahquets, no less a personage than the great Pacahm-woon was introduced to their good offices. He shortly after doffed his fetters to command the grand army.

I may remark, that as the ringed men enjoyed their own superstitions within the prison, so it was a part of their duty to provide materials for the superstitious practices of their superiors without. They were expected to keep a depôt of such articles as might be useful in incantations, especially those which the nature of their craft enabled them to supply with facility. The greater part of the stock of this disgusting museum consisted of various parts of the human body—hair, tongues, teeth, finger-nails, &c., and when any such ingredients were required by the cunning necromancers in authority, an indent for them was made on the prison stock. One of these men once gave me a tongue on a wooden skewer to look at. Not knowing what it was, and mistaking it for a twig of *sticklac*, which, in its dry state it much resembled, I attempted to chip it. The fellow screamed with fury as he snatched it from my hand. It was the last tongue in store, and had just been ordered to the Palace. "If you had broken it, yours should have gone instead," exclaimed the wretch. Possibly it might; or perhaps his own, as it might happen. It is fortunate that these unholy practitioners did not perceive any peculiar virtue in bits of *white* men, or some of us might probably have been anatomized for the museum. Captain Cox tells us that when he was in Ava, a wealthy criminal was executed, and that the King's physician secured the tip of his nose, his ears, tongue, and lips, with a little of his blood, to form a *nostrum* to ensure longevity to any one who received it from His Majesty's hand.* It is to be hoped that homœopathic doses only were administered, or few would have a stomach for longevity under such

* Embassy of Captain Cox, page 342.

treatment. A much more efficacious dose was lately administered by His Majesty to a favourite Woongee in the more elegant form of a title, running "Mengee Maha Thetdau Shai," which, freely interpreted, is taken to mean "Say what you will, and do what you will, your life is safe from the Royal displeasure." Nor is this title an empty honour. I was told that its fortunate possessor has been known more than once to save his head by pleading the Royal pledge. It was recently granted to the Tsa-ya Woongee.

About the end of March, the wonder and joy of the whole city was awakened, by the report of *two* guns from a dispatch boat, announcing, for the first time, that a victory had been gained over the invaders. It was said Bundoola had beaten them off in an attack on Denoobew, and the report proved to be true. General Cotton had failed in an attack on their entrenchments. Great as was the renown of this Chief before, he was now regarded as the bulwark of the State, and invincible. The whole town was in a state of ecstacy—no name was heard but that of Bundoola.

Alas! these transports were short-lived, and served but to deepen the despair which followed. Another fortnight, and Bundoola was no more. He was killed by the explosion of a shell in his fortress of Denoobew, the missile having, of course, been charmed beforehand, which sought his life. On hearing the disaster, his troops hastened to evacuate the stronghold, and dispersed, leaving no army to oppose the progress of the invaders. The panic was complete. The entire population was distracted between terror and fury. Bundoola's brother, who came to the Court *with dispatches*, fell a victim—his head was instantly taken. Even the Court now became alive to the danger, though, as its pride was not yet humbled nor hope destroyed, it did not exhibit the slightest desire to make terms with the enemy.

Bundoola being dead, the Court took a step to supply his place, which, for its temerity and absurdity, was perhaps unparalleled by any Government on record. They selected the man in the *Let-ma-yoon*, just introduced to the reader, under sentence, it was supposed, for treasonable practices—the Pacahm-woon. How the King was recompensed for his simplicity will be seen in the sequel. This man had learned the art of war under Bundoola, whose Lieutenant he was in the conquest of Assam, and to this circumstance he owed his advancement from the prison to the highest post in the kingdom. It was an appointment ominous of evil to us, for his intense hatred of the English was equalled only by the murderous Prince under whose sentence we now lay. This dislike could not be concealed even while he was imprisoned with us, anticipating the same fate as we did ourselves. His scornful countenance, when his glance turned our way, clearly indicated his feelings, and was so disturbing that our apprehensions at his appointment were in some degree modified by our satisfaction at being rid of such undesirable company.

It was not long before the savage tyrant made us feel his power. I have said that the only European now at liberty was the Spaniard, Mr. Lanciego. He had succeeded up to this time, by his alliance with the sister of the second Queen, in maintaining his freedom, but now fell before the hatred of the Pacahm-woon, who, according to custom, was invested with the whole power of the Kingdom. He would have made short work of us by repeating the Menthagee's command, had he not reserved us for a more deliberate and public example, as will be seen hereafter. Mr. Lanciego suffered what I had from the first dreaded, but had marvellously escaped—the torture. I am happy to say I was spared the sight of the infliction of it; but it must have been very severe. A small cord bound the wrists together, and was gradually tightened by the application of a lever. At each wrench he was exhorted to confess and be liberated; but the Spaniard was too old a bird to be caught by that bait. Knowing the consequence of *confession*, as it is called, he courageously endured the torture to the last. And what was he expected to *confess*? That he had sold the Island of Negrais to the English for a sum of money, which he was now called on to give up to the King! The Pacahmwoon must have been sadly at a loss for a plausible pretext when such an absurd one was adopted. The condition of the poor sufferer's hands, when he was ushered in among us, quivering from the effect of the pain inflicted, was terrible to behold. Every finger was as black as pitch, and the points of them swollen to bursting with the extravasated blood. The wrists were cut through and mangled with the cord. The agony he endured must have been excruciating, though this was generally looked upon as one of the mildest methods of questioning a culprit—far less severe in its character than many we had seen practised on others. He was ironed like ourselves, and henceforth must be looked upon as one of our brethren in affliction.

In the mean time we were left, in the sultry months of March and April, without water to cool our feverish bodies—in the gloom of a filthy dungeon—never beholding the light of the sun—heavily laden with five pairs of fetters—in company with a prisonful of felons—and in hourly expectation of being called on to submit to the last work of the gang of wretches outside, who were rejoicing in the anticipation of the work of blood they would have to perform.

When I look back on the almost unexampled sufferings of those two months, how light and insignificant do all the ordinary troubles of life appear! When such arise, I have only to reflect, and be thankful.

CHAPTER XXII.

We are removed from the Let-ma-yoon, and taken to Oung-ben-lai.—Our sufferings on the journey.—My terror.—Dr. Judson.—His intense suffering.—Murder of the Greek.—The ringed men leave us.—Night at Amerapoorah.—We are carted to Oung-ben-lai.—We are in fear of being burned.—The prison described.—We are put in the stocks.—Contrivance for hoisting them.—Musquitos.—We are chained in couples.—My baker's fidelity.—Mrs. Judson follows her husband.—The Governor's warning to her.

DAY by day, and hour by hour, did we watch, with anxious hearts, the proceedings of our inveterate Enemy, newly raised to power, whose known hostility imparted a tone of harshness to the conduct even of the old Governor himself. Every night, as he returned from the Palace, we could hear his stentorian voice, very much like that of a boatswain, bawling from the street as he passed, "Are the white men safe? Keep them tight," as though circumstances had imposed on him increased responsibility. It was rather a superfluous caution. John Bunyan said, when for years he was imprisoned in a room overhanging the muddy bed and slimy banks of the Ouse, that he feared the moss would, in time, grow over his eyebrows. Unless a change speedily came, I had the more reasonable fear of being eaten up alive, eyebrows and all. A change, however, did come, which, at all events, released us from this source of alarm.

On the 2nd of May our party, now eight in number, again found itself assembled around the memorable granite block. What a ghastly group! The matted hair, the hollow eye, the feeble gait, the emaciated frame, the filthy tattered rags—objects such as the sun surely never before shone upon! Around us the Spotted men gathered for the last time. Thank God! I never cast my eye upon one of their detestable ringed cheeks after this day. They were now armed with spears, and each held in his hand a long piece of cord. Our irons were knocked off—for the first time for eleven months I found my limbs free. The sensation was ridiculous. At first I could hardly stand—the equilibrium of the body seemed destroyed by the removal of the fetters I had so long worn on my ancles weighing fully fourteen pounds—the head was too heavy for the feet. This only lasted a short time, and I enjoyed the first stretch of my legs. We were now tied in couples by the waist, one at each end of the rope, a pahquet, with a spear, holding the rein, just as children are seen to drive each other in their sports. Off we went, we knew not whither bound, but conjectured, by the manner of the men and their weapons, we were going to the place of execution.

And here, before starting on our journey, let me stop a moment to inquire what is the reason that a man who has long been living in the hourly expectation of a violent death looks upon it with calmness and fortitude at one time, while at another he is as timid as a startled hare? Circumstances have not changed—his miseries in life, his hopes in death remain the same, yet is the fact as I state it. Few, it is to be hoped none, who read this book, can know it from experience; but they may take my word for the fact. My life is worth no more to me to-day than it was yesterday—perhaps less—yet the tenacity with which I retain it to-day and the fear at parting with it, strangely contrasts with the resigned feelings of yesterday. It is not the fear of bodily suffering, for I had long reasoned myself into the belief that the common mode of execution with the sword is not more painful than the extraction of a tooth; in fact, that if dexterously performed, as it generally is in Burmah, it is not felt at all. Yet the nerves are unstrung, and the whole frame trembles with fright.

I do not pretend to answer the question; but, be the cause what it may, I confess that I never felt more confused or terrified. How thankful I was that our drivers, after having goaded us a few hundred yards towards the place of execution, turned aside from that road and took the one leading to the old town of Amerapoorah. By this time I had recovered my senses a little, as also the use of my legs.

Our road lay across a bridge that spans a rapid river, called the Meet-ngai. The waters were low at this season, and the torrent swept under it fully thirty feet below the parapet to join the Irrawuddi, at the north angle of the town. It was here I overtook Mr. Judson, who was coupled with Mr. Laird.* He was still fully impressed with the belief that we were being driven to our death in some form or other, although we had turned our backs on the usual execution ground, and in this conviction even his fortitude gave way. "Gouger," said

---

* In relating this story to my friends, I have said that Dr. Judson was my companion. I find, however, on reading Mrs. Judson's letters, that I was wrong. The conversation we had on the bridge might have given me that impression, and as no notes could be taken until I had regained my liberty, this erroneous impression may be easily accounted for.

he, "the parapet is low; there can be no sin in our availing ourselves of the opportunity." It was a momentary feeling; but he was evidently in earnest, and I am not sure that, had he not been linked to a sturdy Scotchman whose assent was absolutely necessary, he would not have taken the fatal leap. For myself, I was in no humour to follow such an indication. I was never tempted to self-destruction throughout our trials, nor ever for a moment harboured such a thought. One moment more and the opportunity had passed—the bridge was crossed.

We proceeded on our way to Amerapoorah. The road was over a plain of burning sand and small gravel, interspersed here and there with a tuft of short, parched grass. By the time we were out of the town the sun was fast reaching the meridian; it flashed upon our undefended heads like flames of fire. No one who has not been subjected to a tropical sun at the hottest season of the year can form any idea of its power. Walking on this arid plain was like walking on a sheet of hot iron, and as none of the party had shoes, the soles of the feet were the first parts of the body to complain. They began in blisters, but when these burst, as they very soon did, the pain was excruciating. I suffered little in this respect compared with my companions; indeed, so strangely is the mind of man constituted, after I had got over my first panic I positively, for a time, found enjoyment in looking on the lofty hills of Tsagain, skirting the opposite bank of the Irrawuddi, the noble forest trees, the wide expanse of water, even the burning sky above had its charm after a year spent in a foul dungeon. Besides, I had been fortified by my breakfast, which some had not, and as I was the youngest, and had quite recovered from my illness, it fared not so badly with me.

The Greek was the first to give in. Before we had gone a mile, it was clear he could go no further, and he fell helpless on the sands. For a few minutes, beating and pricking with the spear kept him on, but these persuasions had their limit; it was of no use beating and goading a dying man. On looking back I saw the inhuman wretches dragging him on the sands with the rope which tied him, while the dying man's hands were clasped and raised as if in supplication for mercy to his tormentors, but in vain. There was no possibility of helping him, as we were all hurried forward under terror of the spear. He just reached our halting-place in a cart, and there breathed his last.

After the second mile Judson was on the point of giving in, not so much from want of bodily strength to go forward as from the state of his feet, which had lost every vestige of skin from the scorching of the sands, and the soles of them were now one mass of blood and raw flesh. He could not endure the agony of putting them to the ground, and was just on the eve of resigning himself to his fate, and following the example of the Greek, when a fortunate accident saved him. One of my old servants, hearing that we were driven towards Amerapoorah, came running after us to see the end of his master, and arrived just at this critical moment. Seeing Judson's sufferings, he tore his turban from his head, made it into shreds, and hastily wound them round his wounded feet. With the help of this man, on whose shoulder he rested for the remainder of the journey, and the relief he had gained for his feet, Judson managed to preserve his life. With great difficulty we reached Amerapoorah at last, where we sunk exhausted with pain and fatigue.

Here the Ringed men left us to return to their Elysium at Ava, committing us to the care of other keepers who had hearts, hard though they might be. They soon came to tell us that we had four miles further to go, as our destination —here we heard it for the first time—was Oung-ben-lai, a country village, where another prison was ready to receive us. But neither threats nor entreaties could get us on our legs again, even had the alternative been, our being slaughtered on the spot. They therefore made a virtue of necessity, and permitted us to pass the night there, intending to move forward early in the morning. Some slept in a shed nigh at hand. I got under a cart on the roadside and fell fast asleep till the morning. The next day it was found we were less able to move even than yesterday. Our joints worked as stiffly as rusty locks—there was no flexibility. I believe I was the only one who could walk even a few yards. Happily for us we were not now left to the tender mercies of the pahquets; our more reasonable gaolers saw the impossibility, and provided a cart, into which we mounted, and performed the latter half of our journey in comparative comfort.

It was about two o'clock in the afternoon when the cart put us down on a small plot of low grass, forming part of an extensive plain in rice cultivation. The place had a dreary and deserted appearance. Before us stood a solitary, dilapidated wooden building, without a door, the roof of which had fallen in, a few rotten bamboos and tufts of decayed thatch only remaining. This brought out into full view a massive range of stocks, occupying the entire length of the building. Strange to say, although this piece of furniture was evidently a relic of antiquity, the number of holes tallied exactly with those required for our accommodation, which will give the reader a pretty correct idea of the dimensions of our prison. A few posts arose out of the ground at a little distance, inclining in every direction from the perpendicular, showing that formerly it had been carefully fenced round, but that time, or pilfering, or both, had now destroyed it. No dwelling was to be seen nearer than a quarter of a mile, where a few scattered huts and trees marked the site of the village of Oung-ben-lai. The extent of the plain, as far as the eye could reach, without an object for it to rest on, imparted to the place an air of desolation and melancholy. On one side alone a range of broken hills, at four or five miles distance, occupying a large space in the horizon, afforded an object to look on.

But what most riveted our attention was a heap of dry faggots, stowed with great precision so as to fill the space between the ground and the floor of the building, which might be four or five feet. It was the only thing we saw that bore the appearance of recent labour or preparation. They were so carefully laid that they touched the floor at every point, and formed a continuous wall with the outer planking of the house on every side. It was a strange place to stack *firewood* in! We now recollected that it had been reported in Ava that we were to be burned, a rumour which, with a variety of others, we gave little heed to at the time, but the sight of these faggots brought it painfully to our mind. How easy is it to admit the truth that we should place implicit confidence in the Providence of God!—how difficult to put it in practice! With what anxiety did we argue the question between ourselves, but could arrive at no result; our gaolers forming a remarkable contrast with those of the Let-ma-yoon in their extreme taciturnity; and it was not until the following morning, after passing a night of painful apprehension, that we learned they had been so carefully stacked to prevent our escape through the dilapidated floor. Such a wise precaution would have saved our venerable father of the Let-ma-yoon the disgrace of having lost his gang of ruffians.

Before night, some men came with palm-leaves to repair the thatch, an encouraging sign, which raised our spirits and tended to relieve our alarm.

When it became dark we were motioned inside and submitted our feet to the stocks, as expected. We had gone to *bed* (I cannot restrain a smile while I write the word, the bare plank being our resting-place) with stomachs uncomfortably light, and with minds anything but placid. The gaol-guard was stationed below us in a little apartment resembling a verandah, formed by a continuation of the roof, on a plan which the builders call a "lean-to." As all became still, we began to compose our thoughts as well as we could, in the hope of obtaining a little sleep, when, to our astonishment, we felt the stocks gradually and slowly moving upwards, as if by magic, for there was no one in the room to put them in motion. At first we were so taken by surprise that we did not know what to make of it. Was it going up to the roof? Was it some new species of torture? Its movement was majestically slow, and gave us a little time to think before it reached the height at which it rested, when a very short time discovered the trick. It was certainly very creditable to the ingenuity of the rogues, and was, no doubt, looked upon by them as a prodigy of mechanical contrivance, as I could hear them outside enjoying the fun. There was a kind of crank outside which had escaped our notice, so contrived as to raise or depress the stocks at the will of the operator. When he had worked them to a sufficient height he fixed them, and left us depending, in the fashion of the bamboo at the Let-ma-yoon. And now began, what I before hinted at, the attack of the musquitos, which swarmed in from the stagnant water of the rice-fields, settling unresisted on our bare feet. We could not reach to drive them off, and a rich repast they, no doubt, enjoyed on our flayed soles. At last it became insupportable, and we lustily bawled out for pity from our guard below. I must do them the credit to believe they knew not the extent of the torture they were inflicting, as before midnight they mitigated it by lowering the stocks, when we could hold the enemy at bay.

In the morning we had the satisfaction to find our gaoler, named Koh-bai, who soon became our only attendant, not impracticable, though somewhat morose and surly. Moreover, he had not the damning spot upon his cheeks like those of the death prison. He allowed us to go outside to enjoy the light and air in his verandah, and sometimes to walk about the prison enclosure, which in a day or two was restored to its original condition by a well-made fence.

Being a country prison but rarely used, the stock of fetters was found to be insufficient to bind the whole party, and it became necessary to couple us in the manner before described, when the leprous Greek was my companion. This time I was better off, the kind-hearted but ungainly Scot, John Laird, being my yoke-fellow. Considering how mutually annoying we were of necessity forced to be to each other, we agreed tolerably well, though it must be confessed we were often compelled to curb the irritation of our tempers. I have heard that Sir David Baird, when he was taken prisoner in 1782, by Tippoo Saib, was coupled in a similar manner with another captive. His mother, when she heard, in England, of the misfortune that had befallen her son, knowing that he was not blessed with the most submissive temper, bestowed the first burst of her sympathy upon the party who most needed it—"How I pity the poor man that is chained to my Davie!"

This system of coupling is enough to ruin the most amiable temper on earth. It is impossible to describe the train of petty annoyances that attend it every minute. Do I wish to recline, to stand up, to walk, to sleep, to change my position? I can do none of these things without first obtaining the leave of my companion, who, perhaps, desires exactly the opposite. Knowing the effect on me, I have often wondered what kind of temper the Siamese twins possessed, and how they got on together! One would suppose that, like animals, the stronger would exercise tyranny over the weaker, and thus, at least, peace might be established. Laird and I did not find it so during the few days of our union, however; and, from the little experience I had, I feel convinced two of the most ardent, devoted lovers the world ever saw (much as they may doubt my judgment) need only be chained by the leg together for much less time than a honeymoon, thoroughly and heartily to detest the sight of each other. After two or three days a fresh supply of irons came to our *relief*, and restored our respect for one another.

But to return from this digression. My morning-call of hunger was, for the first time, not responded to. I had implicit faith in my magnanimous baker, if he knew where I was gone; but the suddenness of our removal left our people in complete ignorance for a time. Nevertheless he found me out, and before noon his rapid stride appeared in the distance with a bag of his biscuits to relieve our immediate necessities. It used to astonish me how this noble-hearted fellow found his way from Ava two or three times a week to see me, never failing for nine or ten months to bring me the news of the day and wherewithal to support life. He was remarkably swift of foot, accomplishing the nine miles in less than two hours; but even this, with the same distance to return, occupied the greater part of the day, and yet he found time to ply his trade for our mutual support. The exchequer of the rest was beginning to show signs of weakness; whereas, so long as my protector retained life and health, I had a never-failing supply, and might, in this view, be considered the most wealthy man among them. After all, our charges could not, at the most, have exceeded two shillings a week for each person, which, if driven by necessity, they could have got by *begging*—a paltry vice, be it said to their credit, altogether unknown among the Burmans.

A day intervened before Mrs. Judson (who had been confined some months previously) came out in a cart with her baby, and got liberty to use part of a rice shed for her habitation. Her distress, when she found her husband had been carried off, no one knew whither, and when at last she learned from the Governor of the town our precarious situation, may be best expressed in her own words. "I found the Governor wished to detain me until the dreadful scene in the prison was over. When I left him, one of the servants came running with a ghastly countenance, and told me the white prisoners were carried away. I instantly went back to the Governor, who said he knew it, but did not wish to tell me. I hastily ran into the street, hoping to get a glimpse of them before they were out of sight, but was disappointed. I ran first into one street, then another, inquiring of all I met, but no one would answer me. At length an old woman told me the white prisoners had gone towards the little river. I then ran to the banks of the little river about half a mile, but saw them not, and concluded the old woman had deceived me. Some of the friends of the foreigners went to the place of execution, but found them not. I then returned to the Governor to try to discover the cause of their removal and their future fate. The old man assured me that he was ignorant of the intention to remove them till that morning; that since I went out he had learned the prisoners were to be sent to Amerapoorah, but for what purpose he knew not. 'I will send off a man immediately,' said he, 'to see what is to be done with them. You can do nothing more for your husband,' continued he, '*take care of yourself.*' With a heavy heart I went into my own room, and sank down almost in despair."

Little did the old Governor know the affectionate and faithful heart to which he addressed this warning advice.

CHAPTER XXIII.

Some comforts at Oung-ben-lai.—Our anxious position.—Ignatius Brito, a Roman Catholic priest, is arrested and imprisoned, and goes mad.—A Lioness in prison with us.—Our conjectures and terror.—The Lioness starved to death.—Object of the Pacahm-woon.—Insalubrity of Oung-ben-lai.—Mrs. Judson takes smallpox; Judson fever.—He inhabits the lion's den.—Plague of snakes.—We kill great numbers of the cobra capello.—Nandau snakes.—My marvellous escape from a cobra.

This protracted imprisonment now exhibits a new phase. The scene is altogether changed, much for the better as regards personal comfort, arising more from the causes of misery having been left behind, than from any wish or intention on the part of the Government to alleviate it. The horrid putridity of the inner prison, the smothering crowd of wretched convicts, the ringed brotherhood of the Let-ma-yoon, the tortures, the assassinations, the hourly alarms, could not be transported to Oung-ben-lai. We had fresh air, freedom from vermin, lighter chains, less abuse, water for cleanliness, and after a few days had established confidence in our new keeper, Koh-bai, by showing him that he had not eight tigers to look after, but so many submissive, quiet, and dejected mortals; we enjoyed as much comfort as a Burmese prison-house could be expected to afford. When our wounded feet were sufficiently healed to permit it, we were allowed to hobble about the enclosure for the greater part of the day, feasting our eyes with the sight of the beautiful range of hills in the distance.

My generous baker had bought me a new Burmese cloth. I doffed the filthy remnants of the old one, (my last shirt having rotted piece-meal from my back many months before,) and again luxuriated in a well-cleansed exterior, and pores unchoked with grime. So far the change was salutary and refreshing, but there was that within eating like a canker into our heart's core, and sapping slowly and imperceptibly the constitution, even though it might be naturally strong and robust. I felt my mind, too, was growing weaker and less capable of concentration of thought under the constant pressure of anxiety of which there seemed to be no end. I could not deceive myself into the belief that any of these happy changes were intended for my comfort, nor that my life was one hair's-breadth safer in this country retreat than it was in the midst of the alarms of the town prison. This abiding feeling of insecurity was kept alive by every rumour which successively reached me, all pointing to the fact that we were sent here for some diabolical purpose by the Pacahm-woon, though what that might be was still shrouded in mystery.

Among the most probable of these rumours was one that I hoped might be true; that we were to be sent away to Monai, a town some hundreds of miles to the eastward, on the borders of the country of Lao, whose Princes were tributary to the Burman Monarch. It was hardly to be expected that any one of us in our debilitated condition could reach that place alive, yet the increased distance from these hourly persecutions alone would be a blessing, and even death itself appeared more endurable when it came in a natural form by the exhaustion of vital strength under the canopy of heaven, than when met in the darkness of a prison by the cord of the assassin, or the more public sword of the executioner. Besides, we heard that the Ramoo sepoys had been sent there, which gave a colour of truth to the report.

The zeal of the Pacahm-woon in hunting down foreigners, now brought to our society a new member, whose name even I had never heard until this time.

Ignatius Brito added another ingredient to the already strangely-heterogeneous materials which composed our society. He was a native Burman, of Portuguese extraction, as dark in colour as a native, and by what accident he fell under suspicion no one knew. By profession he was a Roman Catholic priest. The only languages he spoke fluently were his native ones, Burman and Portuguese; therefore, as we were no longer prohibited the free use of English, he joined but little in our conversations. Had he not given way to frequent tirades against my country and countrymen, I should have thought him an agreeable companion. He was fond of music,—he composed a dance, which he called *"deliverance from prison,"* wrote it on the jailor's black book, and he attempted a *pas seul* in his fetters to the tune of his composition with but indifferent success; he had also learned some Latin songs set to plaintive music in honour of the Virgin Mary, which he was never weary of repeating, often breaking the silence of the night when his companions were at rest by singing these melodious airs in good taste and with good voice. Some complained of the disturbance, but, I must confess, to me they had a soothing effect, and I could lie awake and listen to them with the same sort of pleasure as I ever did (and do still, when I can get it) to the midnight

Christmas street-music in England. In two or three
months it was evident that his mind had given way under
his trials, though I have since heard that he recovered,
and became a useful and respected pastor of a small
church in those remote regions. Chance had now thrown
together, in one common calamity, two American Baptist
missionaries, a Portuguese Roman Catholic priest, a
Spaniard, an Armenian, a Scotch mariner, the old adventurer Mr. Rodgers, and myself, the poor Greek having
gone to his rest.

One night, soon after the events lately related, this
motley little family was trying to forget its sorrows in
sleep, when hollow rumbling sounds, like distant thunder,
disturbed its rest. Presently, as it came nearer, we could
distinguish the sound of wheels creaking as if some
clumsy vehicle was supporting a heavy weight, the voices
of men, and, above all, at intervals the loud roarings
of some wild animal, drowning for the moment all
other sounds. The wide, unbroken plain on which
the solitary prison stood, aided by the silence of the
hour, allowed these sounds to reach it from a considerable distance. Few carts passed this unfrequented
road even in the daytime, but at this hour of the night
noises so strange excited the curiosity of every one. Old
Koh-bai, the gaoler, also seemed to be taken by surprise,
evidently not being prepared for any fresh arrival, and
should this prove to be such, he had no instructions to
guide him. The men who formed the escort professed to
know no more than himself; they left their prisoner and
departed.

In the mean time when the object of our enquiry
had reached its destination, curiosity was changed into
error, by hearing that a huge Lioness, confined in a
strong cage, to which wheels had been fixed for facility

of transport, was the cause of all this uproar. With some difficulty the clumsy car was drawn into the prison enclosure, and placed close under our room. All night long did we listen to the hungry roarings of the animal with feelings of horror, eagerly searching for some probable motive that had influenced the Government to send such a creature here, but always in vain; returning in dismay to that which appeared to be the most simple interpretation, that we were to be thrown into the den of the savage to be torn in pieces and devoured. The Royal beast was so near that her breathings might be distinctly heard, and every roar or hungry growl made us tremble in anticipation of the terrible doom that awaited us.

After a night of agony, morning brought us no relief beyond its own cheering light which itself serves to disperse many of the illusive horrors which darkness conjures up to increase the misery even of the most wretched and forlorn. No information could we gain. There stood the Lioness, glaring on us with eyes of fury whenever we approached her cage; here stood the astonished gaoler, who could throw no light on the mystery; no one else was in the enclosure. We did not dare to name our suspicions, fearing the mere surmise might bring on us more rigorous confinement; and whatever Koh-bai's thoughts might have been, he never gave them expression, nor hinted at such a motive as we feared.

The day passed, still no orders came, but our fears gained strength when we saw that the animal was kept without food. The cravings of hunger made it still more ferocious; the whole of the next night was spent in listening to its dreadful bellowings, which might have been heard at intervals across the plain. Little was it to be wondered at that the brain of the worthy Father

Ignatius lost its balance, far more wonderful is it that we any of us preserved our reason. Day after day the starvation continued, and night after night the same fearful howlings were repeated, until in about a week the poor creature began to exhibit signs of diminished strength, and as these appeared, our hopes revived. Could we be mistaken? This unparalleled cruelty continued for about a fortnight, when the noble animal yielded up its breath. The day before she died Koh-bai squeezed a pariah dog through the bars, but it was too late,—the terrified cur retreated to a corner of the cage and showed his teeth with impunity,—the famished Lioness had not strength to rise and seize him.*

Dr. Livingston, in his late travels through South Africa, very much diminishes our respect for the King of beasts, when he says, " the traveller who expects something very noble and majestic will merely see an animal somewhat larger than the biggest dog he ever saw," and that " nothing he ever learned of the Lion would lead him to attribute to it the noble or ferocious character ascribed to it." The Doctor ought to be a very good judge, but if we were to form our opinion from the picture he has favoured us with, where he is represented as lying prostrate under the paw of the beast, and were to take it for a fair representation, our early imagination can scarcely be said to have misled us, either as to size, ferocity, or majesty. At all events, either the lion of Arabia must be a nobler animal than that of South Africa, or my fears must have

---

* I am aware that in Wayland's " Life of Judson " a different account is given of this event, which is incorrect in time, place, and circumstance. This arises most probably from the anecdote being given by Dr. Judson's second wife, who professes to report it only from her recollection of conversations with her husband.

magnified it far beyond the truth, for I could no more compare it with a dog, than I could a tiger with a cat. The Lion is not found in Burmah. The subject of the foregoing obituary notice was a native of Arabia, presented to His Majesty by the Imaum of Muscat.

No reason was ever made public as to the motives of the Government in sending so strange a prisoner to keep us company. Some conjectured that the Lion being the British emblem, it arose from a superstitious desire to degrade it. But this is not probable, for had such been their wish, it would have been sent to the more appropriate Let-ma-yoon, which was much nearer, and where the degradation would have been more complete. My own belief is, that we were right in our first surmise—that we were destined to be thrown to the Lioness to be devoured; but that a change in the mind of the Pacahm-woon interposed to avert the danger, especially as he had another tragedy in view more in accordance with his own superstitious nature, which, thank Heaven! we were yet in happy ignorance of, and did not ascertain until the danger had nearly passed away. But I must not anticipate the event. The affair of the Lioness remained a fearful mystery.

The tract of country upon which the prison stood, although it might be called pure and salubrious by those who came from the pest-house of the Let-ma-yoon, was, nevertheless, generally considered unhealthy, being subject to fevers of an obstinate character. As I have already remarked, it was an extensive low plain under rice cultivation, and, as is usual with these crops, was periodically laid under water, by means of sluices, from a large embanked lake in the neighbourhood. At the time of this irrigation it presented the appearance of a vast sheet of water, the heads of the green crops just peeping above the surface. The prison and the adjacent village were built on a plot of ground slightly rising in the midst of it, just raising them above the level of the surrounding water, but not enough to free them from the damp exhalations hanging over the cultivated land. It was a Royal demesne, under the government of a Minister called the La-myne-woon, to whose custody in chief we were now committed.

Mrs. Judson was the greatest sufferer from the insalubrity of this place. Smallpox broke out in the village. She and her baby took the infection, while her husband was attacked by the prevailing fever in the prison. Fortunately it broke out mildly in her case; she soon recovered, and, from motives of benevolence, she inoculated all the children in the neighbourhood, though she acknowledged she knew nothing of the practice or the treatment. It so happened that success attended her practice, and she passed for a skilful person; but the experiment was dangerous, and might have brought her into trouble. Judson, in his distress, cast a longing eye upon the den of the Lioness, now vacated by its savage tenant, who had caused us so much alarm, and was lying useless. It was invitingly large and airy, well put together, with an excellent floor and roof; and, weakened as he was with his fever, it was a retreat in which he thought he could repose without disturbance. Old Koh-bai, seeing his debilitated state, allowed him to inhabit this ridiculous dwelling. Once installed, he formed such an attachment to it that no one could induce him to leave it, and for several months he retained quiet possession of a habitation which he once regarded with terror as his destined grave.

The elevated site of our habitation had its inconveniences. If it put us out of the reach of the inundation of waters, it subjected us to an inundation of another kind scarcely less disagreeable. When the sluices were opened to irrigate the parched fields, vermin and reptiles of all sorts, which did not wish to be drowned, sought a refuge on this, the only dry spot of land they could find. Rats, and varieties of the serpent tribe, many of the latter possessing very disreputable characters, were our most frequent visitors. So formidable was this invasion that we were allowed to arm ourselves each with a stout stick for protection, and many a deadly foe to our repose fell under our hands. Considering the confined space we occupied, it is surprising we did not fall victims to these unwelcome guests. A tally was kept of the number killed. Of the cobra capello alone, I think it was thirteen. The silent gliding of the snake, giving no warning of its approach, and the power it possesses of contracting its bulk, enables one of considerable size to insinuate itself unperceived into the presence of man.

A friend once told me that he came home from Calcutta in a ship which, on the voyage, took up as a passenger a large boa-constrictor, intended as a specimen for the Zoological Gardens. By some accident the door of its cage was once left open, and the reptile crept out unperceived, though on the upper deck of a crowded ship, in the light of day. The discovery was made by an unusual commotion among the sheep stowed in the launch for the ship's use, where the monster was discovered embracing in its folds the body of one of the flock, whose bones, one after another, snapped with a distinct report, under the tremendous pressure. My informant says the sight was horribly disgusting. The first general impulse was to destroy the huge assailant, but the more prudent Captain gave him permission to finish his meal, which was performed in about an hour, in the usual nasty manner, by reducing it to a pulp, lubricating and swallowing it. The ship's crew then handled the snake without fear, and returned it to its cage in a state of torpor.

My enemies were not of this gigantic sort; but were equally dangerous. The largest was one I killed myself, a very beautiful snake, about seven feet long, having alternate rings of black and bright yellow from the throat to the tail. The Burmese called it "*Nandau-mwai*"— "throne-snake," and said it was harmless; though I confess I distrust the whole tribe. Besides, he was found in bad company, and we were too much terrified to make nice distinctions.

But I have been saying all this about snakes, without yet telling the story that induced me to introduce the subject. Of all the hair-breadth escapes I had encountered this was the one that came nearest to a fatal result.

Koh-bai, when in a good humour, would sometimes invite me, late at night, to enjoy the fresh air, and to smoke my pipe of tobacco with him in his verandah below. This verandah was ten or twelve feet wide, enclosed by mats on two sides, the prison-wall on the third, the fourth being open. The floor, raised two feet above the ground, was made of split bamboos tied together, such as is known to all Indians by the name of a *bamboo mutchan*. In this snug retreat old Koh-bai and I were one night regaling ourselves with our pipes, seated opposite to each other, the everlasting earth oil-lamp occupying its customary position between us, shedding a dim, smoky light over the apartment, when I became aware of something moving noiselessly over my feet and ancles, which were thrown behind me in the well-known sitting posture of the Burmese. Although out of sight I immediately knew it to be a snake, from its cold, glossy skin, as it slowly trailed its

whole length over my bare ancles. I had the presence
of mind to sit quietly, and say nothing to my companion,
hoping the creature would make its escape if unmolested,
for it had me at too great an advantage to warrant an
attack on my part. Presently it wriggled itself into sight,
coming close round my left side. It was a large cobra
capello, nearly four feet long. No sooner did the old man
catch a glimpse of the dangerous intruder, as it glided
between us, than, with a bound of which I thought him
incapable, he cleared the verandah at the open side behind
him, leaving me alone to deal with the enemy, now
alarmed and irritated by the noise. Gladly would I have
followed his example, but I was in fetters, and the combat was not to be avoided. All the chances were in
favour of the beast, for my pipe-stick was my only weapon; but it was a tough, trustworthy one. My adversary
showed the first fight, by rearing its head and shoulders
nearly two feet high, expanded its horrid hood, and was
in the very act of making its fatal dart, when I made my
first blow. Thank God! it took effect. The reptile, disappointed in its spring, fell partially disabled, and, before it
could recover for another attack, my trusty pipe-stick
rained upon it a shower of blows, and gained me the
victory. I believe that, literally, a delay of *one second
of time* would have sealed my fate, for the fang of the
cobra always proves fatal. The construction of the floor
probably saved me: the snake must have received the
first blow on one of the projecting bamboos, which
injured the spine.

CHAPTER XXIV.

British army goes into quarters at Prome.—The Talain race join and assist it.—Preparations of Pacahm-woon. — His intention to bury us alive in Oung-ben-lai.—He is suspected of treason, and put to death. —Causes of his fall.—Doubt about the plot.—We escape by his death.—Summoned to Amerapoorah.—Translation of letters.—Offer to negotiate for peace.—Negotiations.—Judson taken from prison.—Bad faith.— Melloon stormed.—Judson protected by a Chief.—Ava put in a state of defence.—The Burmese are routed at Pagan.—Dr. Sandford deputed to the British General.—Returns to prison.—Burmese incredulity.—Dr. Price is released and employed.

It is time that I returned from the events of my new prison, to take some notice of what was passing at the seat of war.

After the defeat and death of the great Chief Bundoola, at Denobew, the victorious army continued its march unmolested to Prome, where, from the month of May to December, it went into quarters, as the General did not think it prudent to take the field in the rainy season, though the monsoon was much lighter than on the coast. Finding the army of the invaders invariably successful, and that no outrages followed their victories, the whole population of the Southern provinces quietly returned to their homes, gladly supplying our army with provisions and the means of transport when they saw that punctual payment was not withheld. Thousands of labourers were at the command of the British General, and the river was covered with their boats bringing in supplies. Seventy or eighty years only had elapsed since the whole tract of country they had marched through, from Prome to the sea, was an independent Kingdom, inhabited by a race called Talains or Peguers, speaking a different language, and maintaining itself successfully against the encroaching Burmans. Of late their nationality had been fast disappearing, and there was every prospect of the process of amalgamation with the conquering Burmans being complete in two or three generations—but this, the war rudely interrupted. When they found the country freed from their conquerors by the irresistible advance of the British army, the dormant nationality revived with a renewal of the usual hatred of an oppressed people. They had no idea that the British, having once taken possession of the country, would ever be induced to restore it. As such an act of folly, as it appeared to them, could hardly enter their minds, the unfortunate inhabitants compromised themselves by prematurely throwing off the Burman yoke, little dreaming that a day of retribution would arrive when these conquests would revert to their old masters.

The inactivity of our army, while it occupied comfortable quarters so many months at Prome, afforded leisure to the Pacahm-woon to re-organize his forces. Greater efforts were now made than before. Large levies of men, from the tributary States of the Shans, under the command of their own Princes, joined the army; and as the population became rather shy from the danger of the service, excessive bounties from the Royal coffers were distributed among the troops, wonderfully lightening the long range of glittering logs which I had seen in front of the Shwai-dyke. In numerical strength the army was said to be greater than before; but its ardour was much diminished, and the vile wretch, who commanded it, ruled even the Court itself by the arrogant use he made of the almost Regal power confided to him.

I now learned, for the first time, and the discovery did not at all tend to restore my peace of mind, that Oung-ben-lai had the honour of giving birth to this oppressor. That there was some mysterious connection of this fact with the order he had issued for our being conveyed to the place, hardly admitted a doubt, when we considered how he was inflated with the pride of station, and that he had the reputation of being the dupe of superstitious omens and observances.

At last the horrid truth got whispered abroad that on the 31st of May, when the Generalissimo's arrangements would be completed, Head-quarters were to assemble at Oung-ben-lai, where the white prisoners were to be sacrificed by being buried alive at the head of the army. This is the only way I can account for the starving of the Lioness,—the superstitious tyrant had abandoned that idea for one which would redound more to his own personal aggrandizement. By a curious coincidence the name Oung-ben-lai may be translated "field of victory,"* so that it is not unlikely the name may have suggested the idea. The field would be sown with seed likely to yield a rich harvest of slaughter among his enemies. The first

---

* I observe Major Yule gives the translation of the name of this place "*Cocoa Tree rice fields.*" We always regarded it in the sense I have attached to it, as I see Mrs. Judson does also. My recollection of the Burmese language is becoming rather misty, but I think it might read the "Sea of Victory," the extensive lake in its vicinity helping them to the name.

intimation of this appalling destiny was brought by my baker, but happily for our peace—I might say for our Reason—not until the fatal day had so nearly approached that we were spared some weeks of mental agony. I hasten to dismiss this harrowing part of my recital, and to record again the merciful goodness of God in saving us from a frightful end, and the retributive justice which laid low the oppressor, and frustrated all his schemes of cruelty and superstition.

It was on the afternoon of the 28th of May, three days before our expected sacrifice,—a day never to be forgotten by me,—that my trusty baker again reached the prison, panting for breath, and exhausted by his speed; gladness lighted up his countenance, he was evidently the bearer of good tidings; as soon as he could speak, the joyful news burst forth. Our oppressor was dead! he had been hunted to his death like a wild beast. But "where did you get the news? are you *sure* of it?" "I saw it myself,—he was dragged and beaten through the town to the place of execution, and there trodden to death with elephants." I will not attempt to describe a scene which language can but feebly express. Let those who have hearts to sympathize in the joys and sorrows of their fellow-creatures think on the nature of the peril impending over us; let them think of the manner of the escape, and then let them imagine the feelings of the condemned captives.

It was some time before the detail of the circumstances, which brought about this righteous retribution, became known to me. It then appeared that although entrusted with the command of the army, and invested with the almost unlimited influence of the office, the Pacahm-woon had never been cordially restored to the Monarch's favour, but was still regarded with suspicion. On the eventful day in question, he was before the King in Council, when, inflated with his elevation, he pressed for concessions which led to his ruin.

I have said that the tributary Princes of the Shan tribes had to bring their contingents into the field, which it was usual for them to command in person. The Pacahm-woon, probably from sound ideas of military discipline, asked for the Command-in-Chief of these levies, but was refused, on the ground of the impropriety of subjecting Royalty to the control of a subject. The request was no doubt thought arrogant. He next solicited that as the danger was pressing, and the safety of the kingdom depended on his success, the King's body-guard — my old friends the Taing-dau — might be ordered to accompany him to the wars. This was a bold request, and created fresh suspicions; but what sealed his fate was a proposal that before his army marched to encounter the enemy, His Majesty would condescend to proceed to the sacred pagoda at Mengoon,* a few miles from Ava, there to make offerings and prayers for the success of his arms. The words had scarcely escaped his lips, when the enraged Monarch, now apparently convinced of the treasonable designs of his General, broke forth with, "Ha! he would take away my Guard, and then have me leave my Throne!" The words were considered to justify what followed, without any more precise sentence. The wretched

---

* The Mengoon pagoda was held in high estimation from its enormous size, and being the pious work of the King's grandfather; in fact, the extent of the plan was such that it was found necessary to abandon it before its completion. The weight of the bell attached to it ranks it among the largest in the world. It is estimated to contain from 80 to 90 tons' weight of metal.

man was instantly dragged by the hair from the Presence, and met his fate as before related. He had counselled that a bounty of 100 tickals, equal to about £12, should be given to each recruit, and it was said that immense treasures were found in his house, purloined from the sums thus passing through his hands.

The want of deliberation manifested by the chief men about the Court in thus hurrying the Pacahm-woon to his death, without giving time for his examination, or extracting from him a confession of treasonable practices was thought, not without reason, to throw suspicion on others, whose participation would have been discovered by delay. If there really was a plot, the conspirators acted wisely in thus stifling inquiry under the plea of zeal for His Majesty's safety. To me it was a matter of indifference whether there was a conspiracy, or whether it was a groundless suspicion of the King, the happy result being the same. The contemplated spectacle, in which we were to have borne so conspicuous a part, being one altogether of the Pacahm-woon's planning, was abandoned at his death. It was never again thought of, and although for some days I had my uncomfortable misgivings, time convinced me that the idea was dropped. As no second Oung-ben-lai born tyrant appeared to enforce it, the sentence was allowed to die a natural death.

Several months now passed away while the British army was at Prome without any exciting incident. I remained with my companions in dreary seclusion, seemingly as much forgotten as if we were already among the dead. Once indeed our fears were a little excited by the arrival of a band of officers who showed authority to place us in carts, and to drive us to Amerapoorah, for what purpose we were at a loss to discover. On reaching the Governor's house there, we were further confounded by finding ourselves divided, each being placed in a separate apartment alone; but it soon came out that those of our number who spoke Burmese were required to translate a document offering to treat for terms of Peace, sent by Sir A. Campbell, as also a few letters on private affairs from officers in the army to their friends abroad, which had been captured with a post-boat on her passage down the river. The separation from each other was only a piece of cunning to ensure the obtaining true translations by collating them, and thus avoiding the possibility of collusion.

Having done what was required of us, the carts carried us back to our old quarters, there to speculate on the great event of the day. I knew the character of the Court too well by this time to attach any great importance to the considerate overtures of the British General. Their chief value, in my estimation, lay in the additional security afforded for the preservation of our lives, now that the Court had found out our services might be required on future occasions. It would hardly, unless driven to despair at the last extremity, sacrifice those who formed the only means of communication with their enemies. So far the incident was consolatory, but as to listening to such terms as the British General was likely to offer with a sincere desire to accept them, such an idea was not entertained either by myself or my companions. They must suffer further defeats, and find their King and Capital in immediate peril before they could submit to terms of humiliation. So far were they from entertaining the notion of closing the war by Treaty, I had the opportunity of observing, that the effect of Sir A. Campbell's offer was exactly the reverse of what he expected. It was regarded as a sign of weakness, and as the forerunner of a flight from a country which we could conquer, but could not keep. Our long inactivity at Prome deceived them. Ridiculous rumours got abroad,—cholera had broken out, and was destroying our camp; war had broken out elsewhere, and the Governor-General had recalled the army, &c. In this last conjecture they were not far wrong, for a considerable force had been ordered to assemble for the reduction of the strong fortress of Bhurtpore, and I had reason to believe that emissaries from that State had reached Ava, and had encouraged the Court to make a protracted resistance under the promise of a diversion in its favour. This gleam of sunshine therefore failed in any great degree to cheer our depressed spirits.

In the month of December a movement of some importance took place. Negotiations were entered on between the belligerents with all the semblance of sincerity; the one in good faith, with an earnest desire to put an end to hostilities,—the other in a spirit of dissimulation and treachery, with the vain hope to throw the enemy off his guard, and to attack him at a disadvantage when his suspicions had been lulled to sleep.

Dr. Judson was taken from our prison, and carried to Melloon in the capacity of Interpreter. The preliminaries of a treaty of Peace were discussed, its terms agreed to,—it was actually drawn out and signed by both parties, and Sir A. Campbell was assured that it had been sent to Ava to receive the ratification of the King. After a short time unmeaning delays occurred, then prevarication,—suspicions on our part revived, until, convinced of their perfidy, and irritated by it, the British General gave notice that the armistice was at an end, and fighting recommenced. The stockades at Melloon, where the negotiations had been held, were stormed, and to the astonishment of Sir A. Campbell, the draft of the Treaty which the Burmese General assured him had been sent to Ava, was discovered in his quarters, a convincing proof that he had only been trifled with throughout. The General, thinking it a good opportunity to put his adversary to shame for his duplicity, sent him the Treaty thus strangely recovered, with an intimation that, in the precipitation of his flight, he must have inadvertently left the precious document behind him. He received a cool reply, acknowledging the General's politeness in returning to him the Treaty, adding, that at the same time he had forgotten his *military treasure chest*, which he trusted he would also have the goodness to restore.

This phantom of a negotiation having been laid, no farther use was found for Dr. Judson, who was again put in irons, and ordered back to Oung-ben-lai. He was fortunate enough, however, to interest a powerful Chief in his favour, who granted him an asylum in his house at Ava, and he thus had the happiness to avoid a recurrence of the dangers and privations of the prison which he had such good reason to dread. I saw him no more until we both rejoiced in our freedom in the British camp.

In December, the fine army raised by the infamous Pacahm-woon, placed at his death under the command of Men-mya-boh, a half-brother of the King, was totally defeated. A fresh one of inferior quality was raised, and met the same fate at Pagan, led by another Chief of note, Nai-wen-buren, its commander, being instantly beheaded for his want of success. After the new year set in few troops were left to oppose the progress of the victorious

British, the greater part, convinced of the hopelessness of the struggle, having dispersed to their homes, or sought a shelter from oppression below the British lines.

Great efforts were now made to strengthen the defences of the Royal city, where it was determined to make a final stand. Mrs. Judson, who was with her husband at the house of his protector, had the opportunity of seeing the preparations for defence, which I had not. She says,— "The Court did not relax their exertions to fortify the city. Men and beasts were at work night and day, making new stockades, and strengthening old ones; whatever buildings were in the way were torn down. Our house and all that surrounded it was levelled to the ground, and our beautiful little compound turned into a place for cannon. All articles of value were conveyed out of the town, and safely deposited in some other place."

The defeat sustained by the Burmese at Pagan on the 9th of February, brought their powerful enemy within a few marches of the Royal city. Their situation was desperate, but there was a difficulty in the way of putting an end to the war by treaty, arising not so much from the terms offered as from the impracticable character of the people themselves.

Without entering minutely into the terms of the Treaty offered, it is sufficient to state that it stipulated for the payment of an indemnity of one million sterling, which being paid, the British General engaged to restore all his conquests, with some small exceptions on the sea-coast. This was what staggered the Burmans; they could neither believe the promise, nor understand the motive. Such an unheard-of thing as conquering a country and then restoring it was incredible! Measuring British faith and honour by their own standard, they concluded the intention was first to impoverish them, and then to march on the Capital. Under this invincible incredulity there was great reason to fear the negotiation would fail, and the Burmans be driven to fighting in despair, when circumstances occurred which shook their settled opinion, and gave them hopes that this unaccountable race were really in the habit of being so weak as to keep their word. Troubled by these doubts, they proposed to reverse the order of time—that we should first restore the territory, and then claim* the money, but in this they could make no impression.

It so happened that two British officers were at this time in Ava, who had been captured some time previously on their way from the army to Rangoon on sick leave; they were Lieut. Bennett, of H. M. Royals, and Dr. Sandford. I had never seen these gentlemen, but heard of them through my baker. In their falling fortunes, it occurred to the Burmese Court that it would not be amiss to try the persuasive powers of the doctor, being a man of peace, upon the obdurate heart of the British General, in the hope that he might be beguiled into more moderate terms. I presume the worthy doctor was afraid to refuse so simple a request.

---

* It is singular that a people so naturally inquisitive as the Burmese should have shown so little desire to make themselves acquainted with the character and institutions of European nations. Their ignorance of them was extreme, and often exhibited itself in a most ridiculous light. Captain H. Cox tells us that when he took office as Resident at the Court to protect British interests, he was required, as a preliminary, to *swear allegiance to the King*, by swallowing a charmed potation in public before one of their pagodas,—was asked to officiate as accoucheur to one of the Queens, &c. So little had they profited by experience that, even after the war, when Colonel Burney held the same dignified office, His Majesty saw no impropriety in asking him to translate the *Encyclopædia Britannica* into the Burmese language!

With this view our acquaintance, Dr. Price, was taken from prison, and associated with him. The compact was, that if success did not attend the embassy, they were to return as prisoners to Ava. Of Price they were sure, as he had a wife and two children to answer for him; but as to the other doctor, they had about as much expectation of seeing the Governor-General come into voluntary captivity as of witnessing the return of Dr. Sandford. As the reader may well imagine, the silly attempt was abortive, but the astonishment of the Court was beyond all bounds when they saw the British officer, punctual to his promise, return into captivity. When wonder was expressed, they were told it was nothing surprising, that it was the custom of the nation to keep its word inviolate. The incident created confidence, and who can tell how far its influence extended, or how many lives it saved?

Still, not wishing to commit themselves too far, they tried the experiment of sending Dr. Price a second time, in a war-boat laden with treasure, but to a much smaller amount than the instalment demanded, which was one-fourth of the million sterling. This was looked upon as a clever bait—a sure test. Would the white people take it and advance? No such thing—the boat, with the treasure it contained, was indignantly returned. These instances of honesty and good faith, so utterly at variance with all their preconceived notions, puzzled them, but in the end, when found to be consistent with the invariable conduct of the British, could not fail to inspire confidence and command respect. They no doubt had their weight when it became necessary to choose between trusting in the word of their conquerors, and carrying the war to extremity.

CHAPTER XXV.

The British army advances.—Rumours.—The King prepares for flight.—Kindness of Dr. Sandford.—I am supplied with arrack.—Doubtful policy of the Court.—I make preparations to escape.—Koh-bai gained over.—Major Jackson.—His munificent present.—Another strange cage of prisoners.—Liberated on the 16th February, and carried to Ava.—Interview with the Myo-woon.—I embark on a war-boat and start for our camp.—Passage down the river.—Stopped by the Kaulen-mengee.—Remains of the Burmese army.—Its dejected state.—Interview with the Burmese General.—I am allowed to proceed.

NEWS now came pouring in of the daily advance of the army—of the utter prostration of the Burmans, their panic fear, their exasperation, their hopes, their schemes, their negotiations, the preparation of the Royal family for flight, and rumours of all sorts, false and true. After so long inactivity, the constant excitement kept up by the hourly recurrence of something new made me feel as though I were an actor in the scene, having a real part to perform instead of remaining the sport of events over which I could exert no influence whatever. My baker flew backward and forward between Ava and Oung-ben-lai with the rapidity of a weaver's shuttle.

On one of his visits he brought me a token, which, coarse and sensual as it was, looked like the olive-branch of Peace, the assuaging of the waters of strife, one of the luxuries of civilization which I had not known for nearly two years—a cup of arrack! Oh! who can tell the comfort a daily glass of strong waters administers to a frame ready to sink with exhaustion? It is indescribable. For this treat I was indebted to the considerate kindness of Dr. Sandford, who, though a stranger to me, had heard of my destitution, and had given to my baker a small sum for my use out of the money issued to him to bear his expenses to the British camp on the occasion I have mentioned. As Buddhists, the Burmese were prohibited or discouraged from the use of spirits; but, with their usual leniency to foreigners, the Chinese settled at Amerapoorah were not included in this prohibition. How they, being of the same faith, reconciled their consciences to it, I know not; but I now got a daily supply from their shops, through my baker, to my great comfort. In the old King's reign, during his fits of bigotry, when a subject was detected drinking spirits, he was treated in an exaggerated homœopathic style, by having molten lead poured down his throat. The law remained in force; but the reigning Sovereign's government was more lenient. When it became known to the local Governors that slaughtering his subjects was not the way to the King's favour, a man was allowed to take his dram in secret, when he could find one, without much fear for the consequences in case of discovery.

The crisis of my fate had now arrived. If I survived a few days, there could be no doubt I should be free. The question to be decided was this: Will the Court hold out, and compel our army to take the Capital by storm? or will their fears so far overcome their suspicions as to induce them to capitulate and agree to terms of peace? The strengthening of the city fortifications and the preparations for the flight of the King favoured the former idea; while the frequent communications held with Sir A. Campbell, through the medium of the American missionaries, led us to hope the latter. It was the question above all others which puzzled and alarmed me from the moment I got into trouble to the present time. If the city was to be stormed, I estimated my life as of little value; if, on the contrary, peace prevailed, of course I was safe.

But even under the worst aspect of affairs, I was not inclined to give in without a last effort. I ventured to fathom the depth of the integrity of old Koh-bai, and was happy enough to find soundings in very shallow water. Though by nature a surly fellow, our long acquaintance had gained his good-will. Besides, if the city were stormed, he could gain nothing by our slaughter; but, if he aided or connived at our escape, I was lavish of my promises of reward. If it must be, that the Royal city should be stormed, there was little doubt our army would make the assault below the town, on the South or West side, where it would not have any rapid river to cross; but, unfortunately, this would cut off my communication with it. Still, as I estimated the distance at not more than ten miles at the most, and dear life was at stake, I determined to attempt it under cover of the night, if the opportunity should be given me. I reckoned something, too, on meeting parties which I felt sure my countrymen would send to our rescue, now that they were apprized of the place of our captivity. Such of my companions as felt strong enough would join in the flight; but, to give the scheme a fair chance of success, the greatest caution was necessary, especially as to time. One of the captured Sepoys had imprudently attempted it, but failed, and his keepers cut off a foot to prevent a repetition of the offence, as well as to deter the rest. I knew I could depend on my baker for correct information, unless at the approaching crisis they arrested him also. The thing most necessary was to respect the aphorism, that "many a man saves his life by not fearing to lose it, and many a man loses his life by being over anxious to save it." Failure would be worse than inactivity.

I have alluded to Dr. Sandford's considerate gift; but it would be ungrateful to overlook the extravagant munificence of my friend Major Jackson, of the Bengal army, who, without my knowing it, had been acting as Quartermaster-general of the force ever since it took the field. His commanding person, and the active duties he had to perform, soon made him conspicuous to the Burmans, who gave him the sobriquet of "*Myet-hman Boh*," or "Spectacled General," from his habit of constantly using spectacles in the field as well as in the tent; and little did I think, while I was listening to wonderful stories about this active Chief, that the hero was my old friend. With the characteristic generosity of an old Indian, he gave to Dr. Price, on his first visit to the camp, 500 rupees for my use—a sum which, had it been known to the Government, might have revived unpleasant suspicions. My friend Jonathan David, however, with more wit than I gave him credit for, knowing how absurd and even dangerous the possession of such a sum would be to me, did not hesitate to appropriate it to his own use, and repaid the Major at the conclusion of the war. One-hundredth part of the sum would have kept me in luxury for a month. Dr. Sandford's gift had fallen into the hands of an able and judicious purveyor, who was gratified in nourishing me with such comforts as it would purchase, among which not the least acceptable was a warm, black, quilted Shan jacket. The cold had been severe the last month, and trying to ill-clad captives.

At this late hour of the story we heard, for the first time, of another cage of strange birds in a minor prison,—where caught, or how or when, I could not learn. It consisted of a Jew, a Turk, and four or five Persians. It is a pity they were not lodged with us, if only to make the allotment more outrageously ridiculous. The Burmans, however, are accustomed to divide foreigners into two classes. One they call "*kula yeen*," or "tamed strangers," being those who have resided in the country long enough to be reclaimed from a semi-savage state by the civilizing influence of polite intercourse with themselves; the other, "*kula-yaing*," or "wild strangers," being newcomers, ignorant, and so unfortunate as not to have partaken of this civilization. These must have belonged to the latter class, and possibly Sandford and Bennett also, who were never introduced into our *State prison*.

After the news of the battle at Pagan, every day was an age. With a mind oscillating between hope and fear, the situation was more trying than ever. Eight or ten very moderate marches would bring my gallant countrymen before the walls of the city, almost, as my fevered imagination pictured, within the sight of my eyes and the sound of my voice. From the 9th to the 16th of February passed away in fearful uncertainty. It ought to have brought them close up. The delay was well-nigh insupportable, and to my unstrung nerves the glass of grog was as nectar. Still I was left unmolested, and intently dwelling on my plan for escape, when on that happy, glorious day,

THE 16TH OF FEBRUARY, 1826,

my good Genius the baker appeared, in company with a band of liberating officers, who suddenly broke into the prison. They were ruffians of the first water, and performed their pleasing office with such churlish ill-feeling, that it was some time before I could persuade myself of the happy nature of their mission. Other and far-different orders would have been more to their taste. The irons, which had so long galled our limbs, were now struck off from the young Armenian, Arrakeel, and myself, and we were abruptly told to follow our liberators to Ava. Follow them to Ava! Had our heads been the forfeit, the thing was impossible. Our stiffened limbs refused to carry us this short distance, even when life and liberty were its reward. It was now evident, on a trial, what an absurd resolution I had formed, how grievously I had miscalculated my own strength, when I contemplated a nocturnal flight to the army. How fortunate that I was not put to the test, for inevitable destruction would have been the consequence.

As their orders to take us to Ava were imperative, our rough escort seized a cart and oxen in the adjacent village, and while they were searching for it, we had time to join in mutual gratulations. Those who were left behind had their minds at ease, and could now, for the first time, lay down their heads to sleep with the tolerable certainty of finding them on their shoulders the next morning.

It may seem strange that two only were taken and the others left. The explanation is, that the four who remained were considered to be Burmese subjects. Poor Laird was paying the penalty of his vanity in aspiring to become a titled Burmese nobleman and agent to his Royal Highness the Prince of Tharawudi, either of which honours, in

Burmese estimation, would constitute him a Royal slave. He was now wiser, and charged me to remember, when I met the British General, to assure him that under all circumstances he gave the preference to his British nationality, an injunction that I did not forget. The Spaniard had his wife and family to bind him to the country; the Father Ignatius had his little flock, the descendants of a few French and English captured nearly a century ago, and now assimilated to the natives; but poor old Rodgers was a difficult and deplorable case. He remembered how often in his chequered career his life had been in peril—how probable that it might be so again—he had a yearning, too, after his native country—but could he return there with safety? I saw the conflict going on within, and ventured—relying on all the circumstances of his story to be correct—to urge him to authorize me in naming his case to the General, who would not fail to demand the surrender of his wife and family also. He hesitated some time, but to my sorrow finally declined, and ended his days in Burmah not long after.

Leaving the rest of our fellow-sufferers in the hands of Koh-bai, we mounted into the bullock-cart provided for us. The old man, since he became our partizan in the plan to escape, had shown us much kindness; but his position was anomalous, for he could never be certain for an hour that he would not be compelled to throw aside the garb of good-fellowship under an order to cut his friends into mince-meat.

On the journey I had time to make myself acquainted with the true position of affairs, which seemed publicly known to every one, and to ascertain by what means my happy deliverance was brought about. After the rout at

Pagan, the remnant of the Burmese army which was still faithful to the King was too weak in number and too much dispirited by defeat to venture to meet the enemy in the field. The march, therefore, was unopposed; and in the panic created by its steady advance, the Court chose to place its hesitating confidence in the honour of its enemy rather than endanger its existence altogether by defending the city. It was this resolution that saved me. It signified its assent to the terms offered, one of which (and this was extorted as a preliminary to evince its sincerity) was the instant surrender of the British prisoners. Until these arrived in the camp, together with the stipulated instalment of the indemnity, the General would listen to no solicitation to stop the advance of his army,—a wise resolve after the duplicity practised on him at Melloon. He modified this determination, however, by a promise that the advance should be made by slow and deliberate marches, to afford time to the Government to complete its promises. This accounted for the undignified haste of my liberation, and the disappointment I had felt at the tardy movement of my liberators. Such was the state of affairs when I quitted the prison at Oung-ben-lai.

On reaching Ava in the afternoon, I was carried before my old friend the Myo-woon, now a Woongee of the Empire. He seemed very anxious to know what report I should give to my countrymen of the manner of treatment I had met during the war, as though it might have some influence on the making or the marring of the Treaty. He impressed on me the debt of gratitude I owed to the King for saving my life when it was forfeited by Treason and Rebellion. As this seemed to be the only object of the interview, I became apprehensive that any expression of complaint might compromise my safety and prevent my surrender. My conscience did not accuse me, therefore, when I practised a lesson out of their own book and descended to dissimulation. When I went away, he was certainly impressed with the idea that I was grateful to His Majesty for all my sufferings, and that I intended to trumpet aloud the praise of his clemency when I got among my countrymen. To himself, personally, I was sincerely grateful, for, be the motive what it might, his partiality to me had certainly saved my life more than once.

It was late at night when I was put on board a warboat with my friend Arrakeel. On the river bank, before embarking, I encountered Mr. ———, a subaltern officer in H.M.'s 47th Regiment, who was said to have disappeared from his corps and fallen into the hands of the Burmese in a manner not very creditable to his military character, and still less so to his intellect as a man of common sense. He did not appear to be a prisoner at the time, and would have entered into an explanation had our haste permitted it; all he could do was to beg I would call on his commanding officer, Colonel Elrington, and beseech him to see that his name was not omitted in the list of prisoners claimed. This did not look like guilt. I did as he desired, and surrendered he was, but I was sorry to hear, that instead of clearing his fame by a trial, he availed himself of an extraordinary clause inserted in the Treaty which protected rebels and deserters on both sides, in the hope that it might afford protection to the revolted districts of Pegu!

And now, with fifty lusty men at the oars, the boat shot down the smooth stream, each stroke lifting her light stem out of the water and leaping forward as if in unison with the hearts of her passengers, beating with ecstasy in the happy prospect of their emancipation. Oh! for a simile which could convey to the reader an adequate idea of the delicious sensations of that night's voyage! My imagination can find none that would not weaken the impression and fall short of the truth. The night was cold and calm, we had no covering but the canopy of heaven, and I may almost add, no company but the stars above us, at which I lay gazing the greater part of the night, trying to assure myself of the reality of this marvellous change. Few words were spoken. I was too happy in my own thoughts to interrupt the silence by conversation. What a change had been wrought in a few hours! What a contrast with all I had been witness to for the last two years! Dr. Paley somewhere expresses an opinion, that the pleasure enjoyed by the cessation of severe bodily pain is a full compensation for the suffering that pain has inflicted. If it can be supposed to be true of the body, how certainly so of the more lasting and abiding ease of a troubled mind—or of both united! At that moment I should not have been disposed to dispute the doctor's position.

These soothing meditations were interrupted in a most unwelcome manner, about three o'clock in the morning, by a loud hail from some men on the left bank of the river, who had perceived the boat shooting past them. She rounded to, and I once more found myself among— what shall I call them—enemies or friends? It proved to be a picket of the beaten army of the Kaulen-mengee, now encamped at this spot after the retreat from Pagan. I was desired to land and to follow a guide to their Chief, whose quarters, fortunately for me, were not more than ten minutes' walk from the bank. Accustomed as I had been to sudden alarms, I began to fear some obstacle would yet arise between me and liberty. Although the day had not yet dawned, I could distinguish by the starlight the deplorable state of this small body of troops. They were dispersed in small groups, at short distances from each other, some sleeping while others sat smoking or keeping watch by a fire. No protection from the weather was to be seen except here and there some boughs of trees spread upon a few upright sticks, the accommodation of the General being little better than that of the men. I think I saw pretty nearly the whole of them, and (although it is no more than a guess) I judged they might number, at the most, a thousand men.

The encampment bore every sign of disorganization. Arms and accoutrements were strewed about in confusion, there was no regularity in the arrangement of the men, no regularly-posted sentinels to be seen; among the few who were awake, there was a total absence of the hilarity one expects to see in soldiers in the field—a gloomy, dejected silence prevailed, heightened, perhaps, in my imagination by the darkness of the hour. Altogether it had more the appearance of a gipsy camp, or still more, a band of brigands, than a portion of the army of the State. One could not look without a feeling of admiration on this handful of brave men, the few who were faithful to their King after the discouragements of constant defeats, among the countless host that streamed down to the war, but had deserted their colours in the hour of trial. Their fidelity deserved a better fate.

I was kept waiting only just long enough to take a hasty survey of the scene before me, when the Woongee, now awakened, ordered me into his presence. Like the

Myo-woon, he was anxious to fathom my thoughts, and ascertain how far I could be trusted to proceed; like him, too, he was deceived by my disingenuous protestations. He suggested my leaving my four Bengalee servants with him, and even hinted at detaining me also. I replied that I was sent down, without my consent being asked, by the King's order, but that I was quite willing to remain if he ordered it. After an hour's hesitation, during which I was suffering torture, he made up his mind to let me proceed, and I joyfully retraced my steps through the encampment, with the conviction that if this force was their only dependance, the sooner they put themselves under the protection of a Treaty, the better for the country.

CHAPTER XXVI.

Arrive at the British camp.—My joy at regaining my liberty.—Alarm of my crew at the steamer.—I am kindly received by Major Armstrong.—I report myself to Sir A. Campbell.—His hospitality.—The army advances to Yandabo.—Timidity of the Indian Government.—Their anxiety for peace.—Translation of the Treaty.—I save the Government £70,000.—The Commissioners refuse to admit my claims.—Treaty of Peace. I leave Yandabo with Sir A. Campbell.

THE morning dawned as I again took my seat in the prow of the war-boat, thankful to have escaped this last hazard of detention, for the Treaty was not yet made a fact by signature; and in the storm of conflicting passions which influenced the Court at this time, a thousand accidents might happen to imperil it altogether. The half-naked band of gloomy patriots I had just left were far from being safe company under the existing state of things, and it was a solid pleasure to count the hours as they widened the distance between us. But for this agreeable computation and for the inspiring hope of its happy termination, the voyage of this day would have been almost insupportable. The cold temperature of the night was but little felt; but far different the intense heat and glare of the day that followed it. The sun, as is usual at this season, rose without a cloud. For a time it was pleasant enough; but as the day advanced and the sun began to gain its meridian height, the rays reflected from the glassy surface of the water almost drove me mad. I had no idea of the pain the sun's rays can give to eyes which, from long use, have been accustomed to a kind of dingy twilight, and as little fit to encounter a glitter or bright light as those of a bird of night. Shelter in the boat there was none, and but for the loan of a handkerchief to cover my head, soaking it occasionally in the river, I hardly know how I could have supported it.

At this season of the year the waters of the river had subsided, the current was sluggish, and the boat had often to pull a circuit of many miles round a projecting sandbank, which might have been crossed on foot in less than half the time. It seemed to me that the remains of the Burmese army had fled an unaccountable distance from their enemy until this explained it. When noon had passed we began to gaze, more and more eagerly, on the left bank of the river, in the hope of gaining some indication of the object of our search. As the boat rounded each successive point of land and opened out a fresh reach of the river, the whole crew made a careful survey, without any result, until about four o'clock in the afternoon, when at the distance of some miles, at the bottom of a long reach, eyes stronger than mine, though far less interested in the sight, descried the masts of boats they well knew were not those of their own country. I will not attempt to describe my feelings when some of the crew told me foreigners' boats were in sight. In fact, I believe I had none. I was stupified. Nearer and nearer every plunge of the oars brought me to my desired haven of rest— more and more distinct became the welcome sight. I do well remember one thought that possessed me. "There they are, certainly—they are only a mile or two off—but shall I really reach them in safety? Will no ill chance intervene, even yet, to thwart my hope? I have my doubts." Presently a gun from the leading gun-boat—for it was, indeed, no other than the advance division of our flotilla—fired in our direction, aroused the fears of my crew, who seemed as little to like trusting themselves in the power of the English as they did the formidable sort of salutation that greeted them. They did not understand it, and were in the act of realizing my doubt by rounding the boat and fleeing from such rough usage, when I explained to them its cause, and desired them to row direct to the gun-boat that fired the shot. Not without some trepidation and misgivings lest they should be blown to atoms, they complied. But with the sound of that shot, and not before, came to my mind the conviction—*I am free.*

And now, since I am so, let me pause awhile, on completing this eventful passage in the history of my life. Though thirty-five years have rolled away since these terrible scenes were enacted, though I then was young and now am old, they are as fresh in my memory as the occurrences of yesterday; and whenever they recur to my mind, as they often do, shame it would be if they ever arose without being accompanied by the deep feeling of gratitude which my deliverance from them is calculated to inspire. The Almighty, in His wise and merciful government of the affairs of the world, was pleased so to order them, that while dangers of infinite variety, such as to human eyes seemed to lead to certain destruction, threatened me, they were averted by means in which I was not even in the most distant manner an actor. As if to remove every sentiment of self-gratulation or vaunting in the idea that "my own hand hath saved me," and to throw open the mind to unqualified praise and gratitude to God alone, I was not permitted throughout to make a single effort, however weak, for my own preservation. My utter helplessness was a remarkable feature in this long captivity. My position might justly be compared with that of a traveller who encounters an Alpine storm, and sees with terror the threatening clouds, one after another, driven across his path by the fierceness of the tempest, discharging their fury around him, but leaving him unscathed—one disappearing only to be followed by another charged with equal ruin, but in like manner passing harmless away. I had no more to do with my own preservation than the traveller had in escaping the flashes of lightning which glanced past him without injury—turned aside by a beneficent Power which it is our happiness to acknowledge and confide in, though "His ways are unsearchable and past finding out." Many and severe have been the trials in after-life that have fallen to my lot, such, perhaps, as may be thought more common to the whole race of mankind than those I have just related; but if ever they have aroused a feeling of disquietude or discontent, I had only to look back to this period and be thankful.

Among the numerous instances of protracted imprisonment on record, I am not aware that any one presents such a combination of bodily privation and misery, of perils encountered from a variety of sources, and of unceasing and intense anxiety of mind throughout as I have attempted to describe. Again let me express my gratitude to Heaven for my wonderful liberation, and take leave of the subject.

I now quit this digression and return to my war-boat, which I left unwillingly complying with the demand of the signal gun. On reaching the gun-boat I found on board, a lieutenant of H.M.S. *Alligator*, who commanded the advanced division. The gallant officer was not a little astonished when he saw his emaciated countryman sink on the deck before him with hands joined in the humiliating attitude of supplication, instead of rejoicing in the hearty welcome and gratulation he was about to offer. No doubt he thought I was bereft of reason, and he was not very far wrong. The mind was wandering—the excitement had been too great for the spirit, and it was some minutes before the kindness of the officer restored me to my senses and enabled me to realize my change of fortune. Our interview was short. With the promptitude of his profession he ordered me once more to enter the war-boat and to thread the flotilla until it reached a river steam-boat, called the *Diana*, where further orders would be given.

A steamer in those days was not in India the familiar sight it has since become. Its performances had awakened the superstitious fears of the natives, and the terrified boatmen almost rebelled when the command was explained to them. They begged hard for any other boat than that, but the Lieutenant was inexorable. They were now in the toils and must comply, so we took our leave, and in half-an-hour espied the terrible monster riding at anchor. Never did a timid bird approach its fascinating enemy with more fluttering alarm, nor with less chance of escape, than did the Captain of my war-boat, this work of Enchantment.

On board the steamer I found a gallant soldier,* now no more, whose hospitality, when he heard my story and

---

* The late Sir Richard Armstrong, K.C.B., who died in command of the army at Madras.

saw my condition, knew no bounds. I must have the best of dinners, choice wines, and he must vacate his own cabin and couch in order that I might have uninterrupted rest. I believe he was truly disappointed when I assured him that I should, for the present, sleep more soundly on the planks of the deck than on a bed of down; and as to dinners, the little wit I had remaining told me, as if by instinct, that what he called a good dinner, would be my death. He kindly let me have my own way, and a night of refreshing sleep on the deck of the *Diana*, the first one in security for nearly two years, restored mind and body to a certain degree of health and calmness. But what half-forgotten luxuries met my eye in the morning? Let not the reader laugh,—if he does, he sadly wants sympathy in the happiness of others. A razor—a hair-brush—a tooth-brush—a clean towel—a veritable basin of water—a cake of soap! I had indeed leaped all at once into the lap of luxury.

While I had been enjoying my rest, the war-boat had been tied to the stern of the steamer all night. In the morning, when she had got up her steam, we brought some of the boldest of the crew on board. I believe they looked upon her incomprehensible moving machinery as the bowels of some infernal beast called into existence by superior art in sorcery, and would have marvellous tales to tell on their return home. Great was their relief when they received their passport and permission to quit her company.

I was now reminded that it was time I reported myself to Sir Archibald Campbell, the General commanding, whose tent was only a short walk from the river side. We had met before in Calcutta. He recognized me,— but how changed—the mere wreck of former times! My clothes—if such they could be called, where shirt and half the habiliments that cover or adorn the outward man, even down to the shoes and stockings, were wanting—were unfit to appear in even among an army in the field. The General's compassionate eye immediately detected it, and after the example of the good Samaritan, to detect was to relieve. His son, the late Baronet, who fell in the Russian war while gallantly leading the 38th regiment, the same his father commanded before him, was then a youth of eighteen years old, acting as his father's *aide-de-camp*. Fortunately for me, if not for himself, his stature was pretty nearly my own. "Now, John," said the veteran, "your clothes will fit Gouger better than mine, (a laugh, —he was corpulent,) go and divide your stock fairly with him;" and he added, "Gouger, you will take up your quarters with me for the remainder of the campaign. You may probably yet have the pleasure to see Ava again."

The extreme kindness and consideration of the General henceforth did much towards restoring me. As Peace was not yet concluded, we had to make two or three onward marches, which, as I could neither walk nor mount a horse, he provided me with the means to accomplish by water, meeting him in his tent at the close of the day's march. My old friend, Major Jackson, too, the spectacled General, whose munificence I have recorded, greeted me with a hearty welcome. He placed rather a high value on the pleasures of the table, and was the only man in the camp who could boast of a flock of sheep. A fat one was killed to welcome me.

The army continued to advance until it reached the village of Yandabo, a place well known as being the spot on which the belligerents settled their animosities, and concluded the Treaty bearing its name. It will appear strange that after a succession of victories that brought us almost to the very gates of the capital, the Government of India was quite as eager for the conclusion of a treaty of peace as were the beaten enemy. The enormous expenses of the war had alarmed them; the tenacity of the Burmese in their resistance had baffled their calculations, and as the policy of the home Government discouraged an unnecessary extension of territory, and the country was too poor to pay an adequate ransom, they were not prepared with a scheme ready to meet the difficulty if the Court fled further North, and continued the war.

Sir A. Campbell had earnestly and repeatedly solicited permission to declare the independence of the provinces of Pegu, but our timid Government refused his request, fearing it might involve further complications, and render a permanent occupation or assistance to a new Government necessary. Thus, in their ill-timed alarm, they cruelly sacrificed to State policy a people who had rendered them essential services; who, although they could not advance any *specific pledge* made to them, had certainly been allowed to believe they would not again be subjected to the tyranny of their exasperated masters. Fortunately this anxiety on the part of their conquerors to put an end to the war was not known to the enemy, or it might have encouraged a longer resistance. I am not aware that this undignified feeling appears on the face of the published documents. Perhaps it does not. Perhaps it was communicated confidentially to the Civil Commissioner who was deputed by the Indian Government specially to the camp; but that I am right in attributing it to them, no one could doubt who stood behind the scenes at Yandabo. To it alone I owe the refusal of the Civil Commissioner to enforce on the Court of Ava an act of retributive justice to myself when it was proposed to him by Sir A. Campbell. He was terrified lest it should present an obstacle to the duty he had to perform, viz. to make everything bend to the eager desire for peace.

On the 22nd or 23rd February two dignitaries from the Burmese Court arrived in the camp with honest instructions this time to consent to the terms made known to them. The preliminaries had been complied with by the release of the prisoners and by the arrival of a quarter of a million sterling in specie, being one quarter of the stipulated indemnity.

But now a singular difficulty arose. How the British army could have advanced thus far into the country without having a man among them capable of translating a State document into the Burman language, it is not easy to explain. So it was, however, and this clearly shows how slight the intercourse must have been between the two countries before this time. The General's interpreter was a native youth of Chinese extraction, who, of course, *spoke* the Burmese fluently enough, and English indifferently. With this his knowledge ceased; he could neither write nor read the Burmese, and, had not Dr. Judson and myself been at the General's disposal, the impediment would have been a serious one, as the Burmese could not be expected to put their hands to a document written in a language they did not understand; nor, on the other hand, could the British Commissioners trust to a native copy alone. The English Treaty was therefore placed in our hands for translation, and when we produced a Burmese copy, both were to be acknowledged as original documents of equal validity. It gave me great pleasure to make some return for Sir A. Campbell's kindness in this and other ways where my knowledge of the language was required; indeed, by an extraordinary accident, I was the means not only of aiding the General, but also of enriching the exchequer of the East India Company to the amount of nearly £70,000, in a manner that was not the less gratifying to me because it came from the pocket of my late oppressors. The affair is worth recording.

The fifth article of the Treaty has these words—"As part indemnification to the British Government for the expenses of the war, His Majesty the King of Ava agrees to pay the sum of *one crore of rupees.*" It will naturally be asked, What kind of *rupee* is intended? It is not a coin of the country. The Burmese only know it as the coin issued to the British troops, and these being chiefly from the Madras Presidency, the *Madras rupee* was the one issued and passed into general circulation. This was the one commonly known to the Burmese, and one crore, or ten millions, of *these rupees* they would naturally expect to pay—no other could have been reasonably demanded from them. But there was another kind of rupee current in Bengal in those days, denominated the *sicca rupee*, the metallic value of which was between $6\frac{1}{2}$ and 7 per cent. greater than the Madras rupee; and as both the General and the Civil Commissioner came from Bengal, I had reason to think the *sicca rupee* was the one they intended, though they had failed to express it in the words so carelessly used. As the Treaty was not yet signed, I went to communicate my thoughts to Sir A. Campbell. He saw the blunder at once, summoned the Burmese Chiefs instantly to a conference, at which I was present, and explained to them that although the words would be allowed to stand in the Treaty, *sicca rupees* were those intended and would be claimed; and paid they were ultimately, in full tale!* A memorandum was attached to the Treaty expressive of this understanding.

Similar success did not attend me when I brought my own affairs before the British Commissioners. I asked whether I was not entitled, besides the simple restoration of my property, to claim from the King of Ava two years' interest on the sum they had despoiled me of, and was coolly told in reply, that such a thing as interest on the restoration of *confiscated* property was an unheard-of demand, thus ignoring my right by the substitution of the word " confiscation" for " robbery." I was too far worn-out in mind and body to enforce my claim, and too happy in the possession of life and liberty to care much about it, though my loss on this score alone was more than £2000. But by far the heaviest loss I had to complain of was caused by the restitution of a large amount of cotton goods, which had been stored through two rainy seasons in a shed in the Palace-yard, and were now, though comparatively worthless, ruled to be a fitting satisfaction of my claims. This *restoration of property* could hardly be termed " indemnity," yet it was allowed to pass as such. I must do the General the justice to say, that these were not *his* opinions.

The Treaty was signed on the 24th February, and while it was undergoing the necessary ratification at Ava, the

---

* A stronger proof of the utter carelessness and want of thought in the framing of this Treaty can scarcely be adduced than the discovery of so important an error by a casual reader like myself. Considering the means by which this large sum was saved, if the East India Company had devoted a portion of it to the relief and complete indemnification of the few of its subjects who suffered by the war, and whose sufferings, be it said, were, in a great measure, attributable to its own culpable remissness, it would hardly have been thought an instance of overstretched liberality.

Burmese deputies were busily employed in the delightful task of providing boats for the return of the British army. Though it was not likely they could be accused of any want of alacrity in such a service, and though the brave veterans of two campaigns were far from numerous, sufficient water-carriage could not be provided; it was therefore found necessary to divide the Force, some forming land columns to return by different routes, the remainder embarking in native boats and canoes of a motley character. Sir A. Campbell, to save time, preferred to return to Rangoon by water. He kindly offered me a passage in his boat, which was a stout, decked row-boat, of twenty oars, carrying a twelve-pound *carronade* gun in the bow, and the General's palanquin at the stern, in which he slept. As the boat had no accommodation, his son and I spread our mats and pillows under an awning on the deck, and on the 5th of March I turned my back on the scene of suffering, and sped my way again to the habitations of civilized life, where happiness is more surely to be found than in the dark parts of the earth, submerged in ignorance and cruelty.

CHAPTER XXVII.

Voyage from Yandabo to Rangoon.—A dispatch received by Sir A. Campbell to proclaim Pegu independent.—Too late to act on it.—Delightful voyage.—An unexpected adventure.—Capture of a war-boat.—I am appointed Police magistrate for the Pegu district.—Its disturbed state.—Burmans and Peguers.—Instances of Burmese revenge on the revolted Peguers.—Massacre of a boat's crew.—Attack on a Talain village.

PERHAPS my narrative ought to end here. When it first occurred to me to commit it to writing, my intention was to tell a tale of Burmah, *as it was*,—to exhibit an instance of the numerous opportunities which occurred in bygone times to realize fortunes in new paths of commerce—to follow it out in all its bearings—to show the dangers and impediments it was liable to, and how my golden dreams were defeated; to try to interest the reader by the recital of such a story of imprisonment as few can have endured—to make him thankful for his own immunity, and rejoice that his lot is not cast in a land of savage ignorance,—and finally to set forth and acknowledge the beneficence of the great Creator and Disposer of all things in bringing me out of all these troubles and restoring me to the comforts of life. All this having been done, perhaps I ought to close the narrative without further infliction on those who may peruse it; but as the incidents between this time and my quitting the country have an interest to me, I cannot persuade myself that they will be altogether uninteresting to the reader. Besides, the story is not quite complete, so long as we remain in the country of our late enemy.

We are now floating down the Irrawuddi. The General's flag is flying at the mast-head of the row-boat, and he leads the fleet of native canoes filled with soldiers, here and there interspersed with, and protected by, the armed gun-boats of the Flotilla. The weather is glorious, and the sight an animating one; always something in view to demand our attention, either in the movements of the motley fleet itself, or on the banks of the river, now pretty well known to me on this, the fourth time of my passing them.

On the second day a post boat met us, bringing dispatches from the Indian Government to Sir Archibald Campbell, of the highest importance had they reached the hand they were intended for in time to act on them, but useless after hostilities had ceased. Nothing less than the fate of a Nation rested on the timely receipt of that sheet of paper!

I have said that the General had long expressed an urgent desire to proclaim the independence of Pegu, either by re-creating it a separate Kingdom, or by incorporating it with the British dominions. His feelings revolted at the idea of sacrificing a people who had risen in his favour, and rendered his army such signal services, to the tyranny of their exasperated masters. The subsequent course of events proved that it would have been not only an act of humanity, but a measure of sound policy also. The excision of a few sea-board excrescences of the Kingdom, as was effected by the present Treaty, did not deprive it of much power, and left it quite competent to future aggression. The consequence was, that when the freshness of the impression caused by their defeat wore away, the old spirit revived; they again became troublesome, and it was found necessary some years after, by a renewal of the war, to adopt the very measure our Government had so pertinaciously refused—the permanent occupation of Pegu. All this ought to have been foreseen and avoided. The dispatches he now received authorized too late the step he so ardently desired. To me, personally, the tardy assent of our Government was fortunate,—it probably saved my life; but the mortification of the General was great as he threw the dispatch across the table to me, exclaiming, " There, Gouger, if I had received that a fortnight ago, your friends would not have got off so easily !" " True," thought I, "*nor I either!*" There are two sides on which to view every question. It would have been all very well for the Talains, but what would have become of *me!*

It took little more than a week to accomplish the voyage down the river to Rangoon. This is one of the little fragments into which life is broken, that I look back upon with peculiar delight. The weather, early in March, though hot, was charming. Our days and nights were passed upon the deck of the boat, a broad substantial awning shielding us from the sun by day and the dews by night. Our table was well garnished,—the subjects for conversation were never exhausted, and the extreme kindness and sympathy shown me by my warm-hearted friend and protector tended to cheer the dejected and disordered frame of my mind, and to restore both it and the body to a healthy action. There can be no doubt, from the observation of my friends, though I was not aware of it myself, that my mind, for a time, was much weakened and impaired by long inactivity and anxiety. It manifested itself to them by frequent returns of what is called *absence of mind*, often unheeding the remarks made to me, and omitting to reply to questions as though they were unheard, or if answered, it was often incoherently, also by a look of vacuity and a habit of inertness and listlessness. Another year of the same sort of imprisonment would most likely have brought on a state of settled and irrecoverable melancholy, from which I was liberated just in time to save me. As it was, it was merely temporary; mixing once more with my fellow-creatures rapidly restored me, and what contributed much to do so, was the calm serenity of this river voyage, and the cheering company it was my good fortune to enjoy.

The passage to Rangoon, however agreeable, did not abound in adventures. One alone happened worth relating.

The General's boat, as I have before remarked, headed the fleet; but sometimes, as it was powerfully manned, we dropped astern just to see that all was right, then shot ahead again to resume our proper position. I think it was the day we left Prome, as the evening was setting in, we were seated at our table on the deck making vigorous attacks on a noble cold round of beef, when we were surprised by a volley of musket-shots flying over our heads. None of them hit us; they appeared to be aimed some inches too high. We were at that time four or five miles ahead of the fleet. The right bank of the river, from which the shots proceeded, and which were pretty steadily kept up for two or three minutes, was about 150 yards distant, and was lined with high grass, flags, and jungle. As the river was nearly a mile wide, it would have been an easy matter to put the boat out of harm's way in a few minutes by rowing her into the stream, and as Sir A. Campbell did not speak the Hindostanee language, I took the liberty to ask his permission to give the required order for the purpose. But the smell of powder had put the old soldier's blood up. "No, sir! just tell the steersman to put the nose of the boat right in among them."

Now, this may be called bravery—with due submission, I call it downright folly. Here were three men seated at table on the deck of an open boat, offering an inviting butt for concealed marksmen on shore,—one of the three (I beg his pardon), who ought to have known better, absolutely donning his cocked hat in order to present a fairer target, and showing by the flag at the mast-head that it was the boat of the Chief risking his life—for what? For the chance of punishing a gang of marauders, who, if they are good shots, are pretty sure to make him pay dearly for his temerity.

Having done my duty, and not wishing to be a mark for the enemy, I retired behind the screen of the palanquin at the stern, while the General directed two or three discharges of grape among the assailants before the boat touched the shore. At one time his eye fell on me snugly ensconced behind his palanquin. He laughed—"Gouger," said he, "do you think the shots can't go through that palanquin? It is only made of leather." "Certainly they can," was the reply; "but they are not potting at me as they are at you at this moment."

As the boat touched the shore I quitted my screen;—it is only when nothing is to be done that a man seeks for shelter. She was lined with a row of formidable boarding-pikes, enough to arm the whole crew. A line was instantly formed, and we charged our unseen enemy into the jungle,—a mad trick, without knowing their numbers or position,—but fortunately with greater success than our folly deserved. They retired before us some hundreds of yards, and we emerged from the jungle just in time to see a body of men escaping across a creek, the entrance to which had been concealed from our view by the denseness of the jungle on the river face. Following them up, we made an unexpected prize of a fine, large war-boat, lying concealed among the high flags: the crew, our late enemy, finding their lair was discovered, took to their heels and fled, leaving us in possession of the splendid trophy of our victory to carry with us in triumph to Rangoon. What chance of escape should we have had, if these men had been decent marksmen!

Launched once more on the busy world, it became necessary that I should shake off the indolent habits the last two years had encouraged, and address myself again to some occupation. All my sanguine hopes of fortune had been completely overthrown by the overwhelming crowd of adventurers, who, now that the war had disclosed the sources of wealth, rushed into the field that I had hitherto been in the habit of looking upon as a close preserve of my own. These brilliant prospects having vanished, Sir A. Campbell recommended me to offer my services to the Government. By the provisions of the Treaty made at Yandabo, we were to retain Rangoon and 100 miles of territory around it, until the remaining instalments of the indemnity were paid; and, as a considerable time might elapse before this was done, and the tranquillity of the country in the mean time had to be provided for, he expressed a wish that I should undertake the duties of a Police magistrate so long we as held possession. At the General's request I accompanied him to Calcutta to have an interview with the Governor-General, and returned with all speed to enter on my appointment.

It was no sinecure office that I had undertaken. A state of war for two years had, as its usual concomitant, encouraged all sorts of crime. The vices and passions of a people, not naturally vindictive or cruel, had been allowed to acquire strength from the want of means to restrain them, until at length the whole district was in a state of frightful anarchy. In most instances crime went undetected, and when detected often unpunished. Murders and gang robbery were of every-day occurrence; and had it not been for the merciful protection it afforded to the poor deserted Talains, that article of the Treaty which assigned to us the temporary occupation of this large part of Pegu would have been an unmitigated evil to the unfortunate inhabitants. But this prevalence of crime so naturally follows a state of war, that I should not think it worth while to continue this chapter to illustrate so evident a truth, were it not to comment on the cruelty of giving up a people to the tyranny of their former masters in a state of revolt, of which we ourselves had been the occasion, and which in truth we may be said to have encouraged for our own advantage.

I have before said, that previous to the war the two races of Burmans and Peguers were fast amalgamating into one people. Time had almost obliterated the memory of the separate independence of the latter; their Royal stock had long become extinct by the sword of their conquerors, and all idea of again asserting their claim to separate existence as a distinct nation had vanished, when the British invasion once more aroused their hopes, and brought them into a state of revolt. After their first alarm had subsided, they made common cause with the invaders. Although their assistance in the field was not needed, the services they rendered in supplying our army with provisions and the means of transport, were so important, that it may reasonably be doubted whether we could ever have marched through the country, and dictated a peace almost under the walls of the Capital, had their assistance been withheld. This may be admitted when we consider the difficulty of marching some hundreds of miles through jungles and forests, amidst a hostile population, where communications might be easily interrupted, and supplies intercepted,—where carriage could not be obtained, nor guides trusted,—and contrast it with the facilities we enjoyed by the adhesion of the Peguers to our cause. Our march forward was assisted by a friendly population, through whose good-will—barring the opposition of the regular army of the Burmans—it was as easy and safe as one through the plains of India. No instance of treachery was ever charged against them, the approach of our army being always hailed with pleasure.

In proportion to the advantages we derived from the adhesion of the Talains was the exasperation created in the mind of the Burmans by their revolt. Little mercy could they expect, if by any means they should again fall under the iron rule of their former masters; and yet these were the people sacrificed by us to an ungrateful and a mistaken policy.

That a cruel retribution would be inflicted by the Burmese on their revolted subjects was well known to the British authorities. Besides an idle Treaty stipulation that they should have the benefit of a general amnesty, which it was equally well known would not be regarded, the temporary possession of the country in question for a protracted period offered facilities for emigration to those who felt themselves peculiarly obnoxious to the Government. The adjacent province of Tenasserim on the one side, or of Arracan on the other, both ceded to the British, presented a safe asylum, and many, no doubt, saved their lives by a timely flight; but the bulk of the population did not possess the means, otherwise there might have been a much more general exodus. Meanwhile, the Burmese, inflamed with the desire of revenge, saw the chief objects of it eluding their grasp, and chafed at the stipulation which restrained their indignation beyond the boundary line.

The worst cases I had to deal with were the offspring of this national hatred. I will cite one instance out of many, just to give an idea of the treatment these poor creatures had to expect when the protection of our army was withdrawn from Rangoon.

I was seated in my Court—always crowded from sunrise to sunset—when a fine young man of the Talains came before me with the following astounding story:—

He and six other men of his race were in a canoe the previous day fishing,—hoping, as a famine of no slight severity was afflicting the country, to take a fish or two to mix with the leaves of trees to which they were reduced for subsistence. They were inhabitants of a village on the banks of the Panlang river, about thirty miles above Rangoon, where the country was so thinly populated and so little cultivated, that for many miles together nothing could be seen from a boat on the river except a tangled jungle on both banks, almost impervious to a human being. In this wild, secluded spot he and his companions were endeavouring to provide a precarious meal, when a fully-manned war-boat, rowed by fifty or sixty Burmans, came in sight from below, ascending the river. She was the bearer of dispatches to Ava, fully equipped and efficiently armed, each of the boatmen, as usual, having his sword or spear.

The canoe of my informant was hailed and brought alongside, when the Chief of the war-boat demanded why they, being Talains, dared to go about with offensive weapons. The poor men, astonished that the fish-grains fastened to a pole—the only thing of the kind they had in the boat—could be mistaken for offensive weapons, made no reply, and were immediately seized, and their elbows pinioned behind them with ropes. No further questions were asked, but they were made to kneel at the head of the boat, and to bend over so that their heads might fall into the water, and thus, one after the other, they were deliberately decapitated.

My informant beheld his six companions slain in cold blood in the manner I have described, and was himself kneeling to receive the fatal blow, when, the boatman who acted as executioner wishing to exchange the sword for a sharper one, a slight delay occurred. At this moment, feeling that the rope that bound him had become loose, and was giving way, the poor fellow suddenly resolved to make a last effort for life, plunged into the river and made good his escape to the adjacent bank, where, after a few steps, the friendly jungle effectually concealed him from his pursuers. After a fruitless search, the war-boat proceeded on her voyage to Ava, and the fortunate refugee hastened to communicate the intelligence to me.

A month afterwards, on their return, I had the opportunity of arresting this crew of murderers as they were unconsciously regaling themselves at Rangoon. The crime was proved; in fact, it was hardly denied; but, to my regret, the General, fearing to incur responsibility, or an unenviable reputation for cruelty, declined to execute the villains, who remained in my prison until the town was surrendered, and were then released.

Is it possible to imagine a crime of grosser brutality than this, divested, as it is, of every object which usually excites to deeds of blood? No offence, no quarrel, no prospect of plunder, no plea of self-defence or protection, but a feeling of revenge against a people, intense enough to doom the whole race to destruction indiscriminately. If the devoted Talains courted their own destruction by refusing to emigrate, they cannot allege a want of ample forewarning—their enemies practised no disguise.

About the same time my duties called me to a Talain village in the same neighbourhood, which had been attacked and plundered with the usual atrocities. What a melancholy picture is a secluded village after it has been sacked by banditti! The houses demolished—their fragments and contents strewed about—and the whole place silent and deserted! Not a soul was to be seen except in a corner of a broken-down house, a man and his son, ten or eleven years old, who apparently had been overlooked in the confusion. The boy had his arm broken in the attack by a musket-shot; and, as the fracture was a bad one, an army surgeon who was with me advised amputation. I promised to provide for the poor little sufferer for life, if he would submit to the operation; but the feelings of the parent would not allow it, so we bound it in a splint, and left him. Doctors are not infallible.

Passing by the spot some months after, curiosity induced me to inquire after his patient, when I found the little fellow in the full enjoyment of his limb.

I could never learn what became of the inhabitants of this village,—whether dispersed or driven away in a body. The attacking party was reported to be in such strength, that I thought it necessary to ask for fifty European soldiers to capture or destroy them. Although we were on the spot within twenty-four hours of the attack, in the *Diana* steamer, their track could not be discovered. On the passage up from Rangoon to the scene of the attack, two Burmese voluntarily came on board,— one with a severe sword-cut on the *right hand*, which he said was a wound given by himself in cutting wood, an evident subterfuge, as it was easy to discover from his movements that he was not a left-handed man. My suspicion being excited, I soon found they knew all about the fight, and I gave them in charge to a sentry. Unfortunately, the sentry was an Irishman, who put them into an empty cabin, over which he kept strict watch outside the door, but forgot that it had an open window, and that the Burmese were amphibious. Pat's comic astonishment but ill repaid me for the vexation of losing the spies, and with them all chance of revealing the mystery.

I take these facts from a multitude, to point out the condition of the country and the prospects for the unfortunate Talains when we withdrew the protection of our army, and left them to their fate.

CHAPTER XXVIII.

Famine in Pegu.—Depredations of tigers.—One shot in the town of Rangoon.—Payment of the money under Treaty.—Mr. Crawfurd appointed Envoy to Ava.—Dr. Judson accompanies him.—Death of Mrs. Judson.—The Burmese secretly collect arms in Rangoon.—Their seizure.—Crowded state of my gaols.—Woongee arrives in Rangoon.—Sir A. Campbell honours him with a State dinner.—Some account of it.—How the Woonlouk enjoys it.—Other amusements at table.—Embarkation of the troops.—Evacuation of Rangoon.—I proceed to Amherst.—Some notice of it.—I go in search of teak forests.—Depopulation of the country.—Interesting sight of a herd of wild cows.—Conclusion.

FAMINE to a frightful extent prevailed for some months during our occupation of Rangoon. In a land where Nature had been lavish in her gifts, where the earth gave its increase with less labour bestowed on it, and greater certainty than in almost any other part of the world, the wretched inhabitants were starving, and were driven to all manner of violence for the preservation of their lives. The obstruction it offers to the cultivation of the land is one of the heaviest evils inflicted on a country by the desolating hand of War. Rice had risen to such an enormous price as to render it a luxury attainable only by the wealthy, while the poor of the surrounding country were driven to wild roots and the leaves of trees for the means of supporting life. The entire Province must have been depopulated, had not the spirit of commerce stepped in to its relief by supplying it with the superabundance of countries happily free from such a dreadful visitation. Soon after want became apparent, ship after ship began to arrive at Rangoon laden with grain from the opposite coast of India, disposing of their welcome cargoes at almost fabulous prices. Even when the port became well stocked with provision, it was not easy to disseminate the blessing through the interior, for a boat laden with food became the instant prey of bands of hungry marauders. To effect this object in safety, I moved about the rivers with heavily-laden cargo barges under the protection of a gun-boat with a military guard, dispensing my bounty under the muzzle, as it were, of a twelve-pounder gun. The calamity was not altogether removed until the following crop of rice came in, and rescued the half-famished people from their misery.

Whether from this, or some other cause, we were at the same time besieged by an unusually large number of tigers. They were at all times numerous around Rangoon, the extensive jungles and abundance of deer affording ample cover and sustenance for predatory animals, still we had no fear in perambulating the country for a mile or two round the town. It is a well-known fact that, in times of famine, as the human race grows feeble and less capable of defence, the beasts of prey become bold in proportion, carrying their depredations even to the habitations of man. Cattle and human beings were now carried off in such numbers in the immediate suburbs of the town, that I was allowed by Sir A. Campbell to issue "brown Bess" on loan to as many of the natives as knew how to use her, for the purpose of thinning the ranks of these savage skirmishers, as also to promise a handsome reward in money for each head of the enemy brought in.

I should hardly be credited if I said these savage animals were shot even in the streets of Rangoon in broad daylight, but I should not be wandering very far from the truth if I so stated it.

I was once walking very early in the morning (the only time I had for recreation) along the main street of the town in company with a friend,* when we heard a shot or two fired in the direction we were going. The sound was not far distant, and we proceeded until we came to a little piece of waste land in the town lying on one side of the street, perhaps about fifty yards square, where the jungle grass had been allowed to grow till it was from four to six feet high. Here I found that the shots proceeded from the roofs of huts, where two of the heroes I had furnished with muskets were taking their practice, with very indifferent success, at a royal tiger which was perambulating the grass. Knowing that "brown Bess" was not a lady of very great precision of character, especially when handled by those who ill understood how to use her, she alarmed me more than the beast who attracted her notice, and I crept behind a bamboo lattice at the corner, thinking to be more out of the line of fire.

From my frail hiding-place I beheld, to my surprise, a soldier (an Irishman, of course) walk boldly into the grass with his musket, which he levelled at the tiger, not far distant. The faithless flint missed fire,—the veteran retreated a step or two, and deliberately chipped his flint, with as much coolness as though no danger confronted him, the tiger not attempting to charge. Again he came forward—the second shot told, but not fatally; the beast

* The late Captain William Roy, of Perth.

rushed, not at his assailant, but directly to the spot where I was ensconced with my friend, who fortunately had by this time possessed himself of a musket from a bystander, and gave him his *coup de grace*, when he fell two or three paces only from the spot where we stood. He was probably bent on bursting from the cover, and attempting an escape. It was a full-grown tiger, and had but two shots, most likely those of the soldier and my friend.

Soon after my return home, Pat came to claim his reward, when the secret of his heroism came out. He and a comrade who were taking an early walk, saw a native with a musket endeavouring to stalk the tiger stealthily. Abusing him for a sneaking coward, they forcibly took his musket, and boldly faced the enemy in the grass. The enraged brute rushed upon his comrade, tore him terribly, and retreated further into the grass. Pat Conolly (for such was his name) dragged his dying comrade from the scene of conflict, and it was to avenge his death that the second charge was made which I had witnessed. How the tiger got there was a mystery, as the town was surrounded by a close stockade, the gates of which were always kept closed during the night.

The unpleasant process of paying another instalment of the money stipulated by Treaty proceeded slowly, eager as the Burmese were to regain possession of the valuable province held in pledge, and to commence their crusade against their revolted subjects, yet it must be all paid up before we relinquished our hold on Rangoon. It so happened that the sum fixed for indemnity was most judiciously assessed; had it been more it could not have been paid; as it was, many of the Crown jewels, rubies, diamonds, and sapphires of great value, were sent down and sold to make up the required amount. It was indeed a spoiling of the enemy well merited.

While these arrangements were in progress, Mr. Crawfurd arrived in Rangoon, appointed by the Government as our Envoy to the Court of Ava, for the purpose of negotiating a Convention of Commerce between the two countries as stipulated by the Treaty signed at Yandabo. Although, no doubt, it was a grievous error to leave this important question to future negotiation, when it might have been so much better settled while we held our commanding position almost under the walls of the Capital, yet it can hardly be regretted when we reflect that it was the means of giving to the world a far clearer insight into all the internal relations of the country than had yet appeared, in the volumes afterwards published by that intelligent and acute observer.

Mr. Crawfurd kindly made me a tempting offer to accompany him on this mission as an assistant and interpreter, but I had no desire again to visit the scenes of my affliction; the memory of them was too fresh, indeed such it has ever remained, and will remain, since time and change have failed to obliterate it. Besides, Mr. Crawfurd was fortunate enough to secure the services of a much more able assistant in Dr. Judson, who was induced to sacrifice his feelings, and accept the appointment from motives of a far higher character than could be supposed to influence a man of commerce like myself. Mr. Crawfurd promised to use his best endeavours to obtain from the Court the concession of religious toleration, with liberty to preach our holy religion, and make proselytes among the natives without fear of punishment either to the teacher or his convert. It was this, hitherto the great business of Dr. Judson's life, which induced his compliance, and deep was his disappointment when it was found that the bigotry of the Court was proof against the solicitations of the Envoy. What rendered this fruitless instance of self-sacrifice and devotion to the cause peculiarly distressing was, that in his absence the amiable woman, his wife, who had so long and successfully administered to his and our relief in our troubles, passed away from this life, having been carried off by a fever, which her impaired constitution had not strength enough to resist. She was buried in a piece of ground in front of my house, adjoining my garden in the new settlement of Amherst, where her husband had some idea of taking up his abode if Mr. Crawfurd failed in obtaining the desired toleration.

The time now drew near when British faith was to be put to the test by the surrender of the country we had held in pledge. It was difficult for a nation so utterly faithless as the Burmese to credit the fact, yet they had already seen so much to bewilder them in the incomprehensible conduct of their new friends, that they really began to think we should be foolish enough to give them back their country. By the end of November they had completed their part of the contract by paying the money, and a Woongee had arrived from Ava, outside the boundary line, to demand, and take possession of the Province.

But just as the last of the money was being told out, I had the wickedness to enjoy a delightful little panic their own folly gave me the opportunity to create among them.

The Chiefs had been secretly accumulating arms in their quarters to be in readiness to open upon the Talains the moment they assumed the government. This was in contravention of a written agreement attached to the

Treaty, and when it came to my knowledge I thought it my duty to report it to Sir A. Campbell, not because I apprehended any treachery, but as our troops had been gradually withdrawn, and but few remained, caution was necessary. The General saw it in the same light. "I will thank you to go to the Chiefs, Mr. Gouger, take out your watch, and tell them that unless the arms are surrendered within a quarter of an hour, steps will be taken to secure them." I did so— they prevaricated like Burmans. When the time was up I retired, and found every approach to the place already occupied by parties of our soldiers. They kept the streets, while I and one of their officers entered the houses of the Chiefs, and brought to light heaps of trashy muskets, quite as dangerous to themselves as to their enemies. I must confess to a malicious gratification in allowing them for a long time to remain in error as to our motives. They had now no doubt we had outwitted them! We had taken their money, divested them of their arms, and would certainly keep their country! After a sufficient punishment had been inflicted, I restored their peace of mind by assuring them that we intended to leave their country next week, when their valuable stock of arms should be returned to them.

The 9th of December was the day selected for the evacuation of Rangoon by our troops, and restoring it to its old rulers. Its appointed Viceroy, the Woongee, was invited to leave his distant quarters beyond the line of boundary some days before the event, and to take up his residence among us, that we might all rejoice together—he on his accession to power, we on resigning it, both parties, I believe, being sincere in the happiness they expressed. Perhaps no one had better cause for rejoicing than myself; in my department the measure had become a necessity. My gaols were crowded with miscreants of the most ferocious character; they had long been so full of rapine and murder as to leave no room for misdemeanor or petty larceny, and, as executions were not the order of the day, it was not easy to conceive what might have been the result of a longer occupation.

As it was a time of general rejoicing, the Woongee could see no reason why these felons should be excluded from participating in it, and proposed to me a general gaol delivery to hail the auspicious event. I suggested that as His Excellency would so soon have the power to exercise this graceful clemency himself, I would leave the agreeable task to him, as, for my own part, I should prefer being on board ship before the sheepfold was opened and my lambs turned loose.

To celebrate the approaching happy event, Sir Archibald Campbell invited the Woongee and the *élite* of his staff to a formal banquet at his house. The chief of the military and naval officers were invited to meet them; but, although Lady Campbell and several other ladies had joined their husbands, it was thought prudent to dispense with the honour of their company at the table. The arrangements, however, were such as to admit of their being spectators while they themselves were screened from view. The table was of great length, as richly ornamented as circumstances would admit, and every delicacy within reach was liberally provided for the gratification of the most fastidious palate. Great attention had been paid to the decoration of the Hall; and the gay, mixed uniforms of the different services, interspersed here and there with the white drapery of their Burmese guests, produced at the dinner-table a lively and elegant effect. The General had his interpreter, the Chinese youth once before mentioned, behind his chair; but as few of the company could utter a word of the native language, I was made the most of by being placed between two of the chief guests, while the Woongee occupied the post of honour at the General's right hand.

Has the reader any curiosity to know how a Burman of rank could conduct himself at a dinner-table in those days? He shall hear.

On my right hand sat a Woondouk, second in rank to the Woongee. The dinner commences with soup, of course. My neighbour tastes it, but thinks it not so *piquante* as his *nyapwee;* the servant attempts to remove it—but he insists on keeping it before him; a plate of preserved salmon is handed to him—he thinks it may improve his soup, so he takes it from the plate and plunges it in; melted butter, soy, and anchovy sauce follow it—still it is not palatable; a rich stew of duck is handed round—he thinks it may improve his soup, so a spoonful goes into it: the mess is improving, but may still get better. I now beseech him to have it removed, and try his luck again by beginning afresh—he declines, he does not like taking so much trouble for nothing; other dishes come round—a little is always experimentalized with the soup. He sees me drinking claret—tastes, and wonders I can drink such stuff. I tell a servant to bring him a glass of cherry-brandy—that's the thing at last—he must have more of that—the remove comes—my friend turns pale—looks behind him—calls for his silver spitting-pot which holds near a gallon—turns round on his chair, and with surpassing facility discharges the late contents of the soup-plate into the gallon measure. Is my friend satisfied? Not a bit of it; he returns to the charge manfully—hopes for better luck next time. The dinner, which occupied an unusual length of time, afforded abundant scope for other elegant vagaries, but I spare my reader the finale.

In another part of the table a little by-play took place, which was irresistible. Colonel Kelly, of Waterloo celebrity, a man who never could resist a bit of fun, sat between two of the Burmese guests. Before him, as dinner was concluding, stood a dish containing a huge ornamental lump of fresh butter, considered a great delicacy at the time, the quality of which Lady Campbell was justly proud of. "What's that?" said the man on his left. The colonel cut off a considerable slice, and was preparing to place it on the interrogator's plate, when he saw the man open his mouth as though he expected it *there*. The hint was instantly taken, and an ounce of fine solid butter went into the fellow's mouth, which at once closed upon it, the Colonel drawing the unloaded knife through his clenched teeth. He was delighted, telling his friend on Kelly's right how good it was. The same operation was performed upon *him*.

Now, close by, sat a tall, sedate lieutenant in H.M. navy, so solemn in appearance that he did not seem to have a joke in him. He had watched this process intently, when, perhaps thinking it might be some religious ceremony, or at all events a customary mark of politeness, seeing the butter dish come round to him, without moving a muscle of his countenance or asking a question, he excised a slice which might have served a man for breakfast, and, with the utmost gravity, exhibited it before the face of an astonished Burman seated next to him. The man taken by surprise mechanically opened his mouth, and in went the delicious morsel—evidently a mistake on both sides; the one mistaking it for an English custom, the other for a Burmese one.

Notwithstanding such little *contre-temps* as those I have described, the entertainment went off admirably, and our guests were delighted. I must do the Woongee the justice to say that he was an exception to the general want of refinement and propriety. His manners were dignified, calm, and self-possessed.

The following day the last party of soldiers embarked in the transports. Sir Archibald Campbell had kindly allotted to my use one of the gun-boats of the flotilla to carry me to Amherst. When I was fairly afloat, but not till then, the doors of my prison flew open, and a rare lot of villains were let loose on society. The Woongee most likely constituted them a corps of braves, and used them against the Talains, who still stood on their defence, poor fellows, though without the shadow of a chance of success to their cause.

A signal gun was now fired from the General's ship, and, with the sound, the sovereignty of Henzawuddu reverted to its Burmese rulers.

One word, in conclusion, about Amherst. It is situated on the point of an estuary into which the waters of the river Salween discharge themselves, after receiving its large tributaries, the Attaran and the Gyne, near to Maulmain, about twenty-five miles up the river. The climate was salubrious, the land high and bold to the seaward, and the view of the distant hills of Balloo island very captivating. It is not surprising that Mr. Crawfurd, who had made a short visit to this spot, should have selected it as the site for the chief Civil station of our new possessions on the coast. But unfortunately he made too light of the difficulties of the approach to its harbour.

A chain of rocks, some sunken, others appearing above the water, extends nearly a mile into the sea, across which the tide sets with great velocity, rendering the entrance to the harbour extremely hazardous except at high water, and even then, with a leading wind, not entirely free from danger. This eventually proved fatal to its success. I, nevertheless, continued to reside there for some months, in civil charge under the Commissioner of the province, until there was little reason to hope for its prosperity. The Talains at first did not emigrate in such numbers as I had expected; old ties and associations were too strong to be overcome, even when a despotic tyranny was to be exchanged for freedom. Still, numbers flocked to me at Amherst, and dispersed themselves on the coast.

As the country was entirely new to us I again indulged my propensity to roam in search of novelties, and as often as I could get away I passed several days in ascending the rivers I have before mentioned. A ship's jolly-boat, rowed by four natives, who accompanied me from Rangoon, provided with an awning for protection from the weather, afforded all the means of transport I required; but, beyond the features of the country itself, there was really very little to investigate. On some of the rivers—the Gyne, for example—scarcely a hut or an inhabitant was to be found —there were dense jungles, wide plains, deep forests, but all without a vestige of population. The prime object of my search, however, was teak-trees, forests of which, we were led to believe, existed, though no one could tell us exactly where to find them. I did, nevertheless, succeed in discovering them at last, and, setting gangs of my natives at work upon them, I had the honour to be the first Englishman who ever cut a raft of teak timber upon our new possessions.

In one of my rambles in search of teak-trees up the river Gyne,* I had the good fortune to witness one of the most rare and interesting sights the depths of the forests can disclose.

I landed on the right bank of the river with three of my boatmen, leaving the fourth in charge of the jolly-boat. As the forest was dense, and as we had to make a pathway for ourselves through the brushwood, where there was any, we walked in Indian file, one of the men leading the line, in which I followed second, the other two boatmen bringing up the rear. To avoid the danger of losing our way, we took the usual precaution of chipping the bark of the trees and breaking the branches and twigs as we passed, or leaving what other mark we could in our progress, or the probability is, without such a clue, we should never again have found our boat.

We had not proceeded in this way more than a quarter or half a mile, when my leader, an intelligent woodsman, being eight or ten yards ahead, stopped suddenly and dropped on his knee; a backward motion of his hand told me to be quiet. I followed his example, repeated the signal to those behind, and so we all remained still as death, until the leader, without venturing to look round, motioned me forward with a finger. The nature of the ground enabled me to creep in advance without the noise even of my footstep, until I reached the spot where the man was hidden.

A beautiful spectacle now opened upon me. A few

---

* I am not quite sure that this event occurred on the river Gyne—it might possibly have been the Attaran. I write the anecdote from memory only.

Q

bushes screened us from a circle of verdant herbage, which had apparently been covered with water in the rainy season, and in this little shallow basin were to be seen a herd of wild cows quietly grazing on the rich pasture. The herd might have numbered about sixteen or eighteen, and from the placid, unconcerned manner in which they enjoyed their food, appeared to have no sense of danger or knowledge of the proximity of any unusual intruders. Not so the bull. When I first caught sight of him he was motionless as a statue, his bold front turned towards us, and his head and neck stretched so erect towards the sky that his nose was on a perpendicular line with his fore legs. He could not see us, but he evidently smelt us, though there was no wind to carry the scent in his direction. It was a hot day and a dead calm. The sight was beautiful beyond description.

I remained gazing at them in deep silence and admiration for more than half a minute. My double-barrelled gun, laden with balls, was in my hand, and I could easily have brought down the bull, as he was not more than thirty yards off, but the sight was too engaging, and I let him off. On a sudden, the beautiful statue seemed to have come to the decision that there was danger in the wind, as he set off at full gallop into the forest in the opposite direction to me,—the cows, who to the last manifested not the slightest sense of danger, left off feeding in a moment and followed their lord at full speed, the crashing of the brushwood for some time after we lost sight of them attesting their alarm. I did not know at the time what a rare sight I was witnessing,—one which I was afterwards told by an accomplished naturalist had not been enjoyed by any European traveller before me.

This was unfortunate, as, had I known it, my observation would have been more minute. The following facts, however, may be depended upon.

The cows were small in stature, considerably smaller than the breed of Alderney; their shape and figure were light and elegant; they did not possess humps, like the domesticated cattle of India; they were, without exception, of the same colour, a light reddish dun; their beautiful slender legs being all four white below the knee. The bull was rather larger and thicker-set than the cows—he had a respectable dew-lap, which, together with the breast and shoulders, was covered with a longer dark hair, approaching to black. I do not well remember the horns, but I am inclined to think they were not long, or I should most likely have remarked them. Both the bull and the cows were exceedingly sleek in their coats, which shone as though they had been subjected to careful daily brushing.

My intercourse with the Burmese country ends with the failure of the settlement of Amherst. Our expectations of its becoming a Port of thriving and increasing commerce were totally disappointed. I remained there nearly a year, until no hope of its prosperity remained, when, tired of the monotonous life of an idle functionary, I resigned my appointment under the Government, again to engage in the busy world, and to follow the bent of my mercantile inclinations in a wider field than could be found in these depopulated and worthless possessions.

www.ingramcontent.com/pod-product-compliance
Lightning Source LLC
Chambersburg PA
CBHW030306240426
43673CB00040B/1076